INFORMATION SYSTEMS

A Strategic Approach
to Planning and Implementation

D1531210

in loving memory of
my father,
Irwin Jack Kesner

INFORMATION SYSTEMS

A Strategic Approach
to Planning and Implementation

Richard M. Kesner

American Library Association
Chicago and London 1988

Cover and text design by
  Panikis Images
Composed by Impressions, Inc.
  on a Penta-driven APS-μ5
  in Zapf Book
Printed on 50-pound Booktext,
  a pH neutral stock, and
  bound in 10-point Carolina,
  coated-one-side stock by
  BookCrafters

The paper used in this publication meets the minimum requirements of American National Standard for Information Sciences—Permanence of Paper for Printed Library Materials, ANSI Z39.48-1984. ∞

Library of Congress Cataloging-in-Publication Data

Kesner, Richard M.
  Information systems.

  Includes index.
  1. Management information systems.   I. Title.
T58.6.K463   1988   658.4'038   88-10371
ISBN 0-8389-0493-9

Printed in the United States of America

Contents

8. **Machine-Readable Records: Management Issues in an Evolving Office Environment** 219

Figures

Introduction

When I prepared the predecessor to the present volume, *Automation for Archivists and Records Managers: Planning and Implementation Strategies*, I addressed myself to two subgroups of information managers: archivists and records managers.[1] In that work I sought to acquaint these information service professionals with techniques for dealing with and exploiting electronic data processing (EDP) technologies and machine-readable records. I also supplied a series of management tools that I and others have employed to plan, select, install, and implement automated information systems. In summary, the volume addressed the needs of system builders and program administrators whose responsibilities include the direction of information services within larger organizations.

As an underlying theme of the presentation, I repeatedly insisted that information specialists in archival administration, records management, library science, and data processing work in concert. It was and remains my view that over time the influence of new information technologies will meld the responsibilities of these professions. As I have subsequently argued, when this occurs, we will require the services of more broadly experienced information specialists, possessing a common set of skills and a greater familiarity with EDP technologies than is the case today.[2] My original text offered specific training recommendations and included a number of illustrations as to the types of problems confronting information service managers. Furthermore, I argued that if information workers are to serve their constituents, they must first gain a greater understanding of the operational dynamics of their parent organization. These impressions will in turn direct their efforts into areas in greatest need of their skills.

Since the publication of *Automation* in 1984, much has changed and much has remained the same. For its part, the technology marketplace has gone through major gyrations. Just a few years ago,

---

1. Richard M. Kesner, *Automation for Archivists and Records Managers: Planning and Implementation Strategies* (Chicago: American Library Association, 1984), ix–xi.
2. Richard M. Kesner, "Automated Information Management: Is There a Role for the Archivist in the Office of the Future?" *Archivaria* 19 (1984/85): 162–72; and "Whither Archivy?: Some Personal Observations Addressed to Those Who Would Fiddle While Rome Burns," *Archivaria* 20 (1985): 142–48.

International Business Machines (IBM) appeared to be the dominant force in microcomputing. In point of fact, since entering the personal computer (PC) market, IBM has been playing catchup with a number of its major competitors, in the face of declining profits and lower than anticipated sales for both its mainframe and PC-based products. By contrast, Digital Equipment Corporation (DEC) was obliged to jettison (or so it appeared) its microcomputer, only to emerge as the outstanding performer in the recent EDP industry resurgence. As the software industry boomed, Computer Associates purchased UCCEL, creating a single mainframe software system giant. At the same time, Lotus Corporation, Microsoft and other PC software houses expanded and diversified through acquisitions of their own.[3]

To add to all this activity, the full weight of telecommunications industry deregulation has come to bear. Open competition has led to the rapid development of new products and services, lower usage rates, and greater investment in large capital items, such as private branch exchanges (PBXs), digital phone technology, T-1 and Switch-56 digital transmission services, and programmable multiplexor hardware. The potential "connectivity" afforded by these developments has sparked a heated debate over communication standards and the integrated services digital network (ISDN). Since a decision in this area will have a considerable impact on the user's ultimate selection of computer and telecommunications hardware and software, the stakes are high. The discussion continues, with at least a partial resolution anticipated in 1988. Even with standards, the complexity of EDP and communication solutions to business problems will only increase over time.

It therefore comes as no surprise that the past four years have witnessed two new generations of personal computers; the steep decline and only modest resurgence of the United States semiconductor industry; the emergence of compact disk (CD-ROM) technology as the potential replacement for microfilm, the floppy diskette, and the hard disk drive; and the widespread use of communications networking by non-specialist consumers. Certainly many educated users of the new information and telecommunication technologies have become accustomed to rapid changes of these kinds, and indeed have come to expect them.

While all of this receptivity to the transforming EDP environment is most laudable, it underlines the need for works like *Automation*

---

3. For those unacquainted with the wide-ranging developments overtaking the computer and telecommunications industries, I suggest a number of weekly International Data Corporation publications, *Computerworld* and *Infoworld*; and Ziff Publication's *PC Week*. For some insight into computer industry publishing, see Jonathan Goodspeed, "Patrick McGovern: Creating A Global Empire," *High-Tech Marketing* 4,7 (1987): 32–35.

for Archivists and Records Managers and the message it conveys. The present volume, INFORMATION SYSTEMS: A STRATEGIC APPROACH TO PLANNING AND IMPLEMENTATION, carries the task forward with greater focus and clarity. The latter is not a second edition of *Automation* but is, rather, its intellectual heir, drawing from its contents and building upon them.

Both works view rapid change and innovation as characteristics of the late-twentieth century workplace. Information systems provide modern man with the capabilities to cope—at least in part—with this dramatically evolving and transforming environment. However, to be of use in this sense, EDP systems must be engineered, implemented, and managed with care. This is the common challenge confronted by today's information service professionals; yet there are few practical guides to assist them in this process. Much of the so-called trade literature is either too general, too technical in nature, or devoted only to descriptions of existing management information systems (MIS). There is therefore little to offer the beset manager of MIS services in the form of a systematic methodology to problem solving, analysis, and project administration.

Automation sought to fill this void for archivists and records managers. However, its major lessons apply equally well to most related fields. In this regard, INFORMATION SYSTEMS takes up where my earlier work left off. It walks the reader through a series of tried and tested management tools, covering such fundamental areas as needs assessment, project planning, request for proposal preparation, hardware and software selection, and system implementation. I and my staff have applied these approaches to real-life information management situations. In addition, I have added refinements as a result of regular interactions with colleagues at training sessions in the United States, Canada, Europe, and Israel. Thus, most of the material presented here has undergone major revisions since it first appeared in 1984. Furthermore, it is as useful and as necessary now as it was then.

However, as its title suggests, INFORMATION SYSTEMS places my tools and techniques in a broader business context. A well developed strategic plan, complemented by a rigorously administered tactical planning and implementation process, is in my view essential if one is to manage organizational change successfully and maximize the benefits of the new information technologies. The present work therefore emphasizes the importance of incorporating a strategic planning discipline in managing information resources—both paper and electronic. It also considers the general business environment within which these systems must operate in concert with the goals and objectives of the greater organization. Similarly, INFORMATION SYSTEMS examines the role of corporate structure in shaping the parent institution's information services. I dwell on this point because, together, strategic thinking and organizational structure provide the context for the creation of effective and economical information delivery and management systems. These concerns are at the heart of my methodology and are therefore fundamental in shaping the presentation of this volume.

My preface to *Automation* also referred in glowing terms to the promise afforded by technological change to produce a commonly trained group of information service specialists or information managers. While many organizations now boast management information system (MIS) personnel, in terms of their skill base and outlook these people tend to represent the more traditional data processing community. Though records managers, archivists, librarians, and information center administrators may also roam the halls in large institutions, each subgroup tends to retain its separate and usually operationally unrelated responsibilities. As a result, one must still distinguish between various types of information service professionals and the nature of their responsibilities in the workplace.

In INFORMATION SYSTEMS, I do not surrender my vision of where MIS careers are headed, but I confess that it will undoubtedly take longer to get there than I had hoped in 1984. As an expression of my commitment to the concept, I refer to my audience as "information service" or "MIS professionals" in the broadest sense of both designations. I do this as a warning of things to come and as an encouragement. INFORMATION SYSTEMS provides both general and specific recommendations to assist records managers and other information service specialists in harnessing new technologies for their own use. If these professionals are to avoid the reassignment of their responsibilities to operations personnel more in tune with the strategic processes within their organizations, they must take a more participatory and creative (indeed, proactive!) role in their own right. The purpose of this book is to suggest new directions and to provoke greater debate among the managers of information services.

On the other side of the coin, technologists have concentrated solely upon their day-to-day operations and services, without tying these activities into the larger picture. Their focus on computer hardware and software has established a wall between them and less technically oriented users. The jargon-ridden language of the EDP industry has contributed to this trend. Furthermore, they have failed to recognize the fact that machine-readable information is but one set of MIS resources. Paper files remain at the heart of both public and private-sector business functions. Thus, if these MIS professionals are to fulfill their mandate, they too must broaden their definition of their responsibilities.

In making this observation, I do not cast blame on any practitioner. Even so, external pressures are forcing MIS personnel to take a hard look at their operations. For example, attitudes toward general management have become more strategic and EDP technologies are transforming communications in the workplace. Unfortunately, these developments appear to have passed by many MIS professionals. It is my hope that this volume will provide them with new strategies of their own for dealing with these challenges. I also offer some practical tools to assist them in selecting and implementing information systems that relate more directly to the articulated goals and objectives of their parent institutions.

In particular, such professionals as records managers must move beyond their immediate preoccupation with the narrowly defined context of their traditional assignments to a more active approach in the management of "current" records as "living" information.[4] Through the effective use of this book, traditionally defined information service professionals will be in a stronger position to complement their counterparts in data processing and telecommunications. In fact, they will soon discover that they share many of the same objectives, skills, training requirements, and job responsibilities as their MIS colleagues, namely: the quick and economical delivery of well-focused information to end users.

Much must be accomplished before these services merge. In the short term at least, they will undoubtedly remain functionally distinct. Nevertheless, one can envision a common body of professional training and practice serving the overlapping requirements of these communities of information technologists. Indeed, the process has already begun in a very limited way. Umbrella professional organizations, such as the American Library Association, the Special Libraries Association, the Society of American Archivists, the Association of Records Managers and Administrators, the American Society for Information Science, the Association of Canadian Archivists, and

---

4. "Current records" are those in active use by the creating organization. One finds that such files are usually housed in systems that provide rapid and convenient access, and accurate refiling. "Non-current records" are documents retired from the active filing system and placed in economical, temporary storage. The vast majority of these records will be discarded after a period dictated by state or federal law, while a small fraction are retained permanently for their long-term evidential or informational value. "Evidential value" refers to the administrative or original value of documents as they were employed by the creating agency. "Informational value" refers to the intrinsic value and substantive contents of documents considered independently of their place of origin. See T. R. Schellenberg, *Modern Archives: Principles and Techniques* (Chicago: University of Chicago Press, 1985), 11–16; Maynard J. Brichford, *Archives and Manuscripts: Appraisal and Accessioning* (Chicago: Society of American Archivists, 1977), 2–7; and Frank B. Evans, Donald F. Harrison, and Edwin A. Thompson, comps., and William L. Rofes, ed., "A Basic Glossary for Archivists, Manuscript Curators, and Records Managers," *American Archivist* 37,3 (1974): 415–33.

the International Association for Social Science Information Service and Technology, have all, to a greater or lesser extent, recognized the need to integrate new technologies thoroughly into more traditionally defined information services. Workshops, seminars, and conferences offered by these organizations, as well as the contents of their publications, reflect this change in perspective and their growing concern that members be equipped with the tools to meet the challenges of the 1990s and beyond.[5] This is a start. However, much more attention and energy needs to be devoted to this process, if it is to succeed.

In my own way, I hope to provide similar direction through this book. By focusing upon strategic planning and implementation scenarios, this work offers managers an approach to effective exploitation of new technologies as they influence both information services in general and records administration in particular. I have purposely avoided references to specific hardware (equipment) and software (programming) products. The nature of the EDP industry is such that it faces significant changes in direction yearly, if not more frequently. As a result, most product-oriented works tend to be outdated before they reach the reader.[6] I do not mean to suggest that I have neglected references to particular applications altogether, but I have chosen to emphasize the importance of making intelligent choices among options. My readers will find it necessary to adapt these tools in keeping with their own records management requirements.

The decision-making models and development strategies that follow serve as guides and recommendations. They are examples that the reader should tailor to his or her management needs. Do not take them too literally. My tools serve as illustrations of a methodology, not as *the* definitive approach to specific situations. The reader must reshape my models in light of his or her own strategic, organizational,

---

5. Through the years, the Automated Records and Techniques Task Force of the Society of American Archivists has provided information service professionals with a core curriculum for both the management of machine-readable records and the implementation of automated systems in records repositories. In addition, the Task Force and its members have participated in the following relevant publications: H. Thomas Hickerson, *Archives and Manuscripts: An Introduction to Automated Access* (Chicago: Society of American Archivists, 1981); Richard M. Kesner, *Information Management, Machine-Readable Records, and Administration: An Annotated Bibliography* (Chicago: Society of American Archivists, 1983); Carolyn L. Geda, Erik W. Austin, and Francis X. Blouin, Jr., eds., *Archives and Machine-Readable Records* (Chicago: Society of American Archivists, 1980); and Margaret Hedstrom, *Archives and Manuscripts: Machine-Readable Archives* (Chicago: Society of American Archivists, 1983).

6. For those interested in up-to-date product reviews, I recommend any of the currently available loose-leaf publications, such as McGraw Hill's *DataPro Series* or its online equivalents through the Bibliographic Retrieval Service (BRS), Lockheed's DIALOG, et al. A more economical though perhaps more time consuming approach would entail surveying trade magazines, such as *Datamation, Infosystems, Computerworld,* and *BYTE,* to keep abreast of new products and developments.

and operational context. Throughout, I speak as a manager to other managers. I therefore make every effort to recognize those administrative issues associated with bringing MIS services in a timely and economical manner to end users.

How are information service professionals to integrate their efforts into the larger corporate strategy? How are they to maximize their contribution to the team effort? And how are they to make the most of each high technology opportunity that presents itself? INFORMATION SYSTEMS: A STRATEGIC APPROACH TO PLANNING AND IMPLEMENTATION seeks to address each of these points through a series of management tools and operational prototypes. While the text illustrates techniques and suggests particular MIS solutions, it is only meant as a guide which the individual manager must tailor to suit the needs of his or her particular work environment. In my view, the analytical skill base exists among records management, archival, and library professionals to join their technology-oriented colleagues in data processing to make things happen. All we lack at present is a broader definition of responsibilities, greater familiarity with EDP products and services, and certain generic systems planning and implementation tools.

To begin, Chapters One and Two consider the strategic planning process and the role of corporate MIS in more detail. My objective here is to provide a general context for all that follows. I therefore review current strategic planning concepts, the implications of changing information technologies, and organizational dynamics. I then examine the impact of corporate structure on the formulation of information policies and services as they apply to both public and private institutions. With this vantage point, I next discuss typical characteristics of the modern organization's information environment and what these mean to the planning of information delivery systems. Finally, I analyze the positioning of MIS personnel and services within the broader framework of corporate management.

Drawing upon this base, Chapter Three reviews the generic system requirements of information services. Without referring to specific technologies, I consider the administrative issues associated with such processes as the physical management of records, reference services, financial accounting, word processing, information retrieval, file storage, and final records disposition. My purpose throughout is to illustrate how one ought to define and rationalize systems that are already in place as a first step toward automating some or all of their functions. Once the role of MIS within these processes is identified, I provide a methodology for needs assessment and the structuring of systems to best exploit a technology-based approach to the realization of enhanced information services.

Having prepared the way for EDP solutions in Chapter Three, I discuss hardware and software options in Chapter Four. I make no effort to cover the universe of possibilities. Instead, the chapter deals with general categories of products and systems and how they fit together. Again, my focus is on management issues, such as the appropriate allocation of corporate resources, rather than the detailed workings of each EDP component.

With the information system typologies from Chapter Three, and the hardware and software options from Chapter Four firmly in place, I move to the core of my presentation, Chapters Five and Six, which deal respectively with system planning and implementation. In these chapters, I cover specific tools for the selection of information systems, procedures, and products. I also discuss the use of consultants, the financing of electronic data processing equipment and software acquisitions, and the most effective use of EDP industry resources.

The remaining two chapters further illustrate the planning and implementation process through the review of a number of system scenarios. These examples are arranged by application in the following areas: Developing Information Management Systems in the Workplace: Paper-based and Computer-based Scenarios (Chapter Seven), and Machine-Readable Records: Management Issues in an Evolving Office Environment (Chapter Eight). Finally, the Postscript offers a profile of the information services professional and how this worker must be developed for the MIS challenges of the present and future.

Some of the tools offered here derive from my experience as an archivist and records manager both in the administration of my own programs in Michigan and Tennessee and as a consultant for a variety of archival and records management programs throughout the United States and Canada. I developed other techniques more recently as the Vice President of General Services and MIS for Multibank Service Corporation, a Massachusetts banking services organization, and as the Manager of Office Systems and Services for the Faxon Company, a leading international library and information services company. While I cannot point to the widespread use of my models by others, I can attest to their success in my own work and to their use by my associates at Multibank and at Faxon. If information managers approach these models with flexibility, I have no doubt that they will prove equally applicable in any number of other information management settings.

As strongly as I may advocate my views, I am in no position to address all aspects of these complex issues. I have no doubt neglected some areas, due to a lack of experience. In other instances, I have had the forethought to refer to the successful work of colleagues or to exemplary illustrations drawn from cognate disciplines. Where gaps exist in my narrative, I trust that others in the field will come forward to share their thoughts and experiences as I have done. In many respects, the present study is and will continue to be a work in progress. It is hoped that my work may encourage those with keener views and more pervasive knowledge to take up the challenge and to provide guidance for those seeking to wed new information technologies with large management concerns.

The present volume would not have been possible without the support and assistance of many individuals and organizations. First and foremost, I would like to acknowledge the aid—individually and collectively—of the Automated Records and Techniques Task Force of the Society of American Archivists. Through their industry and determination, records managers, archivists, and other information service professionals enjoy access to a wide range of publications, workshops, and conferences pertaining to the use of computers and the management of machine-readable records in MIS. I have benefited in innumerable ways from close association with Task Force members David Bearman, Tom Brown, Charles Dollar, Carolyn Geda, Meyer Fishbein, Margaret Hedstrom, Harold Naugler, and Lisa Weber.

My views on strategic planning and organizational structure have been shaped through my experiences in the field. However, their intellectual base, such as it is, stems from a series of seminars that I regularly attend at the Wharton School of Finance, University of Pennsylvania. I would therefore like to acknowledge my debt to Wharton's Executive Training Faculty and in particular to the staffs of the Strategic Planning and Management Information Systems for Strategic Advantage seminars.

I also wish to thank Earl James and his associates at Deloitte, Haskins and Sells (Boston) for sharing drafts of their hardware/software selection guidelines with me. In addition, I would like to thank the staffs of the Archives of Labor and Urban Affairs, Wayne State University; the Archives of Appalachia, East Tennessee State University; Simmons College Library; Stanford University Libraries; Babson College Library; Wellesley College Library; and the Massachusetts Institute of Technology Libraries for their assistance at various stages in the development of this study. I am also indebted to Nancy Yuill, Margaret Hedstrom, Lisa Weber, and David Horn for their careful review and constructive criticism of earlier drafts of this work.

Multibank Service Corporation has generously given of its resources to allow me to undertake and complete this project on schedule. Furthermore, both Herman A. Hipson, President of MSC, and Selwyn I. Atherton, President of the holding company, Multibank Financial Corporation, are to be commended for their consistent support of this and related professional undertakings that did not entirely coincide with my day-to-day responsibilities at Multibank. I would also like to thank my editor at ALA, Herbert Bloom, whose efforts caused this project to come into being and who has nurtured it to its present form. I would be very much remiss if I did not also thank Una Walters and Lori LaRochelle for their good work at the word processor.

Finally, I wish to thank my wife, Susan Nayer Kesner, for tolerating yet another "special project." She is my best proofreader and soundest critic. To her and the many others who have contributed to this book, I am deeply grateful. My readers have them to thank for what is of worth in the pages that follow, and me to blame for any errors of fact or judgment found herein.

CHAPTER

1

Strategic Planning and the Discipline of Information Management

Today's senior managers and administrators face wrenching changes in the ways they go about their daily work. Global trade has transformed the marketplace, and new computer and telecommunications technologies have permanently altered the nature of human communications, information gathering, and corporate structure. To be effective and efficient in the execution of their duties, government, educational institution, and business leaders must possess an immediate grasp of all relevant data. Thanks to office automation and the computerization of work processes, there is no shortage of raw information. Our paper mountains have also continued to grow, with no end in sight. What we lack are the means to transform these mountains of data into useful knowledge. Thus, as we are about to enter the twenty-first century, mastering this information has become one of the greatest challenges facing the modern organization.

Indeed, it is one of the paradoxes of our age that a society so rich in information tools and data gathering capabilities should face such difficulties in attempting to make practical use of all the information at its disposal. Ironically, it is our very advances in information science that have allowed us to reach this state of affairs. Nevertheless, it should come as no surprise that the senior managers of diversely sized, focused, and structured organizations are turning to management information systems (MIS) for help in extricating themselves from their difficulties.

However, the real success stories in this uphill battle are not necessarily about those companies with the latest and most extensive deployment of the new electronic data processing (EDP) technologies. In fact, it is just as likely that these organizations are the ones in the deepest trouble. The true winners are those institutions that are far-sighted enough to manage the introduction of new MIS products and services as part of their long-term strategic planning process. While a grasp of the potential afforded by automated information systems is essential, it is of even greater importance that organization leaders place the exercise of these tools within a strategic context. They must master the workflow of operations, paper-based document genera-tion and storage, and the retrieval of filed information as well. In this manner, they will be sure to apply their EDP resources where they will yield the greatest benefit.

Broadly defined, the group of professionals that address these requirements within most organizations include electronic data pro-cessing specialists, systems and work analysts, records managers, archivists, librarians, and other information service workers. Unfor-tunately, these same players cannot always contribute to their full potential because they are either intentionally left out of strategic and MIS planning by their superiors or because they fail to assume a proactive role for themselves in those processes. To get involved, MIS personnel must first place their specific assignments in an organi-zation-wide context. In so doing, they will come to recognize op-portunities to maximize their contribution to the team effort.

With this objective in mind, Chapters One and Two provide an analytical framework for the development of a "big picture" per-spective. From the outset, I warn my unwary readers that the con-cepts and terminologies presented here may be alien to their way of thinking about current assignments. It is nevertheless essential that they make this leap and hence conceive of the services that they manage as part of a larger, integrated entity. While I make every attempt to connect strategic planning and general management with MIS services, my audience must—in keeping with their own respon-sibilities and work environments—devise their own operational links between these sets of activities. In so doing, they will evolve into key contributors to the success and prosperity of their parent organi-zations.

Strategic Planning and MIS: The Challenge

The discipline of strategic thinking as practiced by the organization's leadership, and the intellectual rigor of information systems planning and implementation as administered by MIS professionals do not blend easily. Each group comes to common issues with differing perspectives, skills, and vocabularies. Senior managers will need to establish an organizational culture which fosters both. To achieve a satisfactory result, they must also consider the environment and marketplace within which they operate, as well as their entrenched institutional traditions. If they are to be successful in this regard, senior management will require the assistance of information service professionals and "technologists." By working as a team under the aegis of a strategic planning process, these leaders and their MIS counterparts would bring to the table EDP solutions that effectively and economically address the information needs of the larger corporate entity.

Unfortunately, the aforementioned approach assumes a great deal about the structure and culture of an organization which may not in fact be true. In the first place, this recommended scenario is predicated upon the presumption that management operates within and is guided by strategic concerns. A well-defined strategy will articulate commonly held corporate goals and objectives. It will also provide direction and focus to organizational resources. Most importantly for the purposes of this discussion, a strategic plan will stipulate the broad information system requirements of the company. In so doing, it will furnish the organization's technologists with a framework and various points of reference for the construction of complex systems.

Second, if a strong strategic planning process is in place, the short-term development of EDP capabilities as part of a twelve- to eighteen-month tactical plan will accurately reflect the business objectives of the organization. Similarly, resources will be deployed and projects initiated, not because they employ exciting new technologies but because they will increase market share, profitability, quality of service, or any other goal set forth by the corporation. The underlying assumption here is that management, marketing, and MIS operate in concert but under the general direction of senior corporate leadership. For all of this to work, the process must be streamlined, decision oriented, and well communicated.[1]

While the current trend among senior managers in both the public and private sectors has been toward the building of such strategic processes, managers have many times ignored the organization's information strategies in developing such plans. It is one of the postulates of this volume that successful strategic planning requires the

---

1. The literature pertaining to strategic planning is vast. Two works of particular note are Peter Lorange, *Corporate Planning: An Executive Viewpoint* (Englewood Cliffs, N.J.: Prentice-Hall, 1980); and Peter Lorange, Michael F. Scott Morton, and Sumantra Ghoshal *Strategic Control* (St. Paul: West Publishing Company, 1986). For strategic planning in banking, see Douglas V. Austin and Thomas J. Scampini, "Long-Term Strategic Planning," *Bankers Magazine* 167,1 (1984): 61–66.

incorporation of MIS. The reasons for so arguing are threefold. In the first place, information systems tell management what is going on. Without such data, corporate leaders would have no way of measuring present performance against past achievements and projected targets. Second, MIS can facilitate the communication and enforcement from top to bottom of planned goals and objectives. Finally, such systems also allow for timely responses to external changes in environment and to opportunities created through internal efforts and the forces of the marketplace.

Why then does the leadership at times neglect the development of information system strategies? First of all, rarely are senior managers sufficiently conversant in the latest EDP technologies to identify needs and opportunities in terms of MIS-supported products and services. Second, information specialists are often more focused on the technological breakthroughs rather than how these developments might most effectively transform the larger organization. They do not spend enough time or effort in raising the awareness of their counterparts in operations and management nor do they possess adequate knowledge to make business-driven EDP decisions on their own. Finally, corporate leaders, either by design or default, do not often fully involve MIS personnel in the strategic and operational planning that will ultimately decide how information resources are to be consumed by the parent institution.

To exert an influence over this process and to set it on a more productive course, information service professionals must first get involved. They must also develop a greater sensitivity toward the impact of the effective management of paper files and EDP systems on overall performance. For MIS personnel to be successful in this regard, they will require more extensive training and better management tools. Furthermore, corporate leaders will need to integrate MIS participation into the planning process. In the long run, this move may even necessitate a different organization structure that will, in turn, foster a productive exchange of information and expertise between the organization's operations and technology experts.[2]

Who will serve as the corporate technologists in this scenario? Traditionally, data processing personnel and so-called systems analysts have combined with librarians, records managers, and archivists to provide a wide range of information services. Each group has

---

2. A primer for this process is provided by James C. Emery, *Management Information Systems: The Strategic Imperative* (Oxford: Oxford University Press, 1987). The author spends a great deal of time defining and illustrating the types of strategic tools required to employ MIS to greatest advantage. See also F. Warren McFarlan and James L. McKenney, *Corporate Information Systems Management* (Homewood, Ill.: Irwin, 1983).

operated within its own self-defined spheres of responsibility. However, emerging technologies have dramatically altered these relationships. The dynamics of the work environment, as well as user demands, have led to a call for a less fragmented, more comprehensive, and highly integrated approach to information services. Corporate strategic processes have added pressure to this mix by scrutinizing the direction, timing, efficiency, and cost effectiveness of the organization's overall approach to MIS.

Furthermore, EDP technologies themselves are transforming the documents that more traditionally conceived information managers, such as librarians, archivists, and records managers, are obliged to manage. These changes in turn have blurred the distinctions between participants and have raised serious questions concerning the training and preparation of these professionals.[3] Similarly, as organizations turn in increasing numbers to machine-readable formats for their records storage, the management and service issues surrounding these media will become a widespread concern.[4] Corporate leaders will then be obliged to turn to a cadre of qualified and more broadly trained information service professionals to address these expanding MIS requirements.

Records managers, for example, have worked chiefly with paper-based source materials, ranging from the official files of individual workers to the massive operational records of the entire organization. However, more recently modern information technologies have introduced micrographic, magnetic, photographic, and occasionally videodisc media. The prevalence of these types of documentation will increase over time, yet few records managers are trained or empowered to deal with them. The fragmentation of responsibilities in this manner cannot continue. It is already creating waste and confusion

---

3. The more established archival automation programs have received adequate coverage. See Lawrence J. McCrank, ed., *Automating the Archives: Issues and Problems in Computer Applications* (White Plains, N.Y.: Knowledge Industry Publications, 1981); Michael Cook, *Archives and the Computer* (London: Butterworths, 1980); and H. Thomas Hickerson, *Archives and Manuscripts: An Introduction to Automated Access* (Chicago: Society of American Archivists, 1981). A more progressive attitude toward the new information technologies is demonstrated in contemporaneous records management articles. See, for example, William Benedon, "Interdisciplinary Approaches to Records Management," parts 1 and 2, *Modern Office and Data Management* 20,6–7 (1981): 20–22, 23–24; William Benedon, "Automated Scheduling/Records Center Operations," *Records Management Quarterly* 14,2 (1980): 18–26; and A. Patricia Miller and Susan L. Jenkins, "Automated Retrieval of Project Documentation at Marathon Oil," *Records Management Quarterly* 16,3 (1982): 5–8.

4. The implications of growth in the use and importance of machine-readable records is well documented. See Charles M. Dollar, "Machine-Readable Archives—Records Managers Neglect Automated Files," *Records Management Journal* 13,4 (1975): 2–8; Lionel Bell, *The Archival Implications of Machine Readable Records* (Washington, D.C.: VIII International Congress on Archives, 1976); Lionel Bell, "The Archival Implications of Machine-Readable Records," *Archives* 26,1 (1979): 85–92; and Carolyn L. Geda et al., eds., *Archives and Machine-Readable Records* (Chicago: Society of American Archivists, 1980): 233–48.

that are intolerable to organizations operating in a highly competitive marketplace. As a result, some institutions are reorganizing so as to establish a focal point for the management of all their information resources. The responsible senior manager in such a setting is often referred to as the organization's "chief information officer."[5] It is as yet too early to tell if this trend will continue, but even now it is clear that decisions along these lines will become more common as the need for action grows.

If the proliferation of high-technology records formats did not pose enough of a challenge, today's manager is also faced with the staggering growth in the overall amount of data generated by day-to-day activities. The elaborate bureaucracies that run most large organizations encourage this phenomenon through the duplication and distribution of files and corporate databases. Photostatic copiers, laser printers, computer output microfilm systems, personal computers, electronic mail, and, more recently, video text networks encourage this phenomenon and exacerbate the problems engendered by it.

If the growing use of electronic data processing has encouraged this state of affairs, it is also viewed by some as a means of freeing records managers, and other information specialists from the quagmire of voluminous, highly repetitive, and increasingly complex document sources. In so doing, it will, or so it is argued, eliminate their more mundane activities so that they may directly contribute to operations through the provision of timely, economical, and well focused services. For example, they will be called upon to establish so-called "expert systems" and online, interdepartmental databases to assist users in quickly accessing relevant information.[6] Their assignment will then become one of developing "knowledge systems" from sundry data sources throughout the organization.

As admirable and reasonable a proposition as this might appear, the integration of strategic planning with recent innovations in computer and telecommunications technologies is far from a reality. Even as distributed computing, online bibliographic utilities, and automated library services have created a generation of experienced,

---

5. The role of the corporate CIO is examined in Chapter One. For an excellent overview, see the set of articles that appeared under the leader, "Management's Newest Star: The Chief Information Officer," *Business Week* 2968 (October 16, 1986).

6. Most modern organizations produce more raw information than their managers can possibly digest. Expert systems can assist management in identifying salient data. For an introduction to the field expert system functionality and development, see Paul Harmon and David King, *Expert Systems: Artificial Intelligence in Business* (New York: Wiley, 1985). See also E. A. Feigenbaum and P. McCorduck, *The Fifth Generation* (Reading, Mass.: Addison-Wesley, 1983) and Beau Shiel, "Thinking About Artifical Intelligence," *Harvard Business Review* 65,4 (1987): 91–97.

knowledgeable, and impatient users,[7] these services have added to the complexity of our management problems. Thus, while users have grown accustomed to timely and accurate responses to their information inquiries, circumstances have militated against satisfying their requests. Similarly, chief administrators expect more precise management control over the legal, financial, and service-related aspects of both paper and electronic corporate files.[8]

Given these developments, information service professionals are faced with new challenges from all sides. Although they may have responded to these demands somewhat lethargically in the past, they cannot afford to do so in the future. Clearly, advances in microelectronics and systems software offer numerous promising alternatives to the more traditional approaches to information handling. To plot a successful course, MIS personnel must place themselves in the broader context of their parent organization's planning process and work with corporate leaders in integrating their services into the framework of the larger institutional entity. To assist in this process, this volume offers a series of recommendations and management tools for the reader's careful consideration.

Strategic Planning and MIS: Concepts and Perspectives

As a process, strategic planning is as diverse as its practitioners. This study therefore makes no attempt at summarizing its complexity and instead draws the reader's attention to the excellent work of Lorange, McFarlan, Emery and others on this subject.[9] For the purposes of this discussion, let it suffice to say that the strategic planning process provides a long-term perspective on organization activities and objectives. Moreover, it directs human and financial resources in adherence to the plan so as to ensure its realization. A comprehensive

---

7. Regarding the growth of information networks and facilities, see Dimitri Bertsekas and Robert Gallagher, *Data Networks* (New York: Academic Press, 1987); Joe A. Hewill, *OCLC: Impact and Use* (Columbus: Ohio State University Libraries, 1977); Barbara Evans Markuson, "Computer Based Library Networks," *The Midwestern Archivist* 6,2 (1982): 207–22; Susan K. Marton, *Library Networks*, 4th ed., (White Plains, N.Y.: Knowledge Industry Publications, 1982); and Richard M. Kesner, "The Computer and the Library Environment: The Case for Microcomputers," *Journal of Library Administration* 3,2 (1982): 33–50.

8. Indeed, the present concern with accountability and management by objective has permeated down to the lowest administrative levels within many organizations. See, for example, Robert S. Runyon, "Towards the Development of a Library Management Information System," *College and Research Libraries* 42,4 (1981): 539–48; Michael R. W. Bommer and Ronald W. Chorba, *Decision Making for Library Management* (White Plains, N.Y.: Knowledge Industry Publications, 1982); James C. Worthy, "Management Concepts and Archival Administration," *The Midwestern Archivist* 4,2 (1979): 77–88; and Sue E. Holbert, "Comments on 'Management Concepts and Archival Administration,'" *The Midwestern Archivist* 4,2 (1979): 89–94.

9. See notes 1 and 2 above.

strategic analysis looks at the external environment and marketplace within which the organization must compete. It also considers the internal dynamics of production and/or the services rendered to customers. As such, the process is both analytical and decision oriented, involving the identification of goals and the choice of actions to achieve those ends.

The purpose of strategic planning is to define a mission, to position the institution for success against all competitors, and to ensure that all players understand the plan and perform accordingly. The process also looks for ways to improve resource utilization, to build and diversify for the future, and to establish an advantage over new entrants into the marketplace. If senior management sets the course, it cannot do so without accurate and timely information. This data comes from the interchanges between the organization's leadership and its rank-and-file, via its MIS systems. Chapters One and Two of this volume consider this process in more detail.

Tactical or business planning flows from the strategic process and possesses many of the same characteristics. However, tactical planning has a short-term focus, usually twelve to eighteen months. It emphasizes action steps and the development of specific products and services in keeping with the organization's strategic plan. Indeed, one may view the tactical process as a series of connected steps that move the corporation along to the realization of its mission. Both tactical and strategic planning view organizational outputs (i.e., products and services) as part of the larger institutional fabric and in terms of "families."[10] I will address this subject in more detail later in this volume, but it is important to note that this "bundled" orientation to products and services allows corporate leaders to look beyond the day-to-day minutia of operations and at the larger environmental impacts of their decisions.

From the standpoint of effective management, the process outlined above has considerable relevance for all types of organizations—large or small, public or private. Even though the leadership of a government agency or an institution of higher learning may not view themselves as a "business," they nevertheless produce products and services that must compete for tax dollars, donations, tuition fees, or whatever. Like the private sector, they must manage their resources carefully, deal with and (if possible) anticipate changes in the external environment that influence their operations, and adapt to market demand. Admittedly, the typical public sector administrator does not

---

10. The portfolio approach to product management is one of the predominant themes in the strategic planning of marketing. See Phillipe Haspeslagh, "Portfolio Planning—Uses and Limits," *Harvard Business Review* 60,1 (1982): 59–74; and Yoram Wind and Vijay Mahajan, "Designing Product and Business Portfolios," Harvard Business Review 59,1 (1981): 155–65.

conceive of his or her operation as "market driven." However, an objective analysis of the situation would reveal striking similarities between the information management requirements and operational dynamics of for-profit and not-for-profit institutions. It is therefore my view that the tools of strategic management are as necessary for both categories of organization. Simply put, in coping with change, competition, and shrinking financial and human resources, all of these bodies are in the same boat.

Similarly, sound management information systems and practices are essential to the success of the planning process and to overall organizational performance. As employed here, "MIS" refers to any and all aspects of information and data storage, manipulation, and servicing. Thus, my definition includes the activities traditionally assigned to the records manager, archivist, and librarians, as well as the electronic data processing technician, data network operator, and systems analyst. For the sake of simplicity, I describe this more broadly defined group as information service professionals, technologists, and/ or information specialists. Moreover, I posit that though their current responsibilities may not interrelate operationally, they all share a common mission: the timely and efficient delivery of information to the organization's end users. Thus, to provide the necessary user services, the keeper of paper documents must work hand in hand with those responsible for machine-readable records in developing coherent and comprehensive MIS policies.

Certainly from the standpoint of the strategic planning process, all MIS personnel have a contribution to make. In the first place, they manage and support the communication networks that foster the top-down/bottom-up exchange of data on day-to-day performance. They also provide the systems for measuring the success of individual players and the team as a whole. They collect and preserve the records of past decisions, product development, and marketing efforts. Most importantly, information service professionals maintain the facilities through which all of this data is sifted, analyzed, and delivered to decision makers. This latter service is perhaps the most vital (and daunting) challenge faced by today's information specialist.

This statement is particularly true when one considers the volume and diversity of data generated by most modern organizations. Much of this information is redundant or of little long-term value. At the same time, its creation and maintenance consume considerable amounts of resources. Furthermore, these growing numbers of paper and machine-readable files obscure the vital information that senior management requires to make informed decisions. To cut through this morass of data necessitates more than effective information retrieval systems, it calls for a holistic approach to records management and MIS involvement in the total life cycle of user documentation.

In other words, as part of the organization's information management program, MIS personnel must take into account all records formats and media. These will include paper files and publications, microfilm, machine-readable databases, microcomputer floppy diskettes, and even digital optical disks (so-called CD-ROM technology).[11] The planning for information services should integrate all of these components into its program. Given this breadth of vision, it is essential that MIS personnel also devote considerable attention to the initial creation, storage, and use of these records, as well as their long-term retention and disposition. The benefits of this full life-cycle approach to documentation are only too obvious. By involving themselves with information from its inception, MIS personnel can root out redundancy, ensure greater compatibility between sources, and better anticipate records storage and servicing requirements. Most importantly, such a scenario facilitates the development of responsive retrieval mechanisms and knowledge building systems.

To ensure the success of these efforts, information service professionals must be privy to the goals and objectives of the larger organization. They should spend sufficient time with their "constituents" to understand and, indeed, anticipate user needs. This expansive redefinition of MIS's mission also requires that technologists understand the operational aspects of the organization so as to appreciate how EDP and telecommunications technologies might foster better performance. Finally, MIS personnel must manage their own immediate responsibilities strategically and in concert with the greater corporate plan.

The Challenge of the New Technologies

If one accepts my definitions of the information specialist, records life cycle, and MIS responsibilities, it is clear that information service professionals must do more than acquire greater familiarity with modern information systems and equipment. They need to establish roles for themselves in all areas pertaining to the creation and dissemination of data within the parent organization. Since in many instances information specialists have not played an integral part in

---

11. For an excellent overview of CD-ROM technologies and their uses in the workplace, see David Bearman, *Archival Infomatics Technical Report: Optical Media, Their Implications for Archives and Museums* (Pittsburgh: Archives and Museum Infomatics, 1987). See also Jeffrey Bairstow, "CD-ROM: Mass Storage for the Mass Market," *High Technology* 6,10 (1986): 44–51; Dominic Nghiep Cong Bui, "The Videodisk: Technology Applications and Some Implications for Archives," *American Archivist* 47,4 (1984): 418–27; William Saffady, *Optical Disks for Data and Document Storage* (Westport, Conn.: Meckler, 1986); and Judy McQueen and Richard Boss, *Videodisc and Optical Disk Technologies and Their Applications in Libraries: 1986, Update* (Chicago: American Library Association, 1986).

these processes, they must win the acceptance and support of senior management before they proceed. Though they may initially face resistance, the battle will be well worth waging if it results in a larger participatory role for them in the strategic planning process and in the creation, flow, and storage of records. Ultimately, this involvement will greatly simplify document retrieval, data management, and related MIS services.

For information specialists to prosper in this regard, they need to become involved in areas that were previously the domain of others. Indeed, it could be argued that what I am advocating is the creation of a new type of MIS professional. This is true, but only to a point. First and foremost, librarians, archivists, documentalists, data processing (DP) personnel, and records managers need to bring their skills as analysts and service-oriented professionals to this redefined body of tasks. In so doing, they must also become more aware of current information technologies and of their parent institution's internal dynamics—political and otherwise. They must become, in short, true information managers with a catholic view of their duties and what is required of them in the workplace.

To date, few information service professionals have anticipated this redefinition of their jobs or, for that matter, even recognized the need to move away from their more traditional concerns. The way these professionals have approached the use of EDP technologies in their work environments typifies this problem and underscores the pressing need to reconsider the state of MIS training in light of the new emphasis on strategic planning and technological innovation. Records managers, for example, have concentrated on the administration of paper documentation and the use of automation to generate and manage micrographics (i.e., computer output microfilm [COM] and computer-assisted retrieval of microfilm [CAR]). They have rarely employed automated techniques in managing filing systems, routing records, establishing and auditing retention and disposition schedules, and operating records centers.[12] More importantly, they have only rarely worked with their colleagues and users to integrate records management systems with other corporate information systems.

---

12. This point is made in Richard M. Kesner's survey of the professional literature pertaining to records management and automation. See *Information Management, Machine-Readable Records, and Administration* (Chicago: Society of American Archivists, 1983): 1–16, 77–88. See also Robert J. Kalthoff and Leonard S. Lee, Productivity and Records Automation (Englewood Cliffs, N.J.: Prentice-Hall, 1981); and Robert Landau, James H. Bair, and Jean H. Siegman, eds., *Emerging Office Systems* (Norwood, N.J.: Ablex, 1982). It is noteworthy that the latter two volumes do not refer to records managers, but rather to MIS personnel as the key players in information management scenarios.

Given the usual mandate of the records manager to take whatever steps are necessary to economize on the storage and servicing of office files, it is not at all surprising that events have developed in this general direction. However, it is also appropriate to observe that, due to the nature of their work and their concern with current as opposed to historical documents, records managers are now coming into more regular contact with machine-readable records. As a result, some records managers have demonstrated a willingness to work with nonprint media and computers when the opportunity presents itself. When senior management provides the proper incentives, adaptation to a newly defined mission, as suggested above, should not prove too difficult. Indeed, such an approach underlays the concept of management by objective (MBO) whereby task plans tie line managers and staff to specific deliverables within a given time frame. The objectives in question will (or should) relate directly to the parent organization's strategic plan. In this context MIS would be employed to monitor MBO compliance and to measure the success of individual and team players. As a group, librarians and archivists have not actively participated in this approach to project management.[13]

If the need for a common approach among information service professionals has become more pressing, the technologies currently available to assist them provide the basis for concerted action. Fortunately, the actual specifications for information handling systems do not differ markedly from one setting to the next. However, information specialists must keep abreast of developments in EDP and telecommunications if they are to take advantage of these developments. They must also migrate toward automated MIS solutions in relation to changes overtaking their parent organizations. Indeed, end users' expectations toward system performance and support ought to drive the presently separate servicers of corporate information in the same direction.

To "keep current" requires substantial financial support and careful systems planning and implementation. Information service professionals need to study the marketplace with care and to select those systems that best address the requirements of their users. In many instances, these choices will be limited by the resources of

---

13. On library automation, see Richard M. Kesner, "The Computer and the Library Environment: The Case for Microcomputers," *Journal of Library Administration* 3,2 (1982): 33–50; and *Microcomputer Applications in Libraries* (Westport, Conn.: Greenwood, 1984). Both of these works include detailed bibliographic footnotes. In the field of archival administration, automated techniques have made less headway. See Ben DeWhitt, "Archival Uses of Computers in the United States and Canada," *American Archivist* 42,2 (1979): 152–57; Richard M. Kesner, "Automated Records and Techniques in Business Archives," *American Archivist* 46,1 (1983): 92–95; and Richard M. Kesner, *Automation for Archivists and Records Managers* (Chicago: American Library Association, 1984): 1–11, 126–46.

their parent institutions. It therefore becomes incumbent upon MIS personnel to choose EDP options with care. Again, the new technologies, and in particular the microcomputer, have added variety, flexibility, and potentially lower costs to this selection. These developments in turn afford opportunities for the managers of paper-based information systems to move toward automated solutions.

The procedures and recommendations outlined in this book are an attempt to redress the imbalances noted earlier in this introduction. In the first place, MIS management must work more closely with its constituents if the enterprise as a whole is to prosper. Second, if managers are to assist their colleagues in obtaining and retaining a competitive edge, information service professionals must adopt the techniques employed by their more strategically oriented colleagues in operations, marketing, and senior corporate management. Indeed, if they lose sight of these goals, MIS managers will also find themselves incapable of dealing with the flood of print and nonprint material that is already inundating them. To do so would mean a failure on their part to fulfill even their traditional roles as the collectors and servicers of their parent institution's paper records and publications.

The managers of information services, to whom this book is addressed, need not allow technology-based opportunities to pass them by. Through the exercise of their traditional skills, methods, and practices, they are well prepared to proceed. However, they must also show themselves flexible and adaptable to the changing information requirements of their parent organizations. While the present work does not address every point along this developmental path, it raises questions that demand answers and proposes methods for uncovering appropriate responses to at least some of these issues. I encourage the reader to participate in the evolution and refinement of these processes as they apply to his or her information and work environments.

CHAPTER 2

Strategic Planning, Organizational Structure, and the MIS Environment

In today's highly competitive work environment, managers of distinction are those who provide their organizations with an "edge." Depending upon one's specific responsibilities, this advantage over one's competitors might entail the better management of human and financial resources, product innovations, enhanced profitability through reduced operating costs, the exploitation of patents and trademarks, or an increased market share through more effective marketing. It is of no consequence if the executive in question operates in the private or public sectors of the economy. What *does* matter is one's superior performance in relation to the strategic and tactical goals of the parent organization. The planning process should identify specific objectives for each manager, as well as both the quantitative and qualitative measures for the assessment of that player and his or her team.

What distinguishes the winners from the losers in this elaborate scenario? While many factors can contribute to success, three elements stand out as being of paramount importance. These are: (1) strategic planning for the overall direction and control of the enterprise, (2) the judicious use of human resources and organizational structure for the realization of plan objectives, and (3) the exploitation of management information systems (MIS) for the evaluation of corporate and worker performance, and for the communication of vital information throughout the organization. It is the purpose of this chapter to examine the interrelationships between strategic planning, corporate structure, and MIS, and to suggest ways of improving institutional performance through the creative use of emerging information technologies.

It should also be noted that this Chapter will not consider specific computer hardware and software solutions. Indeed, it is my view that any thought of particular EDP products or services at this point would be premature. Instead, this section will examine the organizational and environmental factors that will allow both public- and private-sector institutions to make the most of their MIS capabilities. At the same time, I will identify cultural and structural aspects of the larger corporate entity that will have direct bearing on the development of the information management function. It is essential that the reader take this perspective prior to a consideration of the MIS scenarios offered in the subsequent chapters of this volume. My approach at this stage is broad with the objective of providing a general context from which specific managerial models may be derived. In this regard, Chapter Two, like Chapter One, provides the foundation for the more focused discussions that follow.

Strategic Planning and the Role of MIS

Strategic planning is that process of long-term, structural planning that prepares the organization for superior performance. The business or short-term tactical plan for gaining market share and increasing earnings grows out of the latter stages of the strategic process. Often the prevailing market conditions within a given industry or the overall economy will dictate the process's complexity and rigor. However, it is the strength and resolve of the management team that will ensure its success.[1] This point is as valid with regard to public institutions providing a community service paid for with tax dollars as it is for companies competing in the "open" marketplace.

Simply put, strategic planning focuses upon converting the goals and objectives of the organization into realities. It also provides the mechanisms for communicating the common mission and for monitoring performance and resource management. This does not mean

---

1. For a thorough introduction to strategic planning, see Peter Lorange, *Corporate Planning: An Executive Viewpoint* (Englewood Cliffs, N.J.: Prentice-Hall, 1980); Peter Lorange, Michael F. Scott Morton, and Sumantra Ghoshal, *Strategic Control* (St. Paul: West Publishing Company, 1986); Wickham Skinner, *Manufacturing in Corporate Strategy* (New York: Wiley, 1978); and Russell L. Ackoff, *Creating the Corporate Future: Plan or Be Planned For* (New York: Wiley, 1981). See also F. Warren McFarlan and James L. McKenney, *Corporate Information Systems Management: The Issues Facing Senior Executives* (Homewood, Ill.: Irwin, 1983); and James C. Emery, *Management Information Systems: The Strategic Imperative* (Oxford: Oxford University Press, 1987).

that every agency which embraces a strategic approach will prosper. Nevertheless, a formal planning discipline will encourage the development of a coherent organizational culture and a clearly articulated and communicated course of action. To work effectively, a strong sales orientation must also underlie this process. While not-for-profit institutions may not pursue sales per se, they are (or should be) driven by comparable forces as measured in terms of services delivered to constituents. Those who are served are in this sense their customers. Thus, even in the public sector, marketing and sales—of a sort—have an important place in the measurement of overall organizational performance.

Unfortunately, many managers tend to concentrate their efforts on cost containment rather than sales, or on day-to-day operations rather than the larger strategic picture. These aspects of corporate culture should come as no surprise to anyone who has worked as a middle manager in a typical U.S. business, government agency, or university.[2] For the purposes of the present study, these experiences raise a number of particularly relevant issues. For example, many of us are asked to manage our responsibilities against an expense budget. We are rewarded on the basis of performing all necessary duties, and even some added, unexpected tasks, while remaining within predetermined limits of expenditure. In a stagnant economy, such an approach to resource management may work well, but in today's changeable business climate, it is both impractical and wrongheaded to operate on the basis of expense rather than revenue (or service delivery, in the case of the public sector).

In the first place, the current environment is extremely dynamic. Even such tradition-bound industries as financial services are undergoing what amounts to a revolution as a result of foreign competition, tax reform, and deregulation.[3] An expense-oriented management system does not afford the necessary flexibility to deal with these forces, nor does it encourage corporate leaders to diversify and

---

2. For insights and illustrations, see J. H. Bower, *Managing the Resource Allocation Process: A Study of Corporate Planning and Investment* (Boston: Division of Research, Graduate School of Business Administration, Harvard University, 1970); R. E. Caves, *American Industry: Structure, Culture and Performance* (Englewood Cliffs, N.J.: Prentice-Hall, 1964); T. E. Deal and A. A. Kennedy, *Corporate Culture* (Reading, Mass.: Addison-Wesley, 1982); H. Mintzberg, *The Nature of Managerial Work* (New York: Harper and Row, 1973); and A. M. Pettigrew, *The Politics of Organizational Decision Making* (London: Tavistock, 1973).

3. For a well informed survey of banking industry deregulation and the impact of automation, see Elbert V. Bowden and Judith L. Holbert, *Revolution in Banking*, 2nd ed., (Reston, Va.: Reston Publishing Co., 1984). For a more general discussion of deregulation and its implications for strategic planning, see Balaji S. Chakravarthy, "Strategic Adaptation to Disruptive Change: The Case of Deregulation," *Academy of Management Review* (forthcoming). See also D. C. Waite II, "Deregulation and the Banking Industry," *Bankers Magazine* 165,1 (1982): 26–35.

expand in response to such changes. In short, it is not action oriented and thus limits managerial options in the face of external pressures.

The problems of this approach are compounded when senior management does not communicate or, indeed, develop a strategic response to these dynamics. If corporate leaders do not provide direction, the end result invariably becomes a middle-management fixation on day-to-day responsibilities. This too may prove harmful to the organization's performance, in that it focuses on the short term and does not, therefore, prepare corporate players for new and greater challenges just over the horizon. Furthermore, it directs institutional resources into areas where the long-term return on investment may be minimal or even negative.

On the other hand, an organization that is strategically oriented and whose managers are revenue (rather than cost) driven can more readily adapt to change and promote creative, superior performance. If the demand for their services contracts, expands, or changes direction, they are in a position to bring resources to bear on the problem and to exploit unexpected opportunities. As part of this type of corporate culture, all managers must assume a "sales" orientation toward their duties. Typically, almost everyone views the selling of products and services as a role assigned to a limited number of "marketing" players within the organization. This is not so. Whatever the business or area of responsibility, every manager must act in part as a salesperson, marketing ideas to superiors and services to colleagues. This perspective of one's management responsibilities is particularly attractive in that it exemplifies the action-oriented approach that is, in my view, so necessary to the success of today's public- or private-sector organization.[4]

Thus, for those institutions who would prefer to control their own destiny in a rapidly changing world, a well focused strategic plan is beneficial; and a commitment to sales and service is essential. By proceeding within this management framework, corporate leaders will more effectively direct and motivate both middle management and the organization's rank-and-file. However, to achieve these ends, senior management must first of all articulate the short- and long-term goals of the institution, expressed in terms of sales, market share, services delivered, return on assets, constituents assisted, or some other relevant set of criteria. Secondly, by hiring people from outside their immediate industry, organizational leaders will bring to their operations a fresh perspective and perhaps the type of orientation so crucial to the promotion of a new corporate culture.

---

4. The case in favor of a "marketing" approach to management information systems is made by Curt Hartog and Robert A. Rouse, "A Blueprint for the New IS Professional," *Datamation* 33,20 (1987): 64–69.

Finally and most importantly, they must tailor their reward/compensation systems to encourage their employees to embrace the organization's strategic objectives.

How is all of this to be achieved? Successful strategic planning and implementation efforts start at the top, through the direct involvement of the organization's chief executive officer (CEO) and his or her senior staff.[5] At the outset, emphasis must be placed on establishing easily identifiable and quantifiable goals. Above all, the process must be vital, tangible, and pervasive—and not, as is so often the case, merely an exercise restricted to the upper strata of the institution. The CEO cannot delegate responsibility here. He or she must lead, set the pace, and make (or encourage others to make) the crucial decisions. Once the CEO and his or her team establish this process, the organization will find itself in a position to move forward with a well focused and disciplined program.

While this may sound quite plausible, bringing it to fruition is no small task. To break past management traditions, the typical business, government agency, or university must go through a great deal of self-analysis and redirection. Management will require the tools to lead, control, evaluate, alter course, and reward, as the case may be. To do so, forward looking organizations are turning to the very management information systems that drive their basic product lines and services. (For the purposes of this discussion, MIS will serve as an umbrella term for all of the administrative services, software programs, computer hardware, telecommunications equipment, and technical and systems expertise that constitute modern records and information systems.) It is through the effective use of these MIS tools that such organizations can differentiate themselves from, and outperform, their competitors. In addition, MIS systems provide the means to foster the effective planning and implementation of agency strategies.

To begin, one should recognize the centrality of MIS to many corporate activities. The introduction of computers in most organizations began slowly with the automation of accounting functions. However, since the late 1960s, computerized systems in the administration of business, government, and education have become virtually ubiquitous.[6] One can therefore observe that financial and med-

5. Raymond J. Lane represents the viewpoint that CEOs must play an active role in emerging technologies. See "The Key to Managing Information Technology," *Bankers Magazine* 168,2 (1985): 20–27. See also F. Warren McFarlan and James L. McKenney, *Corporate Information Systems Management: The Issues Facing Senior Executives* (Homewood, Ill.: Irwin, 1983); J. F. Rockart and M. S. Scott Morton, "The CEO Goes On-Line," *Harvard Business Review* 60,1 (1982): 82–88; and Peter Lorange, *Implementation of Strategic Planning* (Englewood Cliffs, N.J.: Prentice-Hall, 1982).

6. Two recent books provide an excellent overview of the computerization of the workplace. See Gordon B. Davis and Margrethe H. Olson, *Management Information*

ical services, most government agencies, all educational institutions, and many other types of organizations currently commit an increasingly large portion of their resources to support information systems of one kind or another. Furthermore, the importance to many companies of modern information technologies lies not only in their ability to deliver traditionally defined services more efficiently and at lower per-unit costs than manual processes, but also in their capacity to provide new, value-added products. For example, student databases in universities and customer databases in the cosmetics industry are necessary for the effective and economical delivery of services. At the same time, they provide one of the most potent tools for the cross-selling of products to established customers.[7]

It is also important to realize that even with the advent of the automated office, paper records play a major role in the operation of all organizations. For the foreseeable future this is not likely to change. It is therefore incumbent upon senior management to ensure that paper-based information services remain responsive to the needs of corporate users. To achieve these ends, MIS personnel, such as records managers, archivists, librarians, and information officers, must constantly review their operations for efficiency and economy, relate them to the strategic plans of the parent organization, and look for ways to employ the computer to save time and expand services. For example, while most users would prefer to work with a hard-copy version of a document, this does not mean that records managers should not store these documents in a digitized form and reproduce them in a paper format only as necessary. Similarly, when vast quantities of documentation must be managed, automated retrieval systems will often improve records center performance and reduce the cost of overall operations.

Finally, as demonstrated by leading-edge financial services organizations, the potential afforded by MIS has emerged in the development of new high technology products.[8] For example, the fam-

---

Systems (New York: McGraw-Hill, 1985); and Henry C. Lucas, Jr., *Information System Concepts for Management* (New York: McGraw-Hill, 1986). See also James A. Senn, *Information Systems in Management* (London: Wadsworth, 1987); and Allen H. Lipis, Thomas R. Marschall, and Jan H. Linker, *Electronic Banking* (New York: Wiley, 1985).

7. For example, an informed discussion of MIS tools and the cross selling of bank products may be found in Linda Richardson, *Bankers in the Selling Role: A Consultative Guide to Cross Selling Financial Services* (New York: Wiley-Interscience, 1986). See also Nathalie D. Frank and John V. Ganly, *Data Sources for Business and Marketing Analysis*, 3rd ed., (Metuchen, N.J.: Scarecrow, 1983).

8. This case is made most clearly in two studies prepared for and published by a Salomon Brothers, Inc. task force. See Thomas H. Hanley, Jeffrey L. Cohn, Carla A. D'Arista, and Neil A. Mitchell, *Electronic Banking: Yesterday, Today and Tomorrow* (New York: Salomon Brothers, April 1984); and *Technology in Banking: A Path to Competitive Advantage* (New York: Salomon Brothers, May 1985). Of particular note are the case studies of what the team considers to be leading-edge U.S. banks, including First Chicago, Citicorp, Mellon Bank Corp., Chase Manhattan, Irving Bank Corp., CoreStates Financial, PNC Financial Corp., Wachovia Corp., and NBD Bancorp.

ily of services commonly referred to as "cash management" came about as a result of the greater functionality and integration of automated and networked banking systems.[9] Similarly, far-flung automatic teller (ATM) networks and the robotized phone tellers allow us to transact bank business virtually anywhere and at any time of the day or night, thanks to voice/data communications capabilities.[10] In a related vein, an alumni database affords university fund raisers the opportunity to draw upon current biographical, geographical, and economic information in directing their approaches to individual contributors; and manufacturing concerns employ computer assisted design (CAD/CAM) to develop new products.[11] These are just a few examples of how information systems have provided the capability to develop new business and enrich established ones. As part of any strategic planning process, these opportunities need to be identified and evaluated.

One may also observe that these same information systems are essential to the strategic planning process itself in two major respects. In the first place, strategic planning is a "top down" process. Senior management needs to communicate decisions, identify and implement programs, and monitor performance. MIS provides the controls or "hooks" through which management can explore opportunities, make choices, and communicate them to the larger organization. To the extent that information systems are pervasive, they can also shape corporate culture and the behavior of individual players. However, to make the most of this scenario, the organization will need to establish "intelligent" systems that provide pre-selected data to key decision makers.[12] At the present time, few leaderships exploit this capability in developing a shared view of goals and responsibilities.

---

9. In general, cash management involves systems that accelerate collection of customer receipts, the disbursement of payments to suppliers for materials or services; and the control of corporate cash accounts. See Linda Williams, "Cash Management Accelerates with the Middle Market," *Computers in Banking* 4,7 (1987): 30–37; and Allen H. Lipis et al., *Electronic Banking,*: 149–98.

10. Michael T. Dibbert, "Measuring the Benefits of ATM's," *Bankers Magazine* 170,1 (1987): 46–50. See also *Payments in the Financial Services Industry of the 1980's* (Westport, Conn.: Quorum, 1984).

11. Computer-assisted design (CAD) and computer assisted manufacturing (CAM) are two of the hottest areas among the so-called super-microcomputer manufacturers. These CAD/CAM systems are transforming everything from the manufacturing of cars and toasters to the design of space capsules and houses. See Carl Machover and Robert E. Blauth, eds., *The CAD/CAM Handbook* (Bedford, Mass.: Computervision, 1980); Donald Greenberg et al., *The Computer Image: Applications of Computer Graphics* (Reading, Mass.: Addison-Wesley, 1982); Mikell P. Groover, *Automation, Production Systems, and Computer-Aided Manufacturing* (Englewood Cliffs, N.J.: Prentice-Hall, 1980); and Steven K. Roberts, *Industrial Design with Microcomputers* (Englewood Cliffs, N.J.: Prentice-Hall, 1982).

12. For an introduction to the field expert systems and artificial intelligence, see Paul Harmon and David King, *Expert Systems: Artificial Intelligence in Business* (New York: Wiley, 1985). See also E. A. Feigenbaum and P. McCorduck, *The Fifth Generation*

Just as MIS should be helpful in the "top-down" participation of management in strategic planning, it is also of great importance in fostering a reciprocal "bottom-up" component. As part of this latter function, vital data is fed up the chain of command to direct and shape senior management knowledge of what is going on in daily operations. It can also influence leadership decisions regarding new products and services. Some of the technological capabilities in question may be as informal as an electronic mail system that encourages line managers, staff, and sales personnel to communicate with their superiors.[13] Other mechanisms may be more structured, such as analytical tools that monitor weekly performance by salesperson, selling location, and product line. In both of these examples, bottom-up data feeds into planning discussions so that senior management may make informed choices.

Unfortunately, the bottom-up communications component in the typical organization's strategic planning process is even less developed than its top down capability. There are many reasons for this deficiency. In the first place, some institutional leaders do not solicit feedback from the rank-and-file. Even fewer organizations promote such information exchanges through their systems of employee evaluation and compensation. As a result, the bottom-up component is not part of corporate culture and is not, therefore, valued by either the worker or his or her boss. Furthermore, the fragmented nature of responsibilities within a large organization, especially as they relate to information services, makes it difficult for senior managers to solicit data from the rank-and-file in a systematic manner. Since I address this latter issue in more detail in section two of this chapter, I will end here with the observation that both top-down and bottom-up communications are essential within any organization if it is to operate efficiently and plan effectively for its future.

These top-down/bottom-up information flows give strategic planning its dynamic and flexible quality. MIS can and should be integral to this process. For this to happen, information systems must be widely accessible to users. They must also possess "intelligent" tools to assist management in turning raw data into usable knowledge. While these truths may be self-evident to the reader, senior managers are not always creative in their handling of MIS resources. The "winners" in the struggle for industry supremacy, tax dollars, or the best

---

(Reading, Mass.: Addison-Wesley, 1983); Ralph H. Sprague, Jr., and Eric D. Carlson, *Building Effective Decision Support Systems* (Englewood Cliffs, N.J.: Prentice-Hall, 1982); and Edward R. Tufte, *The Visual Display of Quantitative Information,* (Cheshire, Conn.: Graphics Press, 1983).

13. See Steve Davis and Candy Travis, *The Electric Mailbox: A User's Guide to Electronic Mail Services* (Dallas: Steve David, 1986). See also Stephen Connell and Ian A. Galbraith, *Electronic Mail: A Revolution in Business Communications* (White Plains, N.Y.: Knowledge Industry, 1982).

students will map out their own MIS strategies, like their business strategies, in keeping with their individual markets, corporate cultures, and sales capabilities. If structured properly, MIS planning will place computer and telecommunication resources where they are most needed. It will also avoid a great deal of the waste and inefficiency that has from time to time tainted efforts in automation.[14]

In saying this, I do not mean to suggest that information service professionals ought to play a subordinate role in corporate management. On the contrary, even though they must be user driven, the corporation's MIS leadership ought to be proactive throughout planning discussions. Leaders need to understand the relative importance of all strategic choices confronted by the leadership and the supporting role of MIS in that process. It is also essential that they be familiar with the products and services offered by the industry in which their organization must compete for customers or resources. With this knowledge in hand, they can better recognize technology-based opportunities that might facilitate the realization of corporate objectives.[15] In fact, this ought to be a joint effort between senior and MIS management. If they are to make the most of the situation, both groups must approach these discussions with an open and receptive mind, and with a willingness to change established practices in light of improved technological options. To succeed this process requires a serious commitment and an adaptive, cooperative attitude on the part of all players.

The Corporate Environment and MIS Planning

The following section presents a summary of those major environmental and industry characteristics that shape the context of corporate structure, organization, and planning. The specific areas under consideration include (1) organizational typologies and corporate culture, (2) institutional structure and the delivery of MIS services, and (3) information environment characteristics and resources. This

---

14. For example, Manufacturers Hanover Corporation attempted to establish a worldwide voice/data communications network, which ended up costing MHB hundreds of millions of dollars but did not meet its needs. See "Manufacturers Hanover Corporation—Worldwide Network" *Harvard Business School Case Study 9-185-018* (Boston: Harvard Business School, 1986). See also Henry C. Lucas, *Implementation: The Key to Successful Information Systems* (New York: Columbia University Press, 1981); and Robert J. Thierauf, *Decision Support Systems for Effective Planning and Control: A Case Study Approach* (Englewood Cliffs, N.J.: Prentice-Hall, 1983).

15. See note 1 above. See also William R. Synnott and William H. Gruber, *Information Resource Management* (New York: Wiley, 1981); Robert V. Head, *Strategic Planning for Information Systems* (Wellesley, Mass.: QED Information Sciences, 1982); and Ralph H. Sprague and Barbara C. McNurlin, *Information Systems Management in Practice* (Englewood Cliffs, N.J.: Prentice-Hall, 1986).

chapter will then conclude with a series of recommendations as to how MIS planning and resource management might be better integrated into the larger corporation-wide decision-making process.

1. Organizational Typologies and Corporate Culture

Corporate culture and organizational structure are intimately related. In turn, these factors should provide direction and focus to those designing the corporation's information systems. For example, most large organizations are highly hierarchical and bureaucratic.[16] Chains of command are rigorously defined and tenaciously defended. From the standpoint of running a dynamic and flexible business, these circumstances are both beneficial and problematic. On the one hand, all employees know where they stand and to whom they are responsible. Lines of communication are clearly defined so that top-down, bottom-up feedback ought readily to flow through the system. These developments in turn ought to facilitate the management of workflow and the paper documentation generated by these processes. On the other hand, a hierarchical and bureaucratic structure discourages exchanges outside accepted channels, and can lead to a highly territorialized perspective of one's role within the larger organization. Since the access to relevant information is a measure of power and authority in most organizations, the aforementioned process will only succeed if information flows freely up and down within the structure.

The MIS response to this situation should be to establish a communications environment, say through automated document retrieval systems, an electronic mail network, and shared informational databases that would facilitate exchanges across and between discrete areas of responsibility. In so doing, these systems would create greater opportunities for dialog and remove artificial barriers between corporate players.[17] They would also improve end user access to those organizational records required in their work.

Similarly, MIS can play an important role by providing electronic links between the organization's numerous operational and financial EDP systems. In and of themselves, these interfaces will reduce corporate expenses by automating labor-intensive functions and

---

16. Jay Galbraith, *Designing Complex Organizations* (Reading, Mass.: Addison-Wesley, 1973; H. E. Aldrich, *Organizations and Environment* (Englewood Cliffs, N.J.: Prentice-Hall, 1979); S. B. Bacharach and E. J. Lawler, *Power and Politics in Organizations* (San Francisco: Jossey-Bass, 1980); Bernard M. Bass, *Organizational Decision Making* (Homewood, Ill.: Irwin, 1983); and H. Mintzberg, *Power in and Around Organizations* (Englewood Cliffs, N.J.: Prentice-Hall, 1983).

17. The sociology of office automation and its implications for human interaction was one of the primary themes of a symposium at Stanford University in 1980. The conference proceedings were published as *Emerging Office Systems*, Robert M. Landau et al., eds. (Norwood, N.J.: Ablex, 1982).

streamlining operating procedures. They will reduce management's reliance on paper files and, hence, the costs associated with their maintenance. Beyond that, system linkages will facilitate the establishment of a cost accounting capability and other mechanisms of performance measurement. These same systems will disburse knowledge more widely. As a byproduct, well informed workers will more readily buy into the organization's strategic plan because they will better understand it and will in all likelihood have an opportunity to contribute to its evolution.

To make the most of its information resources, the organization might also establish a common "customer" file and other shared databases from which all of its functional units can draw information. While reducing duplication and the cost of redundantly entered and stored data, such tools afford additional sales opportunities. For example, some financial services companies have carried integrated data processing systems into the field through so-called platform automation.[18] The U.S. Internal Revenue Service has pooled tax, census, and government loan records to track down evaders and defaulters.[19] Many other illustrations may be found to underline the point that even as organizations desire greater flexibility, their MIS units are under pressure to provide enhanced records management, communications, and systems integration while reducing related paper and microfilm expenses. Corporate information users will increasingly demand the "knowledge power" afforded by these automated products so that they may compete more effectively.

Yet another characteristic of many organizations is a move toward "matrix" management.[20] In a matrixed arrangement, players from different hierarchically and bureaucratically defined units come together to work on a specific project. Designing a new product for

---

18. The "platform" refers to the nonteller sales locations in banks. Platform automation ties the loan or account opening process directly into the bank's computerized system through remote terminals in the branches. See Dave Stoner, "Choosing the Right Platform Automation System," *The Bankers Magazine* 170,3 (1987): 12–16. See also Allen H. Lipis et al., *Electronic Banking;* and Linda Richardson, *Bankers in the Selling Role: A Consultative Guide to Cross Selling Financial Services* (New York: Wiley-Interscience, 1986).

19. See "IRS Enlists System's Help in Leaning on Tax Cheats," *Computerworld* 19 (February 11, 1985): 23; and Bob Davis, "Abusive Computers: As Government Keeps More Tabs on People, False Accusations Rise," *Wall Street Journal* 210,37 (August 20, 1987): 1, 12. On the other hand, the Federal Government has its problems in planning for its MIS future. See Jake Kirchner, "Federal Computing: The Good and the Bad," *Datamation* 32,16 (1986): 62–72; and Wendy Goldman Rohn, "White House Information Systems" *Infosystems* 34,5 (1987): 26–32.

20. Matrix management is by no means a "new" concept. It has been around for some time but like many other approaches to people management, it does tend to go in and out of fashion. Two of the classics in this field are Jay Galbraith, *Designing Complex Organizations* (Reading, Mass.: Addison-Wesley, 1973); and Stanley Davis and Paul Lawrence, *Matrix* (Reading, Mass.: Addison-Wesley, 1977). See also David I. Cleland, *Matrix Management Systems Handbook* (New York: Van Nostrand Reinhold, 1983).

release into the marketplace is an excellent example of the type of project that lends itself to matrix management. Typically, engineering, manufacturing, marketing and sales, distribution, and MIS personnel would participate in the development process. It is therefore highly unlikely that the project leader will have direct authority over all team players. Instead, the leader must balance the "turf" and political issues raised by his or her staff against the need to complete a specific assignment. More often than not, the project director acts as a facilitator and a consensus builder rather than as a manager, in the more traditional sense of that role. These circumstances apply even within the corporation's MIS structure where records management, telecommunications, and data processing may all report to different heads but must work in concert to address the needs of the parent organization.

MIS personnel should assist in this process by providing the types of tools to complement a matrix management culture. As mentioned above, such services might include "high-touch" communications capabilities, like electronic or voice mail, and interactive modeling systems. Certainly, an integrated approach to customer information would prove essential. Similarly, distributed information processing, through the use of departmentally controlled mini- and microcomputers, lends itself to the flexible, localized environment one associates with matrix management. By contrast, the "citadel" image of the computer center (and all its admitted synergies) may need to be minimized if its perceived role conflicts with this aspect of the corporation's management style. While a decentralized approach may at first appear to be more costly, its long-term benefits to the organization reside in its effective support of matrixed projects and in the monitoring of team performance.

Still other cultural shifts within the larger organization can have major implications for MIS. For example, many agencies and institutions have historically been cost driven rather than revenue driven. As a result, their accounting systems and management concerns have concentrated on expense reduction. It should therefore come as no surprise that the financial systems associated with these traditions lack cost accounting and product profitability analysis capabilities. However, with the growing significance of foreign competition, shrinking corporate resources, and deregulation, some of these requirements have changed radically. Systems once considered uneconomical and even frivolous are now viewed with growing interest by some and as absolute necessities by others. MIS must respond to these changes in attitude and circumstance by building systems that both manage information and measure the utility of its exploitation.

The growing interest in cost accounting systems exemplifies this point nicely. It has become increasingly necessary to compete through product differentiation and pricing. This is as true for universities, and hospitals, as it is for International Business Machines (IBM) and Ford Motor Corporation. However, this is extremely difficult to do unless one knows the unit costs of each and every product, the effect of volume variability on unit costs, salesperson and sales location performance, and the more general dynamics of the market(s) into which one has ventured. In addition to knowing current conditions, management will require historical data and the means to extrapolate from this base when projecting sales results. It would therefore appear prudent for MIS personnel to take these factors into account when planning the development of their own services. Admittedly, this particular capability is of little use to a not-for-profit government agency, where a service orientation takes precedence over a "sales" orientation. Even so, a cost accounting mechanism, facilitated by automated tools, could be employed with great effect in public- as well as private-sector institutions both to control expense and raise new revenues. It should therefore come as no surprise that major software companies are building useful tools in response to this emerging set of requirements.[21]

The final environmental characteristic to be considered here concerns itself with customer service. While most organizations have always been to a greater or lesser degree service oriented, the meaning and significance of customer service have grown with the intensity of competition or, in some industries, since deregulation. In many business settings, pure price competitiveness has given way to value-added services packaged to complement the basic product. To maintain market share, some companies have defined special niches for themselves, either by product or geographical location. At times, they have also provided "bundled" services to customers, cementing loyalties and at the same time raising the client's switching costs. While these players may not have been innovators, they are sensitive enough to shifts in the market to respond promptly to customer demands with new or enhanced products and services.

More recently, one notes a trend among large, leading-edge institutions to market themselves as niche players. They claim to offer personalized service as well as a wide range of choices and competitive rates. What they are in fact doing is availing themselves of MIS capabilities to be all things to all people. Their systems draw relevant information down to meet specific customer needs. This approach appeals to the public who believe that they are getting the best of both worlds—namely, the stability and economies of scale of

---

21. For example, UCCEL's Infopoint System includes an "Enterprise" subsystem which has an array of cost accounting, profitability analysis, and performance measurement tools. For a product survey, see "Is Integrated Software Ready for Banks?" *Banking Software Review* 12 (1987): 27–41.

an industry leader with the personalized service and quality control usually associated with a smaller local provider. Even if they do not wish to respond directly to this sort of marketing challenge, the more traditional organization must rely on MIS to develop products and services in keeping with its plans. As the advertising campaigns of large institutions shape customer perceptions as to what products and services ought to include, all players will be required to turn to their information processing capabilities if they are to remain competitive. Here again, environmental forces will work on corporate strategies, which will in turn express themselves as fresh MIS assignments.

For example, a state-run university decides that it wishes to compete with smaller liberal arts colleges for quality students. To do this, the administration calls upon its MIS unit to develop a system that will allow students to self-select their own curricula and method of course evaluation. In the same manner, if a bank commits to the sale of loans and other banking services on customer premises, MIS will be required to develop a dial-up link between numerous point-of-sale locations and the bank's computer center. Sales personnel will need portable terminals and appropriate software for taking their promotion of products out of the bank and into the field. Similarly, a construction company needs systems that respond to changing consumer tastes in office and residential buildings, by selecting materials and developing designs in keeping with market demand. In telecommunications, carriers have employed various MIS-based products, such as billing systems, voice/data network connectivity, and automated trouble shooting, to differentiate their services from those of their competitors.

In each of the cases cited above, the greater corporate mission depended for its success upon the support and, indeed, the creativity of information service professionals. To realize these ends, MIS looked to the deployment of new technologies to meet the immediate and long-term business needs of their constituents. Alternatively, information managers showed their operations counterparts more cost-effective ways of performing old tasks. Ultimately, the success of these new products and services depends upon the ability of MIS personnel to deliver timely and accurate information—in either paper or electronic form—to those dealing with the customer. The information services professional responsible for the storage and retrieval of this data is a key player in this process. As we go forward in this volume, it will become clear to the reader that the shaping of records management and other vital MIS functions do not operate in a vacuum. To meet the requirements of the overall strategy, senior management and operations must provide direction, leadership, and motivation. In response, MIS personnel must make informed choices among computer hardware and software options to address the needs of the parent organization.

2. Institutional Structure and the Delivery of MIS Services

For their part, information managers must understand the underlying dynamics of the parent institution's operations. At the same time, they should have a thorough grasp of the organization's structure and how this affects systems planning and development. The reasons for such knowledge should be obvious. Corporate structure defines who creates what type of data and how that information is disseminated throughout the larger entity. It also identifies responsibilities for the maintenance and servicing of data—in either paper or electronic formats. Finally, an institution's reporting lines ought to suggest areas where MIS services may be applied to realize the largest benefit. Thus, if an institution's strategic plans provide the general direction for internal MIS development, its organizational charts serve as the information manager's roadmap.

By way of illustration, I draw the reader's attention to the schematic chart (figure 1). This drawing represents a typical organizational structure and its information service components. It goes without saying that this generic model is for the purposes of our discussion and is not meant to represent any specific company, government agency, or educational institution. However, I am certain that the reader will find at least some similarities between figure 1 and his or her organization's structure. Indeed, when running MIS seminars around the United States, I have found that this model typifies both public- and private-sector institutions. While the titles of officers and the labels of departments may vary from one locale to another, their organizational functions and responsibilities have much in common. Thus, for the purposes of this discussion figure 1 serves well as a focus for our analysis.

Our model begins at the top of the organization, with its chief executive officer (CEO). Below the CEO, a number of boxes represent typical corporate divisions, such as administration and finance, marketing, information systems, and operations. Under each divisional heading, I have listed various departmental functions. The final level of the chart is devoted to the types of information sources and/or data managed by that department. Government agencies differ from this format in that they may not have a marketing division or a sales force. On the other hand, they probably have a customer relations/ compliance unit that provides comparable types of services to the parent organization. Similarly, a college or university may not have "operations" divisions, but *does* run various schools and departments, each with its own "family of products." My point here is to

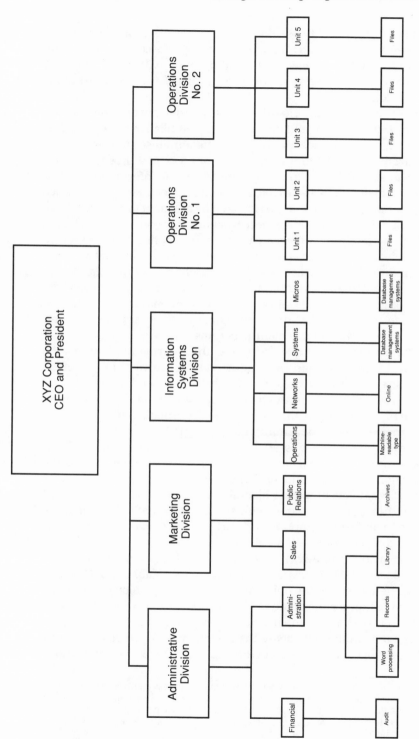

Figure 1. Typical Organizational Structure Highlighting Information Service Components

emphasize the need for senior managers to view their immediate responsibilities in a broader and more generic context. From this perspective, what applies in one setting may, with only minor adjustments, work well elsewhere. This premise lies at the heart of my methodology.

Returning to figure 1, we see that it is not uncommon that the Finance Department maintains audit and compliance records as well as the corporation's accounting files. The administrative arm of the organization often includes such functions as word processing, records management, and the corporate library or information center. Administration might also manage telecommunications services (voice only), although these could just as often be assigned to Network Management within the Information Systems Division. The Marketing Division no doubt maintains a variety of special databases, either on PCs or via the computer center's mainframe system, as well as paper and multimedia files. Occasionally, the archives of the organization are also delegated to Marketing so that the firm's history may be exploited to further sales. Most other corporations run archives programs, to the extent that they have them at all, as adjuncts to their library or records management programs.[22]

The arrangement indicated under the Information Systems (IS) Division heading is typical of traditionally conceived MIS organizations. Here we are speaking of a unit that is responsible for EDP and related activities, and *not* the more broadly defined set of functions described elsewhere in this volume as "information services." The departments within the Information Systems Division therefore include data processing operations; computer output paper and microfilm; network management, which encompasses all data communications functions and perhaps voice communications as well; systems, which encompasses all of the programming, analytical, and support functions associated with the implementation and maintenance of mainframe computer software; and microcomputing, which embraces all corporate PC services.

Within this framework, operations maintains most if not all of the corporation's mainframe-based machine-readable files. Network management oversees the online network through which users pump data into computer information banks and through which their colleagues receive data essential for day-to-day operations. Systems personnel maintain these database management systems (DBMS) as well as DP product and service documentation. Finally, the microcom-

---

22. At least this was the case when my survey of business archives was published in 1983. See Richard M. Kesner, "Automated Records and Techniques in Business Archives: A Survey Report," *American Archivist* 46,1 (1983): 92–95. See also *Directory of Business Archives in the United States and Canada* (Chicago: Society of American Archivists, 1980).

puting group assists users in establishing their own PC systems. Once these microcomputers are in place, users, rather than Information Systems personnel, tend to control the EDP files and computer output so generated. Even if they do not create the data themselves, the IS Division of most large organizations services these areas for users.

Finally, our model includes representative operating units, such as production or processing locations in the case of a manufacturing entity, and servicing regions in the case of a medical facility or government agency. Each Division, in turn, has a number of departments that both create documents on their own and employ the information systems managed by personnel within the Administrative, Marketing, and IS Divisions. One may rightly surmise from this illustration that a great deal of duplication exists between Operation files and those of the support Divisions. On the other hand, this model may wrongly suggest to some that the typical organization will rigorously segregate information servicing functions. On the contrary, here too there is considerable redundancy, fostered by the use of departmental mini- and microcomputers and by differences over corporate turf and priority setting. Indeed, operating units may often fight over "ownership" and access to data rather than work together to make such information widely available to other in-house users.

While strategic planning can root out some of these problems, others are simply endemic to a matrixed approach to information management within a large organization. It is not possible or even desirable to centralize storage and servicing of all corporate data. Though there are undeniable benefits to be gained from access to common databases, this utility does not obviate the need for distributed information systems and the local manipulation of data.[23] Similarly, by permitting wider accessibility—a necessary and positive characteristic of modern MIS systems—one makes local servicing a necessity. Thus, while there may be a corporate records repository, each operating unit may also retain its own records management staff to coordinate document retention and disposition between its Division and the centralized service entity. In larger organizations, it is just as likely that operating areas will, in addition, maintain their own systems analysts, PC specialists, and word processing personnel.

None of this apparent human duplication is wasted if it is managed properly. In some instances, this may mean allowing senior corporate players to go their own way, requiring only that they abide

---

23. I address the issue of distributed processing in Chapter Four of this volume. For a brief introduction to the field, see Bennet P. Lientz, *An Introduction to Distributed Systems* (Reading, Mass.: Addison-Wesley, 1981); James Martin, *Computer Networks and Distributed Processing* (Englewood Cliffs, N.J.: Prentice-Hall, 1981); and C. Bradley Tashenberg, *Design and Implementation of Distributed Processing Systems* (New York: American Management Association, 1984).

by certain EDP standards and cost-justify their decisions. Organizations that run their operating units along entrepreneurial lines are likely to administer the process in this loose fashion. Since the culture of this type of corporation is to run "lean and mean," MIS personnel are often kept to a minimum. Unfortunately, this strategy does not necessarily rule out the possibility of serious errors in judgment when it comes to selecting and implementing information systems, or for that matter products and services based upon poorly conceived and interpreted data. Even in aggressive, fast-paced companies, a strategic approach to these types of decisions will benefit from the systematic' use of MIS resources.

On the other hand, some organizations have gone over to the other extreme and have centralized all information management under a senior corporate player. Often referred to as the "chief information officer" (CIO), this person holds the responsibility for all MIS functions within the organization, including data processing operations, network management, systems and programming, distributed computer systems (i.e. minis and micros), documentation (e.g. audit, word processing, and records management), and information services (e.g., the library, archives or information center). Figure 2 illustrates what a fully integrated Information Systems and Services Division might look like. While this model is merely representational, it reflects a growing trend among organizations of all types and descriptions to put their MIS eggs in a single basket.[24] Certainly, such a structure would—or so it is argued—facilitate standardization, economies of scope and scale, and the often illusive "synergies" of core team productivity.

From my point of view, the CIO model is in many respects more attractive than a free-flowing entrepreneurial approach to MIS planning. Unfortunately, it is not a practical alternative in that corporate information is too important for its control to be entirely centralized. In a real world setting, key users will demand ready access and control over data vital to their operations. For example, active office files must remain close at hand. To these constituents, data processing should provide certain common, basic services. The remainder, at least to my way of thinking, need to be coordinated by some strategic planning committee, but distributed down to the end user. Organizations that have pursued the CIO course have found themselves in this state by default, because key users establish redundant MIS capabilities when "official" MIS services are centralized. As a result,

---

24. For a discussion of the issues, see Fred L. Forman, "Who Should Run IS," *Infosystems* 33,12 (1986): 24–26; Connie Winkler, "Battling for New Roles," *Datamation* 32,20 (1986): 82–88; James F. Collins, Jr., "Climbing the Management Mountain," *Datamation* 33,3 (1987): 75–78; and Janet Crane, "The Changing Role of the DP Manager," *Datamation* 28,1 (1982): 96–108.

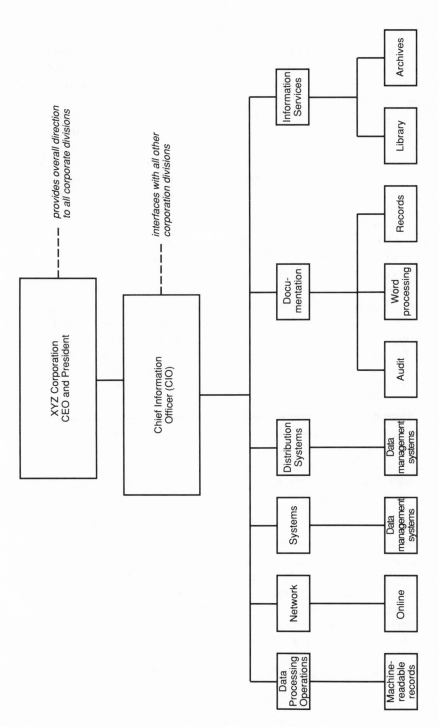

Figure 2.   Typical Structure of an Integrated Information Systems and Services Division

this approach to information resource management may make things less efficient and economical than is currently the case.

Rather than fight the natural instincts of one's own management team, I would recommend a middle course. First of all, MIS personnel must work with the corporate leadership to identify all existing and emerging information services within the corporation. They should then determine those products and services that by their very nature must be centralized and standardized (e.g., voice/data communications). The rest would be spun off to appropriate user departments. Figures 1 and 2 are useful in that the former illustrates the key information resources within the typical organization while the latter suggests a strategy—albeit flawed—for dealing with their management. Each organization will need to structure itself in a manner that best complements its operational and business objectives. I cannot, alas, offer my readers a chart of the ideal MIS structure. None exists.

Instead, I would posit that as part of the planning process, senior management and MIS conduct their own analysis. In performing this assignment, they will be well served to consider the full life cycle of their corporate records, and the product and service requirements of both internal end users and customers. Matrixed MIS services ought to provide the most satisfactory and economical results. Even if the study suggested here is limited to the functions under an existing CIO or Director of MIS, it will assist the organization's information services professionals to better understand where they fit in and how they might best maximize their contribution. With this information in hand, MIS personnel will be in an improved position to support their parent institution's agenda. I will return to this subject in more detail at the close of this chapter. For now, I would like to move on to other aspects of the corporate MIS environment that will influence the development of information services.

3. Information Environment Characteristics and Resources

Since it is framed over an extended period of time (usually five or ten years), the organization's strategic plan will address long-term issues. In turn, these decisions will have a direct bearing on the formation of an MIS strategy. For example, the plan may identify new geographical markets into which information systems will need to extend the parent institution's service delivery system. It may call for acquisitions and/or divestitures that will, in turn, necessitate major system conversions and consolidations. Yet another possibility might involve the offering of new products and services, and possibly the startup of a new corporate subsidiary.

None of these scenarios could come to fruition without a substantial commitment of MIS resources to establish and maintain a responsive information environment for the corporation. Unfortunately, the integrated information services capability so essential for success is not as yet available in most organizations. Instead, one observes a variety of piecemeal efforts that fail to draw upon all available resources. Why is this so? In the first place, senior management has in many instances responded in a highly fragmented manner to environmental and market challenges. Rather than take the broad view of their offerings as related "families" of products, most have focused upon the separate pieces. They therefore lose sight of competitive advantages and synergies to be had from "bundling" what they sell. Second, MIS personnel have concerned themselves with keeping systems current and in compliance with the rapidly changing regulatory and tax environment. In so doing, they have neglected the "sales" component of their own responsibilities to promote greater systems consolidation, standardization, and integration. Finally, individual users have been more concerned with building their own personal working files than in assisting in the construction of commonly employed databases and other information sources.

To correct this situation, senior management must use the strategic planning process to concentrate corporate effort on the long-term administration of coherent product groups. In so doing, they must identify the type of information environment necessary to achieve their goals as well as its associated MIS costs. The benefits of a bundled approach to the selling and cross selling of products and services have been discussed elsewhere.[25] Let it suffice here to say that by viewing interrelated products as a family, development and enhancement issues will be placed in a less fragmented context. At the very least, this arrangement should quicken project turnaround time and improve resource utilization in accordance with corporate objectives. MIS personnel can assist in this process by facilitating the timely and effective exploitation of corporate paper, EDP, and telecommunications resources.

For example, change is now as endemic to many public-and private-sector organizations as stability and uniformity once were. The competitive edge will go to those whose MIS capabilities can promptly seize opportunities as they emerge. Furthermore, in responding to the dynamism of their environment, MIS personnel must be flexible, constantly looking for new ways to perform old tasks. This is a particularly difficult undertaking inasmuch as it forces people to rethink their established work patterns. Since such changes are naturally

---

25. See Phillipe Haspeslagh, "Portfolio Planning—Uses and Limits," *Harvard Business Review* 60,1 (1982): 59–74; and Yoram Wind and Vijay Mahajan, "Designing Product and Business Portfolios," *Harvard Business Review* 59,1 (1981): 155–65.

resisted by even the most sophisticated of workforces, information managers must become promoters of change within their own organizations. To further achieve this end, information service specialists must develop themselves as trainers, communicators, and salespeople in their own right. With these tools in hand, they can begin the arduous process of preparing their colleagues for new work procedures.

The systems installed by MIS must also demonstrate flexibility. Otherwise, when user demands change, MIS will find itself incapable of delivering a competitive product in a timely manner. Beyond this, information systems should also possess the more generic qualities of good computer software—that is, portability, expandability, and "migratability."[26] It should also be well documented and user friendly. Can one find or build such systems? Yes, but at a price. The point to be made here is that the success of the systems—be they manual or automated—will depend to a large extent upon the working relationship between key users and MIS personnel. Only through the more direct involvement of nontechnical management in system specifications, design, and overall functionality definitions can the organization obtain a satisfactory information services end product.

From the user's point of view, the key characteristic that differentiates modern information systems from their paper-based predecessors has to be access. Experienced users have grown to expect online, interactive information facilities. In some instances, this attitude has even permeated the organization's customer base. Nowhere is this perhaps truer than in the banking industry. Here, the customer is no longer content with the receipt of services during regular office hours. Instead, the public now demands access to their accounts and personal financial data twenty-four hours a day, seven days a week. Even corporate customers are increasingly insistent upon the availability of terminals that link the in-house accounting department to their bank's money desk and data center.

As a result of these market pressures, one observes the proliferation of ATM networks, and automated or manually operated "bank-by-phone" services. Large corporate cash management accounts also tend to have direct voice/data links with their banks. In short, enhanced access has become a central theme in the planning and delivery of financial services. Furthermore, this experience is to a greater

---

26. "Portability" refers to the ability of computer software to operate on a variety of compatible computers. "Expandability" is employed in reference to a system's ability to grow as one's data processing needs increase. "Migratability" refers to a system's capability to move easily from older to newer, more sophisticated versions of that product. See Gordon B. Davis, *Management Information Systems: Conceptual Foundations, Structure and Development* (New York: McGraw-Hill, 1978); and B. C. Glasson *EDP System Development Guidelines* (Wellesley, Mass.: QED Information Sciences, 1984).

or lesser degree shared by many other types of operations. For example, major manufacturers have tied their parts suppliers into their inventory control systems, and have in fact added shipment tracking so that they trace vital components from various vendors to their own assembly lines. More generally "just-in-time" (JIT's) inventory systems can reduce operating costs without adversely effecting corporate performance. In some hospitals, medical personnel communicate with a database to check on patient status and to order medications that are in turn drawn from in-house inventories. Even universities are joining this trend by providing high access terminals to faculty and administration so that they may schedule classrooms and other school resources. Similarly, patrons of research library and online database services are now demanding services that are only possible due to the advent of automated retrieval and delivery systems.

It should therefore come as no surprise that these developments have tremendous implications for MIS departments. Information systems personnel must maintain complex, regional, and even international networks that balance data security with freedom of user access. Furthermore, many constituents are no longer satisfied with simply the entré to raw data. They desire value-added products and services that provide them with a comprehensive picture of their operational area and its fiscal performance. More sophisticated users would also like to see prognosticative tools made available to them, as well as telecommunications links to service entities and markets outside those of their parent organization. Institutions that deliver comprehensive, integrated, and highly accessible services will become or remain industry leaders. However, as the tepid response to recent banking-at-home experiments has demonstrated, customers are not always willing to pay for convenience and value-added services.[27] Those who venture forward with information-based products but without sufficient marketing analysis may pay dearly for being at the leading edge of their industry.[28]

---

27. In the late 1970s a number of banks experimented with home banking, but they found that an insufficient number of customers were willing to invest in the microcomputer and hence obtain access to the service. See John F. Fisher, "In-Home Banking Today and Tomorrow," *Journal of Retail Banking* 4,2 (1982): 23–30. See also James Martin, "Banking and Finance," *Viewdata and the Information Society* (Englewood Cliffs, N.J.: Prentice-Hall, 1982): 238–43.

28. For example, Merrill Lynch developed the Cash Management Account (CMA), which bundled some of its typical investment services with more traditional banking services, such as checking and a credit card. The product was quickly imitated. What is noteworthy is that those who followed Merrill into the field learned from the big brokerage firm's mistakes and therefore created more cost effective products. Thus the strategic advantage of the CMA account nearly vanished overnight, to be replaced by a strategic necessity that has adversely affected Merrill's bottom line ever since. The CMA has yet to deliver on its promise as a draw for new investors. Similarly, as their acceptance and use became more widespread, the deployment of ATMs machine moved rapidly from a strategic edge to a burdensome necessity.

To succeed in capturing and retaining market share, organizations must emphasize the services and support that they will provide along with new offerings. In addition, senior management must make a long-term strategic commitment and therefore invest in user acceptance through inventive marketing coupled with systematic customer training. How does one provide all of this enhanced functionality without greatly increasing costs? The answer again lies in intelligently automating operations, in improving overall workflow, and in effectively marketing the value-added nature of newly expanded services. Unfortunately, when introducing new technologies, many managers tend to overlook the steps that must precede automation. In particular, they have not always exerted sufficient pressure to force the adoption of new work procedures. To achieve such changes, senior management should provide its staff with additional encouragement and training. Indeed, senior managers must also become the leading agents of change within the organization, promoting work simplification and the use of new technologies for efficiency, economy, and better sales performance.

Information systems and services personnel can assist in this process by providing the necessary tools. To be truly effective in this regard, MIS must also extend its purview over all information sources within the organization, including individual paper files, the records center or archives holdings, departmental microfilm files, standalone mini- and microcomputer records, and mainframe-based machine-readable records and databases. This is not to say that MIS should control all of these information resources. Rather, to do its job properly, MIS must come to understand the full life cycle of corporate records and its implications for the way work is executed within the organization.[29] Such a comprehensive picture involves the consideration of all company record formats and data entry vehicles, the purposes behind the creation of specific data, the business uses of documents, their storage and preservation requirements, the legal and operational issues governing retention, and the ultimate disposition or elimination of the information. In short, the full range of what I would refer to as the corporate records management function. With this knowledge in hand, the MIS team will be in a position to identify opportunities for paper reduction and labor savings.

---

29. For a more detailed discussion of record life cycle management and its implications for MIS, see William M. Holden, Edie Hedlin, and Thomas E. Weir, Jr., "MARC and Life-Cycle Tracking in the National Archives: Project Final Report," *American Archivist* 49,3 (1986): 305–09; William R. Synnott and William H. Gruber, *Information Resource Management* (New York: Wiley, 1981); and Suzanne L. Gill, *File Management and Information Retrieval Systems* (Littleton, Colo.: Libraries Unlimited, 1981). See also William Benedon, Records Management (New York: Prentice-Hall, 1969), which remains a classic in the field.

From a strictly information systems perspective, this same analysis should provide the foundation for planning software enhancements. For example, if operations personnel are overburdened with the researching and photocopying of customer files, a computerized microfilm retrieval system might prove cost-justifiable. Similarly, automating customer billing, inventory control, distribution management, and even customer inquiry functions may improve performance while reducing overall expense. Such solutions could in fact involve only changes in procedures. Even so, there is an important role for MIS to play in providing the analysis and in assisting in the implementation of any enhancements.

At the same time that MIS is addressing individual corporate requirements, it must also keep in mind the overall architecture of the organization's information systems. The customer often looks to the company for the convenience of services sold as a comprehensive package—so-called bundled services. A student, for example, looks to his or her university for a full education—a degree "package"; patients go to a health maintenance organization (HMO) for all of their medical needs; and an investor signs up with a particular financial institution to manager his or her investments. For that matter, corporate marketing would no doubt prefer to sell its products in a similar fashion. This means that systems integration is essential. To the extent that long-term planning anticipates these requirements, information services personnel can respond quickly and economically by building from a preexisting software base.

The MIS environment, which is established as part of the overall corporate plan, should facilitate that process. It is nevertheless quite common for an institution to fall into the trap of buying a particular product because of price or availability rather than its "fit" within the organization's greater MIS strategy. Home-grown interfaces between disparate systems afford a short-term solution, but these are never happy marriages in the long run. Instead, senior management would be wise to settle upon the systems course that addresses long-term business objectives. In so doing, managers may incur greater initial costs or they may find themselves obliged to delay a product release pending a system delivery. On the other hand, if they have properly prepared their plan, the leadership can at least be assured that individual system decisions will tie correctly into the organization's core mission and make the best use of its resources.

MIS Planning and Resource Management

Faced with momentous changes in the way one manages and conducts one's operations, MIS planning serves a threefold purpose. In the first place, it provides the tools with which the organization can service its constituents, namely, accounting and billing systems, file retrieval and retention systems, customer databases, inventory control systems (JIT's), computer assisted design (CAD) programs, and so forth. Second, MIS allows management to monitor individual worker and overall corporate performance and to redirect resources in response to shifts in the environment or challenges from competitors. Finally, information systems may be employed in the strategic process itself to measure where the corporation has gone and to project where it is headed. Do corporate executives employ their MIS resources—both people and machines—to the fullest possible extent? Perhaps the fairest response to this question is that some senior managers have done a better job than others. In concluding this chapter, I offer the following recommendations as to how corporate leaders and their information management counterparts might make better use of their MIS resources for competitive advantage.

First and foremost, institutions must build bridges between management, operations, and MIS. To achieve this objective, corporations should centralize only those aspects of data processing and MIS that could not possibly operate in a decentralized mode. I would include in this category such areas as mainframe computer operations, network control, large-scale printing, repography, and microfiche production, data security, and DP technical support. Similarly, I would consolidate all activities where there are quantifiable financial and operational benefits. For example, the establishment of a centralized records storage facility might qualify as long as the removal of files from immediate access does not seriously compromise end user performance. These and any other consolidated MIS functions would continue to be accessed by users in ways similar to those already in place. They would constitute the organization's "core" information services. To the extent that workflow, information documentation and dissemination, and records retention and disposition practices are universal within the organization, the management and servicing of these functions should also operate in a centralized manner.

The remaining MIS functions would then be reorganized by product line or family of products and assigned to staff within specific operating entities of the parent organization. Thus, a given institution might have a financial systems team, a communication/publications team, a product design and development team, a products marketing team, and so on. Each unit would report to the operations head for that product area. As so constituted, these MIS subunits might include records, systems, and EDP hardware specialists as appropriate. In suggesting this approach, I assume that the operations manager is not a technologist but is an expert in a particular family of product or service functions. Each MIS subgroup would in effect look to its respective senior user for direction. This person, in turn, would co-ordinate the activities of his or her operations and MIS groups in conjunction with related product areas. Senior management would oversee this process and ensure that the various units work together.

There are many advantages to this approach. In the first place, each MIS subgroup would work directly with users on a day-to-day basis. This arrangement would keep information service profession-als in close touch with customer needs, market conditions, and in-dustry-wide product developments. It would force them to be more responsive and market or revenue driven. More importantly, by in-volving themselves in the actual operating environment, they will more readily identify opportunities for the introduction of promising new EDP and telecommunications technologies into the management of document creation and dissemination.

At the same time, information service personnel would continue to labor alongside the remaining "core" technologists. These inter-actions would be of two basic types. First of all, MIS would need to communicate data handling, hardware, software, and system capac-ity requirements to centralized data processing (DP) and networking so that the core group can build sufficient capabilities to absorb the added work. Second, core DP services would need to communicate standards so that whatever an MIS subgroup plans in response to user directives will fit the corporation's overall information environ-ment. In this regard, the responsibilities of MIS would be matrixed. On the one hand, they would be held accountable by their respective user areas for specific projects. On the other hand, they would con-stantly interface with DP so as to ensure that their systems and hard-ware recommendations are in compliance with corporate standards.

In the aforementioned scenario, senior management makes all of the major strategic decisions concerning the direction of corporate marketing and product offerings. The operational heads, who in turn control their own MIS resources, would then coordinate systems development in line with these directives. Concomitantly, each MIS subgroup would provide the links between operational users, core technologists, and the body of corporate information (in all its forms) that constitute the organization's knowledge base. To make all of this work, one must add a single, yet essential, component: an "advanced technologies" group.[30]

The advanced technologies team would consist of a small group of entrepreneurally oriented core information service professionals and strategic planners. This team would scan developments in in-

---

30. The use of an "advanced technologies" team as part of a corporate strategy to manage MIS planning is exemplified in Ray Hoving, "Air Products and Chemicals, Inc.: The Emerging Technologies Department," *Harvard Business School Case Study 9-185-015* (Boston: Harvard Business School, 1984).

formation science, records management, automation, and telecommunications in search of opportunities. It would review these developments in the context of the institution's strategic plan. When it identifies a match between an organizational objective and an emerging technology, the group would bring this to the attention of senior management. The team would also work directly with the appropriate MIS subgroups to bring particular information management applications to fruition.

In the same vein, the team's mandate would include oversight of operating procedures and the use of existing systems. Perhaps a work management team might be assigned to the technology group to work with operational areas to ensure that the organization streamlines its use of information systems and EDP hardware. The same professionals should also review manual document handling and records management practices with a view toward their reduction or elimination. The advantage of employing the technologies team in this regard is its distance from immediate problems, its lack of commitment toward office traditions, and objectivity. Where the team identifies potential improvements in performance through changes in procedures or enhancements to existing systems, it would work with the MIS team responsible for that particular product or service area.

Because of the territorial issues that will undoubtedly arise from the establishment of a crack team of MIS specialists, the group should report to the organization's senior operations officer. Its recommendations ought then to receive the visibility, attention, and political clout that they need and deserve. It will be this officer's responsibility to ensure that the views of the group reach senior management and surface at the appropriate time(s) in the planning process. Furthermore, it will be his or her assignment to communicate shifts in the corporate mission and business objectives to the technology team. For their part, the CEO and his or her staff must formally acknowledge the significant role of the advanced technologies group in the strategic planning process. This too will enhance the team's credibility and facilitate the success of its efforts.

As I see it, the benefits to any institution of this innovation are twofold. In the first place, such a group provides the organization with a research and development (R&D) capacity hitherto lacking, particularly in the public sector and in most middle-tier service industry companies. If one accepts, as is argued here, that the offerings of these bodies are largely information based, it is necessary and unavoidable that these institutions have some capability to study and apply new technologies as they come on the market. Indeed, the failure to invest in some form of R&D manifests itself in the tardiness of some to adopt and enjoy the benefits of advances in automation.

It also helps to explain why many organizations do not exploit to full advantage the information systems already at their disposal and why they are so slow to upgrade even manual workflow and document handling procedures.

Second, the new technology group can serve as the watchdog of standards and performance efficiencies. A single body must, in my view, oversee the overall architecture of the corporation's information environment and keep it in balance. This is a formidable and yet vital task. It would appear that the advanced technologies group is well suited to this assignment in that its focus is both on the objective review of existing applications and the introduction of new systems capabilities. In saying this, I do not suggest that the group serves as the final arbiter of disputes but, rather, that it identifies the implications of MIS directions for senior management and acts as the champion of effectively administered technological change within the corporation. However, the final decisions in such matters would remain with the company's leadership.

Unfortunately, no amount of computer technology will save a poorly managed organization from failure. While management information systems are necessary for product development, for directing marketing and sales, and for monitoring the performance of the corporation as a whole, they are no replacement for a comprehensive strategic planning process and well focused decision making. Successful institutions must continue to employ such methodologies in realizing their strategic objectives and in employing their information resources for competitive advantage. This final point applies to private sector firms competing in the open market, but it is also salient for not-for-profit organizations that must win and retain constituent support and approval for their services.

In closing, I would only like to reaffirm the paramount importance of investing in MIS planning. As I have indicated, this will require a reallocation of MIS resources and the establishment of a research and development capability. To justify such a move, corporate management must first come to grips with the fact that its products and services need to keep pace with a customer base increasingly familiar with information technologies. It is the expectation of users and their demand for flexibility, speed, convenience, and access that will drive business development in the years ahead. The winners in the marketplace will be those who deliver the best service while remaining cost effective. Information technologies offer some of the answers, but only if managers have the will and capacity to exploit them fully.

CHAPTER
3

Information Systems Typologies

As indicated in the preceding chapter, information delivery systems are essential to the operation of any organization. The institution's culture, structure, and planning processes will determine how these services are deployed and the extensiveness of their funding. In general, corporate leaders recognize the importance of MIS, even if they are at a loss as to how they might maximize its benefits. I, therefore, concluded Chapter Two with a number of strategic recommendations concerning the placement of information service professionals within the larger organization and the definition of MIS's role as it affects the corporation's product and service development. The purpose of Chapter Three is to take this discussion one step further by identifying the nature of MIS responsibilities, management tools, services, and user end products.

To do this, I will first enumerate the key characteristics—from the standpoint of information management—that differentiate public- and private-sector organizations. In this regard, I will briefly summarize their distinct corporate missions as these influence their MIS requirements. Second, I will define and consider the administrative issues associated with the handling of various forms of documentation, including paper files, microfilm, and machine-readable records. Finally, I will review information system typologies that will serve as the basis for further comment on the planning and implementation

of MIS systems in the chapters to follow.

Thus, like Chapter Two, the present section provides the reader with context. While the scope of my subject is vast, I treat it here only schematically. My objective is to facilitate self-analysis of one's work environment and managerial challenges and objectives. I am cursory in the belief that the reader is in an excellent position to complete each scenario with details specific to his or her situation. Within these summary descriptions, information services and records management programs are defined as those functions dealing with creating, identifying, describing, collecting, preserving, and servicing a wide range of raw data and documentary information. The processes employed are often technical and complex. While there may be a role for automation at various levels within this array of activities, one must first understand how these MIS pieces fit together in conjunction with more manual paper handling processes.

With this in mind, I have also fashioned a variety of simple modeling techniques that allow the reader to analyze his or her information services from the standpoint of organizational structure, record type and format, and information delivery system or service. Each of these aspects is then discussed as it relates to more general systems administration. As employed here, the "system" in "information system" refers to those routine procedures that define a specific MIS service or activity. For example, accessioning, retention and disposition schedule preparation, collection description, and research services may be described as "systems" that operate within information center and records management programs. Careful analysis will no doubt lead to much finer levels of distinction. Through this evaluation process, the information service professional identifies daily workflows, as well as how these activities relate to the larger picture. Only after this research is complete will the MIS manager be in a position to proceed with the planning for and implementation of corporate-wide automated information services.

Admittedly, some administrators have integrated computers into their operations without reference to any particular implementation methodology. However, the current economic climate calls for a more rigorous approach to the introduction of automation. Furthermore, if an information services manager wishes to derive the maximum benefit from new technologies, the methods recommended here will prove helpful. These techniques will also aid those program administrators who have no intention—at least in the short term—of relying on computers to assist them in carrying out their responsibilities but who, nevertheless, wish to render their operations more efficient. If executed properly, a critical appraisal of in-house processes will identify those manual systems in need of further rationalization, restructuring, or elimination. By reducing redundant data entry and economizing on forms and labor-intensive procedures, MIS programs as a whole will prove more cost effective and provide better service to the parent organization.

To begin such a study, the information services manager must identify two important factors: the type of organization and the primary constituencies served by the MIS program. Along with this analysis of the larger bureaucratic structure, the information manager must categorize the types of records managed, both in terms of their office of origin and in terms of their physical and intellectual composition. Finally and most fundamentally, the corporation's information service professionals must study those procedures, systems, and operational guidelines that direct employees in their use of paper- and computer-based information tools. In this regard, the greatest challenge to MIS managers—and administrators of corporate resources in general—is getting workers at all levels within the organization to maximize the utility of the tools provided for them to do their jobs. This type of analysis must continue. Furthermore, senior management must encourage a highly critical approach to the work process so that each employee participates in its refinement.

Most DP technologists and more traditionally defined MIS professionals may not actually acknowledge the existence of nonautomated information systems within the scope of their responsibilities. This is a mistake, but it is also an unfortunate reality which this volume seeks in part to correct. For it is undoubtedly the case that paper-based information systems exist and, indeed, flourish in organizations of all kinds and descriptions. The models that comprise the remainder of this chapter will attempt to clarify these systems according to the manner in which information service professionals should approach their work. In so doing, my recommendations provide a common basis for analysis and, if fully exploited, a methodology for the more rigorous integration of manual and automated MIS services.

Institutional Typologies

By their very nature, information services tend to function independently of the primary operations of the parent institution. However, their specific products and systems will (or at least should) depend largely upon the requirements of the greater organization. Under these circumstances, the characteristics of the corporation—bureaucratic, political, and fiscal—as well as the types of documents it generates, dictate the direction and scope of activities within its MIS programs. For the purposes of this discussion, parent institutions may be grouped into four distinct categories: government agencies, educational institutions, not-for-profit organizations, and private sector corporations.

While all of these organizations may have unique information management requirements, they share certain common needs that drive their respective MIS and records programs. For example, they all maintain accounting systems for the administration of their finances and so that their managers may exercise control over specific operations in terms of expense. Similarly, each type of organization requires some kind of performance measurement system to evaluate worker productivity and overall corporate success. They need to communicate among themselves and with outside parties. All organizations therefore have telecommunications, word processing, and filing systems of one kind or another. To the extent that they deal with customer service complaints and inquiries, public relations, marketing and sales, and pure research, these institutions have also developed information service capabilities to perform these functions. Finally, all of these bodies employ some form of data processing activity—be it one microcomputer or a vast, international DP network.

One could therefore argue that many of the MIS issues which confront the modern organization have much in common. The preceding chapter examined some of these similarities. Our purpose here is to look at those qualities that distinguish one type of institution from another. In particular, I will focus upon the organization's view of information creation and exploitation as these processes relate to their overall corporate mission. I do this to draw the reader's attention to the importance of recognizing those unique institutional qualities that will ultimately define and direct the provision of MIS services.

The first of these categories, government agencies, encompasses Federal, state, and local organizations. Though they exercise different responsibilities, governmental institutions have a great deal in common from an information management perspective. As public-sector entities, they are obliged to preserve a considerable portion of their records.[1] Indeed, much of this data is viewed as public property. It should therefore come as no surprise that most of their information management practices is governed by statute, with very specific regulations controlling the retention and disposition of noncurrent files. Thus, access, protection of privacy, and reference services are some of the primary concerns of those who manage government records.[2]

1. See, for example, H. G. Jones, *Local Government Records* (Nashville, Tenn.: American Association for State and Local History, 1980); Donald R. McCoy, *The National Archives: America's Ministry of Documents, 1934–1968* (Chapel Hill, N.C.: University of North Carolina Press, 1978); Michael J. Fox and Kathleen A. McDonough, *Wisconsin Municipal Records Manual* (Madison: State Historical Society of Wisconsin and the Wisconsin Department of Development, 1980); and Committee on the Records of Government, *Report* (Washington, D.C.: Government Printing Office, 1985).

2. Recent Federal legislation in both the United States and Canada has focused on the rights of the public for access to information collected by government agencies. Concomitant concerns over the need to protect the privacy of individuals has also led

Governmental bodies generate a considerable amount of information. They monitor both public and private enterprises, manage a vast array of services, employ (directly or indirectly) approximately one fifth of the total U.S. work force, and conduct research pertaining to matters of public concern. As a corpus of records, government files tend to include the most comprehensive mix of information concerning human activity. Thus, while these records are essential to the conduct of day-to-day business in their originating offices, they also contain much information that is of long-term research value. Through time, these factors have encouraged the evolution of practices that ensure the survival of vital documentation for the dual purpose of public accountability and historical analysis. As a result, government agencies—at least at the Federal and state levels—have developed some common database, archives, and records management programs that meet their diverse legal and informational requirements. They are also the largest group of EDP and telecommunications technology users. Their MIS needs are diverse and complex, and their resulting management problems are similarly considerable.

Though many educational institutions are financed through tax dollars, their responsibilities and needs are different from the perspective of information management, from those of government agencies.[3] First, schools are centers of learning. State laws may govern the management of their official records as they do the files of other public agencies, but for the most part, these institutions are free to operate according to their own self-defined requirements as these relate to the collection of outside information. For example, records management programs are few on college campuses,[4] but archives

to legislation in that area. See Richard J. Bazillion, "Access to Departmental Records, Cabinet Documents, and Ministerial Papers in Canada," *American Archivist* 43,2 (1980): 151–60; Alonzo J. Hamby and Edward Weldson, eds., *Access to the Papers of Recent Public Figures: The New Harmony Conference* (Bloomington, Ind.: American Society for State and Local History, Organization of American Historians, and Society of American Archivists, 1977); Jake V. Th. Knoppers, "Freedom of Information and Privacy," parts 1 and 2, *Records Management Quarterly* 14,4 15,2 (1980, 1981): 28–34, 55–56; Trudy Huskamp Peterson, "After Five Years: An Assessment of the Amended U.S. Freedom of Information Act," *American Archivist* 43,2 (1980): 61–68; and Walter R. Rundell, "Historians, Archivists, and the Privacy Issue," *Georgia Archive* 3,1 (1975): 3–15.

3. See, for example, Nicholas C. Burckel, "The Expanding Role of College and University Archives," *The Midwestern Archivist* 1,1 (1976): 3–15; "Core Mission and Minimum Standards for University Archives in the University of Wisconsin System, "*The Midwestern Archivist* 3,2 (1978): 39–58; and the SAA College and University Professional Affinity Group, *Forms Manual* (Chicago: Society of American Archivists, 1982). See also *College and University Archives: Selected Readings* (Chicago: Society of American Archivists, 1979).

4. As institutions of higher learning struggle to cover their operating costs, university administrators have often viewed expensive and underused archives programs as expendable. At the same time, they have acknowledged the real savings to be gained

programs proliferate, and, in fact, comprise the single largest subgroup within the Society of American Archivists.[5] The emphasis of these bodies is on the preservation of documentary information for research purposes. Faculty and alumni papers, as well as the papers of distinguished persons and significant organizations, therefore complement the administrative records found in most college and university repositories. Collection development is usually based upon some focal point, such as a geographic region, a particular historical theme, or an ethnic or cultural group.

Second, unlike government programs in which the sheer volume of paper records and the need for public accountability tend to control the nature of information management activities, college and university programs roam far afield, selectively gathering materials that fulfill specific research criteria. Ironically, college and university repositories only rarely obtain physical control over all records generated by their parent institutions, even though they may exercise extensive control over the files generated by agencies totally outside their school's administrative structure. As a result, the information management services in educational institutions tend to be highly fragmented, with considerable resources devoted to research collections and much less to administrative and EDP records. MIS professionals must address this imbalance while developing systems which attend to the requirements dictated by the educational institution's mission and scope of activities.

Religious and professional organizations, historical societies, museums, and other not-for-profit institutions possess certain characteristics of both government and collegiate organizations. For example, many state archives began as privately run and endowed historical societies.[6] Some of these programs now function as government entities, while others still remain private philanthropies. In most instances, these archives collect both government (i.e. public)

---

from the introduction of effective records management programs on their campuses. For a theoretical approach to this problem, see Michael Bott and J. A. Edwards, *Records Management in British Universities* (Reading, U.K.: The Library, University of Reading, 1978).

5. While archival programs are making little headway in the corporate sector and have been significantly reduced at both the Federal and state level in government, college and university archives continue to flourish and expand. See College and University Archives Committee, Society of American Archivists, *Directory of College and University Archives in the United States and Canada* (Chicago: Society of American Archivists, 1980).

6. Ernst Posner traces the history and legal status of each state archives and historical society in his *American State Archives* (Chicago: University of Chicago Press, 1964). See also O. Lawrence Burnette, Jr., *Beneath the Footnotes* (Madison: State Historical Society of Wisconsin, 1967) for a comparison of archival programs throughout the United States, and Bruce W. Dearstyne, "Local Historical Records: Programs for Historical Agencies" (American Association for State and Local History Technical Leaflet 121), *History News* 34,11 (1979).

and private papers, encompassing the files of organizations as well as the personal papers of individuals. To simplify administration, public records tend to be housed and serviced separately from private papers, especially since the laws governing use and access vary considerably for these two record categories. Like college and university archives, historical societies tend to emphasis research services, often collecting materials to complement a particular institutional mission. As already indicated, these programs also hold public records and, therefore, the responsibility for servicing these types of materials.

Within many historical societies, it is not uncommon to find not only an archives, but also a library and museum operating in tandem. The archives manages primary source material (i.e., original documentation); the library provides access to secondary book and periodical literature; and the museum serves as the curatorial service for artifacts. If museums have records of their own, they usually relate either to their holdings or to the creators of those holdings. Like the historical society as a whole, its museum component operates around a specific theme or set of themes and serves both as a center for scholarly research and as a place of public education and entertainment.

Other not-for-profit agencies also maintain archives and, at times, records management programs.[7] Though many of these agencies provide research-related services, their functions tend to be more limited than those of educational institutions. In most instances, their primary user constituencies are their own members. For example, the records of professional societies tend to be employed mainly by the administrative staffs of those societies and only infrequently by their respective memberships. Occasionally an independent researcher or a federal auditor may seek access to these files, but this is a rare occurrence. Generally, no laws other than some Internal Revenue Service regulations govern the preservation and accessibility of information stored by these agencies. Therefore the information management procedures of these not-for-profits tend to vary considerably from those of educational and other research-oriented bodies, which by definition maintain more widely accessible documentary information. By contrast, not-for-profit agencies often retain only those records required for administrative purposes. Their MIS services are similarly sparse and often underfunded, except as they relate to the specific needs of their members.

---

7. See Linda J. Henry, "Collecting Policies of Special Subject Repositories," *American Archivist* 43,1 (1980): 57–63 and appropriate citations within the *Directory of Archives and Manuscript Repositories* (Washington, D.C.: National Historical Publications and Records Commission, 1978).

Religious groups are also active in the field of archival administration. Like any organization of similar size, the larger ones have in addition turned to records management to facilitate the most efficient and economical use of their resources.[8] As with most not-for-profit institutions, religious bodies employ these MIS services primarily for internal research, fundraising, and administrative purposes. However, the dimension of historical study is so important to the exercise of faith in some bodies, such as the Church of Latter-Day Saints, that their archives play a much more significant role in the provision of information services to members and constituents. Where religion is closely tied to ethnicity (as it is throughout much of the United States), church archives at times serve as the equivalent of local historical societies, documenting the evolution of the surrounding community. Thus, religious archives tend to be a center for public research, even if access to them is limited to members of a particular faith. They tend, therefore, to develop information services in line with their expanding mission but in keeping with traditions.

The last and potentially most significant category of information system users are found among the private sector.[9] This grouping of organizations ranges from small family and entrepreneurial concerns, with MIS problems similar to those of a small not-for-profit agency, to vast multinational corporations, whose information needs may be compared with those of the federal government. This stands to reason, when one recognizes that in the United States, where much activity remains in the private sector, businesses generate a vast amount of data—albeit largely for internal use. Such entities also spend more than any other group on extensive and highly developed automated MIS systems.

It therefore stands to reason that business corporations command the resources and expertise to act as leaders in the emerging field of information management services. However, the perspective taken within business circles is that information is not only a valuable asset, it is a proprietary one as well. As a result, corporations are usually slow, and at times even resistant, to share developments in their MIS programs with those outside the organization. Furthermore, they tend to invest significant sums in activities, such as records manage-

---

8. Though there are many fine church archivists, few published works are available in this area. See David E. Horn, "A Church Archives: The United Methodist Church in Indiana," *Georgia Archive* 8,2 (1980): 42–53; and August R. Suelflow, *Religious Archives: An Introduction* (Chicago: Society of American Archivists, 1980).

9. See Edie Hedlin, *Business Archives: An Introduction* (Chicago: Society of American Archivists, 1978); and Nicholas C. Burckel, "A Business Records Survey: Procedures and Results," *Georgia Archive* 8,2 (1980): 15–29. For a more extensive list of references, see Karen M. Benedict, ed., *A Select Bibliography on Business Archives and Records Management* (Chicago: Society of American Archivists, 1981).

ment, that not only diminish operating costs and enhance control, but also limit access to information. Only rarely are outsiders given permission to review the contents of business documents. Those files that ultimately survive a rigorous appraisal process are kept away from even curious in-house users. One might say that the MIS policies of most business concerns are governed by a "need to know" principle.

Private-sector organizations are obliged to maintain certain records in compliance with Internal Revenue Service regulations for audit purposes. However, in most instances, these records are destroyed as soon as it is legally permissible. Historical materials are kept for their legal, promotional, artifact, and, occasionally, research value. It is safe to say, though, that businesses generally take a very limited view of what may be of value and show little interest in the preservation of paper records. On the other hand, corporations often have well developed, state-of-the-art data processing capabilities. Their MIS managers tend to emphasize the delivery of current records and their economical storage, coupled with the prompt disposal of non-current files. Not surprisingly, if the service does not relate to and foster their business objectives, few private sector organizations will invest resources in them.

Up to this point, I have reviewed the functional purpose of various organizations and how their respective corporate mission's or areas of responsibility impact their MIS concerns. Figure 3 summarizes my findings thus far. This illustration may also be employed by the reader to position his or her organization within the context of this discussion. My simple matrix includes the four major types of institutions as depicted in this chapter. The horizontal axis distinguishes the office of origin or source of documentation requiring management by information services personnel. Note that the figure differentiates between "archival" records, which refers to the files of organizations other than the parent's, and "manuscript" records, which refers to the private papers of individuals. EDP sources are also included, even though at the present time only a minority of the organizations have effective management programs in place for these types of records.

Government agency programs, for example, concentrate upon the servicing of government records, but state and local agencies also collect organizational and personal papers of relevance to the history of a locale. Colleges and universities, by contrast, tend to service research collections built around a particular theme or purpose. They also manage the papers of their own institution, though these services tend to be deemphasized by MIS management in favor of research collections. Furthermore, if they are funded by tax dollars, university administrative files are technically government records and thus

Document Office of Origin

Type of Parent Institution	Government Records	Parent Institutions	Archival Records	Manuscript Records	EDP Records
Government	p		s	s	h
Educational Institutions	s	p	p	p	g
Not-for-Profit Agencies	s	p			g
Private Sector Corporations		p			h

p=primary record holding or information source
s=secondary record holding or information source
h=high incidence of machine-readable records
g=growing incidence of machine-readable records

Figure 3. Analysis Matrix: Records Holdings by Category of Organization and Document Office of Origin.

bound by laws concerning the disposition and accessibility of these materials.

The records of not-for-profit institutions tend to be more focused but also more diverse. Historical societies that serve as de facto state archives may hold government records. More generally, they, like colleges and universities, collect documents around a particular theme, as well as maintain the papers of their parent organization. Other not-for-profit agencies tend to manage their own records and only occasionally seek outside archives and manuscripts. In the latter case, it will be found that the out-of-house materials are either the records of a regional or local chapter, an affiliated or parallel organization, or the personal papers of a figure significant to the historical development of that agency. Private sector-based information sources tend to be the most diverse and high-technology oriented. While they may be as copious as those generated by government, these records are not administered with the same concerns toward accessibility and accountability.

Figure 3 indicates the variety of institutional settings and user orientations found among MIS programs. As a first step in the process of self-evaluation, the reader should locate his or her institution within this matrix, compare it with the models presented here, and consider the implications of these findings when proceeding to the analysis of information systems that follows. At this point, note that the program's parent organization will often set down certain responsibilities and service requirements which will in turn direct information service professionals in the development of objectives and priorities for their work. This approach necessarily affects any efforts to introduce new EDP and telecommunication technologies as well.

Document Typologies

Beyond the consideration of specific procedures and systems, another dimension in the establishment of information services is the actual record formats and media in which data resides. Despite all the talk about the "paperless office," paper remains the primary medium for recording and preserving information.[10] Though it is true that other media are now playing a larger role and that systems which electronically store and retrieve data are coming into increasing use, they still take a distant second place to paper records. Even so, each record medium and type raises its own problems of storage, preservation, access, and serving. Taken together, they pose a considerable challenge for the information manager concerned with their integration into one common MIS program.

The more traditional paper records include such books as ledgers, letter books, diaries; office files of varying types and descriptions; loose papers, including correspondence, memoranda, notes, diagrams, maps, and drawings; and computer printouts. This list may be incomplete, but it illustrates the diversity of record types in almost any office setting. Furthermore, those readers who have worked as records managers can attest to the fact that recordkeeping practices tend to be highly personalized. It is not uncommon, therefore, to discover different filing systems within the same institution. Uniformity in format, file size, paper size, and so forth is difficult to establish and maintain even in the most cooperative or authoritarian of office environments. This is especially true because most filing

---

10. Certainly, electronic data processing (EDP) has replaced many paper-intensive manual operations, but it has also necessitated the creation of other forms of documentation essential for access to these automated systems. In my view, the pad and pen will remain essential tools in the office for many years to come. See Monroe S. Kuttner, *Managing the Paperwork Pipeline: Achieving Cost-Effective Paperwork and Information Processing* (New York: Wiley, 1978); Nancy MacLellan Edwards and Carmine Shaw, *Office Automation: A Glossary and Guide* (White Plains, N.Y.: Knowledge Industry Publications, 1982); David Barcomb, *Office Automation: A Survey of Tools and Technology* (Bedford, Mass.: Digital Equipment Corp., 1981); S. C. Newton, *Office Automation and Records Management: Report of a Working Party, Society of Archivists* (Sheffield, U.K.: Sheffield City Libraries, 1981); and F. W. Lancaster, *Towards Paperless Information Systems* (New York: Academic Press, 1978).

systems reflect the idiosyncracies of their creators. Nevertheless, a good records management program, especially if it controls forms and office supplies procurement, can restrict the number of options affecting the physical aspects of storage.[11]

However, little more can or probably should be done to routinize and standardize paper-based information organization. Therefore, new MIS systems need to be responsive to individualized data storage and retrieval structures. By its very nature, however, automation has facilitated the rationalization of data capture and presentation by forcing users to rely upon certain standard formats for paper and micrographic output. For example, the vast majority of computer-generated paper records are fourteen-by-eleven inches, with eight-and-one-half-by-eleven inches serving as an increasingly popular alternative. These printouts, along with other textual records, comprise the bulk of most stored and preserved documentation. Unfortunately, the fact that the physical format of these computer printouts does not mix well with traditional office files further complicates records management problems.

Automation affords the user flexibility and ease in terms of data manipulation and access. As digitized document storage becomes more common, the use of paper records will continue to decline and eventually disappear, but this will be a slow, evolutionary process. For example, computers are playing an increasingly important role in the area of finance. The last few decades have witnessed a demonstrable shift by accounting departments away from bound ledgers to computer printouts and, ultimately, to online information systems. The repetitious, formula-driven transactions of the accounting process are very well suited to automation. As this became obvious to programmers in the 1950s, financial software began to appear on the market. Today, thousands of such systems are available. Many are interactive online packages that greatly minimize the need for paper recordkeeping. Though this trend is growing, successfully automated accounting practices will not eliminate the need to preserve vital financial records in some medium, such as microfilm or optical videodisc, for future auditing and research requirements. Furthermore, there will always be times when hardcopies will prove necessary, even if they are ultimately archived in some other format.

In addition to paper documents, traditional audiovisual records raise numerous preservation and servicing problems for records

---

11. A working group within the Association of Records Managers and Administrators, named ELF (Eliminate Legal-Size Files), is organizing the records management profession to support the elimination of legal-size records. Details pertaining to this effort are available through ARMA. See *Project ELF: The 25% Solution to Business Expenses!* (Prairie Village, Kan.: Association of Records Managers and Administrators, 1982).

managers. Photographs and photographic negatives require a special environment to ensure their long-term survival; color slides, maps, and architectural drawings pose even greater conservation problems. As audio and audio-visual equipment comes into wider use, information service professionals will find themselves faced with the challenge of preserving audio recordings and videotapes, which exist in notoriously unstable magnetic formats.[12] Even if the issue of their shelflife is resolved, these document types pose complex information retrieval problems for the MIS team.

Micrographics, which includes aperture cards, microfiche, microfilm, and computer output microfilm (COM), is yet another significant group of document formats. Like audiovisual records, micrographics requires special environmental conditions for storage and viewing equipment for access. Many organizations now employ microfilm as the permanent storage medium for their records. Still others use COM to bypass the generation of hardcopy computer printouts. In terms of space savings and accessibility, microfilm is an economical and reliable storage medium. At least in the private sector, it may soon reach a parity with paper for recordkeeping applications.[13]

The last two media that may concern MIS personnel are magnetic and optical machine-readable records. These record types include magnetic tapes, magnetic hard disks, diskettes of various sizes, and optical, digital videodiscs. Magnetic storage has been with us for some time. In its most common form—magnetic tape—this medium serves as the archives for automated information systems. It is not uncommon for a typical machine-readable records management program to handle two or three generations of backup tapes as part of its responsibilities. Because the data on these tapes is so densely packed and because magnetic media are inherently unstable, they require a considerable degree of maintenance, thorough documentation, and

---

12. The preservation of audio-visual records of all types poses special problems for the records administrator. See, for example, Jerry McWilliams, *The Preservation and Restoration of Sound Recordings* (Nashville: American Association for State and Local History, 1979); Richard Noble, "Archival Preservation of Motion Pictures: A Summary of Current Findings" (American Association for State and Local History Technical Leaflet 126), *History News* 35,4 (1980); Ralph N. Sargent, *Preserving the Moving Image* (Washington, D.C.: Corporation for Public Broadcasting and National Endowment for the Arts, 1974); and Robert A. Weinstein and Larry Booth, *Collection, Use and Care of Historical Photographs* (Nashville: American Association for State and Local History, 1977).

13. The professional literature pertaining to micrographics and records management is considerable. Chapter Seven of this book deals with this special relationship in some detail. For a general introduction to COM, see William Saffady, *Computer-Output Microfilm: Its Library Applications* (Chicago: American Library Association, 1978). For a thorough bibliographic review of the literature, see Richard M. Kesner, *Information Management, Machine-Readable Records, and Administration: An Annotated Bibliography* (Chicago: Society of American Archivists, 1983), 77–88.

careful attention. Data retrieval from magnetic media requires more sophisticated processes and is inherently more difficult than accessing paper and micrographic media, raising a number of complex management issues to be discussed in Chapter Seven of this volume.[14]

By comparison, optical videodiscs are just coming into their own as an information storage medium. Though still too expensive for most organizations, optical disc systems and related image processing technologies are the "hottest" and most promising MIS products on the market at present. I anticipate the widespread use of these devices within the next five years. The stability of data stored on a digital videodisc, as well as the latter's impressive information storage capacity, suggests that highly automated operations will employ this medium for much of their records storage and information retrieval needs. Digital Equipment Corporation and other major computer manufacturers have already offered read/write videodisc systems that operate in conjunction with microcomputers.[15] Though videodisc formats do not at first blush appear as difficult to manage as magnetic media, they will not replace these other sources entirely. Instead, they will become one of many other established formats, including paper, audiovisual, micrographic, and magnetic records, which information service professionals must learn to deal with as part of their broadened responsibilities. As they come into wider use, optical media will raise complex management issues of their own, especially if data retrieval is limited to pre-determined indexing schemes.

The second step in identifying and sizing one's MIS requirements is to catalog all those record media within one's parent organization. To facilitate this process, I have provided a simple analysis matrix

---

14. The stability of magnetic tape as a medium for permanent information storage is somewhat suspect. See, for example, Sidney B. Geller, *Care and Handling of Computer Magnetic Storage Media* (Washington, D.C.: National Bureau of Standards, U.S. Department of Commerce, 1983); Howard P. Lowell, "Preserving Recorded Information," *Records Management Quarterly* 16,2 (1982): 38–42. There is, however, no question about the importance of proper and complete documentation of machine-readable data files if they are to be useful to researchers. See Charles M. Dollar, "Appraising Machine-Readable Records," *American Archivist* 41,4 (1978): 423–30; and Meyer H. Fishbein, *Guidelines for Administering Machine-Readable Archives* (Washington, D.C.: ADP Committee of the International Council on Archives, 1980). See also Meyer H. Fishbein, "The Traditional Archivist and the Appraisal of Machine-Readable Records," *Archives and Machine-Readable Records,* Carolyn L. Geda et al., eds., (Chicago, Ill.: Society of American Archivists, 1980): 56–61; and Margaret L. Hedstrom, *Archives and Manuscripts: Machine-Readable Records* (Chicago, Ill.: Society of American Archivists, 1984).

15. See James Burke, "Optical Archive," *Systems International* 9,12 (1981): 27–30; David Lubar, "Dawn of the Disc," *Creative Computing* 7,1 (1981): 50–54; Dennis Mole, "The Videodisc as a Pilot Project of the Public Archives of Canada," *Videodisc/Videotext* 1,3 (1981): 154–61; and Dick Moberg and Ira M. Laefsky, "Videodiscs and Optical Data Storage," *BYTE* 7,6 (1982): 142–68. For an up-to-date survey, see also David Bearman, *Archival Infomatics Technical Report: Optical Media, Their Implications for Archives and Museums* (Pittsburgh: Archives and Museum Infomatics, 1987).

Document Office of Origin

Type of Parent Institution	Government Records	Parent Institution	Archival Records	Manuscript Records	Data Center
Paper, Bound					
Paper, Files					
Paper, Loose					
Photographs					
Maps, Drawings					
Audio/Visual					
Micrographics					
M-R Magnetic					
M-R CD-ROM					

M-R = Machine Readable Records
CD-ROM = Optical/Video Disk Technologies

Figure 4. Analysis Matrix: Records Holdings by Category of Document Medium and Document Office of Origin.

that the reader should adapt to his or her needs (see figure 4). When employing this tool, place the various types of records by office of origin along the horizontal axis of the matrix. List the record media discussed above along the vertical axis, and then indicate those record types and media that relate directly to your institutional setting. The records manager will, in all likelihood, wish to employ a more detailed listing of offices by department, jurisdiction, or some other appropriate organizational category. Users of this matrix may also wish to differentiate more explicitly between record formats by application.

This simple process will assist the reader in preparing for project planning and implementation as covered in Chapters Five and Six of this volume. Most of all, it will prove useful in terms of establishing criteria for the selection of automated MIS systems. Even for those who do not intend to further automate services at this time, figure 4 provides a checklist. Records management personnel in particular may employ this list to ensure that their services are reaching all in need and that they are equipped and trained to deal with all of the different types of records employed within their organization.

Information Systems Typologies

As the culminating preliminary step to the needs assessment process discussed in Chapter Four, the reader should prepare a list of all those manual and automated information systems services already in place within his or her organization. Some of these functions may fall under the aegis of MIS and others may not. It is nevertheless important to map out all existing information services before approaching the introduction of new technologies. The reasons for this step are twofold. First, the preparation of such a list encourages MIS personnel to appraise their current operations. As part of this process, procedures that are redundant, underutilized, ineffective, or unnecessary may be identified. Even if a certain procedure is not ultimately automated, this period of critical evaluation can help to strengthen and improve existing operations. Second, the survey will focus attention on those areas within the corporate MIS program that are ripe for computerization. By establishing priorities for all manual systems in terms of the need for and ease of mechanization, MIS personnel will facilitate the planning and implementation processes that will evolve from this initial inquiry.

When identifying information systems, the MIS manager needs to think in terms of ongoing procedures, work routines, and daily activities. The models in question should reflect current, and not projected, operations. It is important to compose an accurate and succinct picture of what the MIS program actually does in the course of fulfilling its responsibilities to the parent institution. Each information manager will know best how to describe these operations. No two will be entirely alike. For the purposes of demonstrating various assessment tools, the remainder of this chapter will present a simple model of an integrated MIS and records management program. Information services professionals may then elaborate on and adapt this illustration to meet the needs of their work environments.

In preparing this model, I differentiated between various types of corporate information services by function. To begin, I asked myself this question: What purpose is served by a particular set of services within a given area of responsibility, such as document collection, record storage and retrieval, and reference services? In analyzing one's own shop, the reader should think in terms of the total record life cycle and the role of one's MIS unit in the creation, maintenance, and/or servicing of these information resources. Next, prepare a list of the discrete operations that fall within each of these functions.

For the purposes of my example, I have established seven general categories of MIS activity. They include (1) information resource gathering systems, (2) physical-control systems, (3) intellectual-control systems, (4) user (reference) services systems, (5) access (security) control systems, (6) general administrative systems, and (7) information dissemination (publication production) systems. Each of these functional areas in turn encompasses a subset of MIS-related activities. For the purposes of this discussion, "system" refers to a set of related activities associated with the delivery of a specific MIS service. Thus, all of the functions relating to file retrieval may be succinctly described as part of a reference services system, while the budgeting process falls under general administration and repography falls under information dissemination.

As employed throughout this volume, the terms "collection," "dataset," and "database" refer to logical groupings of information in either paper or machine-readable formats. For example, the records of a government department, the databases of the sales division of a company, the personal files of a chief administrator, or the documents of a strategic planning team might constitute separate datasets or collections of information. It is the management and servicing of these datasets that constitutes the primary focus of the aforementioned MIS systems. By classifying these functions in terms of their operational characteristics, one takes the first major step in the process of institutional needs assessment. Since this particular activity is so important to the success of any information management project, I would like to spend a little more time delving into the nature of my seven information system categories.

To begin, information resource gathering includes all those activities associated with the consolidation of data drawn from various corporate sources, the identification of records for transfer to MIS personnel, the negotiations with the office of origin for that transfer, and the documentation required to establish legal and administrative control over the materials in question. Though this is not always the case, I assume that the MIS management has defined (or the parent organization has defined for management) the scope and criteria for record collection. Once these operating principles are clearly and firmly established, program administrators could then conduct surveys to identify documentation for transferral to the care of the MIS program.[16] Whether the program is concerned solely with data gen-

---

16. The role of surveys in records administration has been admirably handled

erated from within the parent organization or it seeks materials from outside sources, specific procedures must be followed. Each of these key components serves in turn as an object of analysis by MIS personnel, to be streamlined and enhanced as part of the assessment process.

In many instances, information services may establish a resource gathering focus but may not necessarily have the authority to collect. Thus, when the survey uncovers various likely acquisitions, a period of negotiations usually follows, documented by some type of "lead file." This lead file contains pertinent data about the office of origin and any related provenance information, correspondence between the "owner" or creator of the files and MIS personnel, and notes concerning the progress of negotiations. The purpose of the lead file is to document how a particular collection of records came into the possession of MIS and any legal, financial, or operational obligations associated with that transfer.

With the satisfactory conclusion of discussions, the files in question are transferred to information services and the lead file now becomes a "case file." The case file includes the complete lead file as well as the legal documents, such as deeds of gift, bills of sale, and transmittals, that authorize the transfer of materials from the former owner to the record center or MIS unit.[17] When the "transferred" records are in fact a database residing on a computer, negotiations focus more on administrative rather than actual physical control of the information. Nevertheless, it is important to note that many of the related procedures are structured and repetitive, and should therefore lend themselves to automation.

Where appropriate, physical transfer of the records follows the finalization of negotiations between MIS and those whom they service. Here, another set of procedures, pertaining to the physical control of the documentation, takes over. Delivery receipts acknowledge the date, time, and size of the transfer, as well as the personnel involved in initially bringing the records into the records center or in transferring administrative authority for machine-readable files to MIS. Information service personnel would then create an accession

---

by John A. Fleckner, *Archives and Manuscripts: Surveys* (Chicago: Society of American Archivists, 1977). See also Virginia R. Steward, "A Primer on Manuscript Field Work," *The Midwestern Archivist* 1,2 (1976): 3–20. For the process of records retention and disposition schedules, see Suzanne L. Gill, *File Management and Information Retrieval Systems* (Littleton, Colo.: Libraries Unlimited, 1981); and Phyllis M. Lybarger, *Records Retention Scheduling* (Prairie Valley, Kan.: Association of Records Managers and Administrators, 1980).

17. See Richard M. Kesner, "Archival Collection Development: Building a Successful Acquisitions Program," *The Midwestern Archivist* 5,2 (1981): 101–12. See also Trudy Huskamp Peterson, "The Gift and the Deed," *American Archivist* 42,1 (1979): 61–66; and Carolyn A. Wallace, "Archivists and the New Copyright Law," *Georgia Archive* 6,2 (1978): 1–17.

record which would indicate where the collection was placed in storage. Without sufficient and accurate documentation, it is possible that even large collections could be misplaced, resulting in poor service to end users and the waste of MIS resources in reconstructing backup information. Other aspects of physical control are discussed in the retention and disposition (R&D) schedule that accompanies some collections. The R&D schedule indicates record status in terms of "current," "noncurrent," and "archival."[18]

If records are scheduled for noncurrent storage and ultimately for destruction, little else may be done with them by the records center. On the other hand, those files with long-term research or administrative value may proceed through another, more elaborate set of procedures designed to enhance intellectual control. First, the collection or data file may require reorganization, in which case a staff member removes extraneous materials, weeds out duplicates, and arranges the files according to some rational plan.[19] Machine-readable records may in fact be restructured to facilitate their use in ways beyond those intended by the original creator. Such decisions will emerge from the more in-depth appraisal of the information source which takes place at some point during the intellectual control process. All unwanted materials are removed from the collection, and it is prepared for the final stages of processing prior to release to the user community.[20]

---

18. Model retention schedules may be found in the works of Gill and Lybarger (cited in note 16). William Benedon deals with the subject in some detail in *Records Management* (Englewood Cliffs, N.J.: Prentice-Hall, 1969): 29–64, and in "Automated Scheduling/Records Center Operations," *Records Management Quarterly* 14,2 (1980): 18–26. For guidelines and models of retention/disposition schedules, see State and Local Records Committee of the SAA, *Records Retention and Disposition Schedules: A Survey Report* (Chicago: Society of American Archivists, 1977); Association of Records Managers and Administrators, *Records Management Workshop* (Prairie Valley, Kan.: Association of Records Managers and Administrators, 1976), 12–28; and American Bankers Association, *The Retention of Bank Records* (Washington, D.C.: American Bankers Association, 1987).

19. As an established practice, both archivists and records managers tend to process collections while attempting to preserve the arrangement of the files as maintained by the office of origin. More recently, information specialists have come to question the wisdom of this approach, referred to in the profession as "respect of original order" or the rule of "provenance." See Richard H. Lytle, "Intellectual Access to Archives: I. Provenance and Content Indexing Methods of Subject Retrieval," *American Archivist* 43,2 (1980): 191–206.

20. The appraisal process is the most intellectually taxing responsibility of records administration. See, for example, Maynard J. Brichford, *Archives and Manuscripts: Appraisal and Accessioning* (Chicago: Society of American Archivists, 1977): 1–20. Others have complemented Brichford's work with efforts pertaining to specific types of records. See Francis Blouin, "A New Perspective on the Appraisal of Business Records," *American Archivist* 42,3 (1979): 312–20; Meyer H. Fishbein, "A Viewpoint on the Appraisal of National Records," *American Archivist* 33,2 (1970): 175–87; Richard M. Kesner, "Labor Union Grievance Records: An Appraisal Strategy," *Archivaria* 8 (1979): 102–14; and Michael V. Lewellyn, "The Yellow Square of Paper: The Archival Appraisal of Accounting Records," *Georgia Archive* 7,2 (1979): 23–31.

During these last steps, MIS personnel may prepare some type of finding aid that serves to facilitate access to the collection. The end products of these efforts vary widely in comprehensiveness, detail, and format. For example, a simple inventory of file folder headings or of•storage box labels might be prepared. If more detail is required, a collection guide with a cross-referenced index or even a calendar with descriptions at the individual document level would provide additional information. The MIS unit might also employ card catalogs similar to those used in libraries for their book and periodical holdings. Machine-readable records might already come with their own query systems or some other type of computerized information retrieval product. CD-ROM datasets may also come self-indexed. Even so, MIS personnel may be obliged to build on these existing finding aids to render them more useful to a wider constituency.[21]

Once chosen, the mode or modes of intellectual control over collections should be employed uniformly throughout the organization. Files retained in short-term storage do not require the rigorous level of description that one would necessarily employ in preparing research or reference collections. Each institution must therefore develop systems that best suit its needs. However, individualism, if taken too far, will complicate the intra- and interorganization exchange of information. This is particularly true in the public sector, where government agencies must often share data and cooperate in the delivery of services. On the other hand, the widespread use of so-called flat files for the storage of machine-readable data provides a de facto standard, facilitating the exchange of digitized information.[22]

The establishment of intellectual control by MIS over the records and datasets of the parent organization provides the basis for the subsequent development of user or reference services. Since it is the

---

21. The professional literature in this area is quite substantial. See, for example, Society of American Archivists, *Inventories and Registers: A Handbook of Techniques and Examples* (Chicago: Society of American Archivists, 1976); Richard C. Berner, "Toward National Archival Priorities: A Suggested Basis for Discussion," *American Archivist* 45,2 (1982): 164–74; Arie Arad and Lionel Bell, "Archival Description—A General System," *ADPA* 2,3 (1978): 2–9; and M. E. Carroll, "NATIS, an International Information System: Impossible Dream or Attainable Reality?" *American Archivist* 39,3 (1976): 337–41.

22. Modern database software stores data independently from the systems employed in retrieval and data manipulation. While individual data fields are tagged, they can be read by most other systems (hence the "flat file" designation). Under favorable circumstances, one may change data base management systems without rekeying all of the raw data. Unfortunately, mosts DBMS's impose tags on the data that limit the transfer of information and may in fact render the database software dependent. In such instances, the user will need to write a conversion program to move the data from one system to another. See Grayce M. Booth, *The Design of Complex Information Systems* (New York: McGraw-Hill, 1983): 107–234; and Jay-Louise Weldon, "Trade-offs in Data Base Design," *A Practical Guide to Data Base Management*, James Hannan, ed. (Pennsauken, N.J.: Auerbach, 1982).

primary function of information services professionals to deliver relevant data to their corporate managers in a timely and economical fashion, it is not surprising to find that most MIS programs devote substantial resources to this category of services. The specific character of these systems will be dictated by user needs and MIS resources. In general, staff members will provide reference services in the form of manual or computerized retrieval tools, retention and disposition schedules, user handbooks, study guides, and reading lists. Increasingly, senior management is calling upon MIS to provide the actual information, rather than the tools with which the latter might do its own digging. The degree to which any given program gets involved in such services will depend to a large extent upon how it defines its constituency and mission. Furthermore, certain aspects of user (reference) services, especially those entailing human interaction, do not lend themselves to automation. They, nevertheless, remain at the heart of what MIS is all about.[23]

On the other hand, some of the administrative components of reference work are highly repetitive and, therefore, could be computerized. For example, most information centers require the registration of researchers. In records repositories, where the user does not appear in person, a transmittal form is required before files are released to constituents. Through these and similar procedures, the information service professional keeps track of who has obtained access to the materials, as well as the exact location of those records in use. Other, related procedures are in place so as to ensure document security and file integrity.[24] Automated systems may be employed to track file activity and, as necessary, restrict user access. Some of these MIS products also provide statistical data with which records center personnel can better manage staff assignments and anticipate user needs.

For example, researcher registration and the tracking of collection use by constituents tend to be manual, cumbersome, confusing,

---

23. The Society of American Archivists has been particularly active in promoting publications in this area. See Sue E. Holbert, *Archives and Manuscripts: Reference and Access* (Chicago: Society of American Archivists, 1977); Ann E. Pederson and Gail Farr Casterline, *Archives and Manuscripts: Exhibits* (Chicago: Society of American Archivists, 1980); and Carolyn Hoover Sung, *Archives and Manuscripts: Reprography* (Chicago: Society of American Archivists, 1982).

24. Physical security is another issue about which records administrators are particularly sensitive. See Philip P. Mason, "Archival Security: New Solutions to an Old Problem," *American Archivist* 34,4 (1975): 477–92; Timothy Walch, *Archives and Manuscripts: Security* (Chicago: Society of American Archivists, 1977); and Katherine F. Martin, "Security and the Administration of Manuscript Holdings at Southern Academic Libraries, Part I: Administration, Staff and Physical Security," *Georgia Archive* 8,1 (1980): 1–55; and "Security and the Administration of Manuscript Holdings at Southern Academic Libraries, Part II: Security Procedures and the Patron," *Georgia Archive* 8,2 (1980): 61–76.

and largely ineffective processes. More dynamic and intelligent mechanisms of control are required. The computer can provide the management tools necessary to enhance these operations, research trend analysis, and even the analysis of unit service costs. In addition, many organizations now have in place more sophisticated data security products that restrict access to both online systems and machine-readable records stored in the data center's tape library.[25] These tools are programmable and can therefore limit use by specific transactions, user identification number, or data file name. In so doing, these access control systems protect corporate information from unwarranted use, without limiting authorized users from getting at their data. Automation reduces the tedium in these tasks while freeing MIS personnel for more creative assignments.

General administration includes all those routine activities that keep the bureaucratic components of the information services area afloat. These functions include the creation of memoranda, reports, internal and external correspondence, financial statements, and budgets. In addition, many programs maintain mailing lists of collection donors, external sources of information, financial contributors, researchers, and scholars in the field. Some agencies raise their own funds; others are obliged to prepare reports for local, state, or federal government agencies; and almost all produce quarterly or annual reports for their parent institutions. Many of these functions are well suited for computerization, employing word processing, project management, electronic publishing, and/or accounting software.

In addition, MIS units that conduct special projects—either by contract or through a grant from an outside agency—must prepare various documents in compliance with their funding arrangements. For example, if the grant or contract is obtained through a formal application process, this involves the preparation of forms, budget proposals, and execution scenarios. Once the grant is received, its implementation often must comply with specific monitoring and reporting procedures set down by the grantor. At the end of this process, the grantee must prepare a final report that catalogs the accomplishments of the project as an ex post facto justification for the funds already expended.[26] The recipient MIS or records center man-

---

25. In this age of online data processing systems, data security has become a hot topic and a big industry. Both DataPro (McGraw-Hill) and Auerbach offer excellent loose-leaf publications on data security management. Other typical publications include R. C. Summers, "An Overview of Computer Security," *IBM Systems Journal* 23,4 (1984): 309–25; and Robert P. Campell, et al., *A Framework for Data Security* (Rolling Meadows, Ill.: Bank Administration Institute, 1985). Most EDP trade journals, such as *Datamation* and *InfoSystems*, also carry regular articles on the subject.

26. See William T. Alderson, "Securing Grant Support: Effective Planning and Preparation" (American Association for State and Local History Technical Leaflet 62), *History News* 27,12 (1972); Larry J. Hackman, "Introductory Bibilography: Fundraising

ager must ensure that his or her office carefully observes all provisions of the agreement. Since each step in this process is highly standardized, grants administration lends itself to automated tracking and management.

Finally, many information service and records management programs occasionally need to produce publications of their own. These works might be finding aids, directories of services, newsletters, brochures, user handbooks, booklets, full monographs, news releases, or posters. Some are planned for internal consumption, while others are expressly designed to impress, draw attention, and win financial or political support from outside sources. Like routine correspondence, many of these publications can be produced in-house with the benefit of word processing, desktop publishing, and computerized photocomposition tools.

MIS Systems and Services Matrix

The preceding commentary on information services functions is by no means comprehensive. It seeks only to illustrate a method for viewing MIS product typologies. All information service units—be they associated with private- or public-sector organizations—provide these and a great many other things to their user constituencies. As the reader has observed, these services range from data collection to its control and description, to its processing and delivery. Some of these activities are labor intensive, requiring a human interface, while others may be readily automated. To conclude this chapter, I offer the following management tool to assist information services professionals as they evaluate the nature and relative importance of specific MIS functions in terms of resource consumption and overall corporate planning.

Figure 5 suggests a methodology for the grouping and description of various MIS and records administration functions. It will serve as a useful self-analysis tool. However, I would also caution that figure 5, like all of the other examples presented in this work, is meant only as an illustration. It must be adapted to the specific needs of one's MIS program.

To begin, this evaluation matrix should list all of those major groups of activities currently offered by your program. Estimate the percentage of management and staff time devoted to each set of functions. Where appropriate, provide greater detail as to the sub-

---

for Archivists," *Society of American Archivists Newsletter* (May, 1978), 6–7; and Hedy A. Hartman, comp., *Funding Sources and Technical Assistance for Museums and Historical Agencies: A Guide to Public Programs* (Nashville: American Association for State and Local History, 1979).

Systems and Subsystems	Resource Allocations	% MIS Manager's Time	% Staff Time	Labor-Related Costs	Material Costs	Over-head Costs	Total Costs	Priority Ranking
Information Resource Gathering								
Record Surveys								
Lead File Maintenance								
Case File Maintenance								
Physical Control								
Accessioning								
R&D Scheduling								
Intellectual Control								
Reorganization								

Figure 5. Analysis Matrix: MIS Systems by Resource Allocation.

Systems and Subsystems	Resource Allocations	% MIS Manager's Time	% Staff Time	Labor-Related Costs	Material Costs	Over-head Costs	Total Costs	Priority Ranking
Appraisal								
Final Processing								
Description								
User/Reference Services								
User Services								
Reference Tools								
Research								
Access Control								
Physical Security								

Figure 5. (Cont.)

Systems and Subsystems	Resource Allocations	% MIS Manager's Time	% Staff Time	Labor-Related Costs	Material Costs	Over-head Costs	Total Costs	Priority Ranking
Data Security								
General Administration								
Word Processing								
Financial Administration								
Grants Administration								
Communications								
Publication Planning								
Publication Production								

Figure 5. (Cont.)

ordinate services within each activity grouping. Next, assign dollar amounts for staff time, materials, and overhead. Finally, prioritize these products and services as they relate to the strategic plan and business objectives of your parent organization. These priorities ought to correspond with those of your own program. However, if your strategies are at variance with those of your parent organization, you may wish to add an "in-house" priorities column to my matrix. Senior MIS management will need to address these differences. For the purposes of needs assessment, it is necessary at this point to note discrepancies in priorities and resource allocations.

Once completed, this matrix will indicate in the sharpest possible terms how your unit's resources are distributed. It will also point out those areas in need of further attention and development, and perhaps suggest where activities might be curtailed in an effort to reduce expenditures or reallocate scarce funds and staff-hours. More important, it will put into focus any disparities that may exist between your operational objectives and the overall corporate mission of your parent organization. If your information management services complement your institution's strategic planning process, you should find that your resource allocations and your priorities complement one another. If this is not the case, it should raise a number of questions that require resolution.

In the first place, are you aware of the goals and objectives of your parent organization? Have you developed your own planning to reflect this corporate purpose and to foster its realization? Do you balance your resource limitations against the expressed needs of your constituents? Do you, in fact, know what your users require by way of MIS products and services? Finally, are you working toward a situation whereby MIS maintains programs in keeping with those of the larger organization, and is therefore positioned so as to respond quickly to changing organizational requirements?

Perhaps, figure 5 will raise more questions in the mind of the typical MIS manager than it can possibly answer. This is all for the good. In subsequent sections of this book, I will build upon the model presented here to analyze MIS operations in greater detail. My purpose is not just to question present practices but to identify future opportunities. While certain labor-intensive capabilities, such as user services, may not prove adaptable to automated solutions, other functions may be computerized, freeing resources for reallocation where they are most needed. The procedures recommended here prepare the ground for making these types of management decision. By first understanding the extent to which these capabilities draw upon the unit's human and financial resources, one has taken a major step toward designing automated systems to enhance MIS performance.

With this observation, I complete the pre-planning stage of my approach to the strategic management of MIS. These procedures prepare the way for the planning and implementation methodologies which appear in Chapters Five and Six respectively. To obtain the greatest benefit from these sections, I suggest that the reader develop the aforementioned pre-planning matrices as they apply to his or her organization. As a next step, it is necessary that I review the nature of electronic data processing and, hence, the EDP options that lie open to the information services professional in planning for automated MIS solutions.

CHAPTER
4

EDP Options

Change is endemic to modern society and certainly to corporate operations. Nowhere is this characteristic more evident than in the areas of electronic data processing (EDP) and telecommunications. Industry watchers have speculated that, by the end of the century, a majority of the workforce in the industrialized West will be occupied with some aspect of computer- or information-related production and services. While all of this dynamism bodes well for those knowledgeable in EDP and voice/data technologies, these same forces raise major challenges for the general manager. Even those with information systems and service responsibilities must develop a greater sensitivity and awareness. In particular, they will need to recognize how their work is influenced by these environmental factors.

In saying this, I do not mean to suggest that all managers must become technologists to prosper. Given the scope of activities that encompass computers, and voice/data communications, this is not even a reasonable objective. On the other hand, each and every manager needs to be cognizant of the EDP and MIS resources at his or her disposal, the range of choices within each DP category, their relative costs, and the skill base required to maximize their benefit to corporate operations. At the very least, administrators ought to become more aware of how they might exploit the talents of their MIS staff. Concomitantly, it is the responsibility of an organization's information service professionals to ensure that senior management receives the support it needs. Furthermore, it ought to be the charge of MIS personnel to identify the potential benefits of new technologies and to bring these to the attention of their organization's leadership.

This is a formidable assignment, especially to those inexperienced in the use of data processing and telecommunications equipment (hardware) and information systems (software). Assuming that the reader is not an expert in these fields, where does he or she turn for the broad base of general knowledge required to achieve satisfactory results? Fortunately, there are many formal and informal training paths that one might choose. As a minimum requirement, users must act as educated consumers; they must become computer literate. Beyond that, they should be familiar with the disciplines of good management, namely, the ability to successfully plan and implement complex projects, and the willingness to recast existing operations and procedures so as to take advantage of new information technologies.

To become more aware of the latest developments in EDP and telecommunications, one may turn to any number of readily available educational sources. For example, the "explosion" in new hardware and software products has also prompted the creation of periodicals, training manuals, and a wealth of monographs that address user needs.[1] However, simply to be well informed may not suffice. The swiftness of change in the computer industry has exacerbated the efforts of many corporate leaders in their attempts to arrive at judicious choices among numerous options. Thus, though an organization's management team may be committed to the role of automation in achieving operational improvements, it may not know where to turn for assistance. If the past is any indication of the future, these problems are not likely to diminish over time. As a result, both short- and long-term MIS planning will prove increasingly important to the success of information managers and those whom they serve.

---

1. A number of publishers, including McGraw-Hill's Datapro Research Division, produce monthly looseleaf services that provide timely and informative data on activities within the computer, telecommunications, and information management industries. The Datapro publications, for example, fall into two general categories: directories, which are compilations of product reviews and analyses, and management or solution reports, which focus upon problem solving, and planning and implementation scenarios. The subject areas are broad, as evidenced by Datapro publication titles, which include: *Electronic Data Processing, Office Systems, Communications, Data Communications, Microcomputer Software, Automated Office, and Management of Small Computer Systems.* The market for up-to-date information on the availability of computer hardware and software products has grown so rapidly in the last few years that bibliographic utilities are now starting to sell similar product information in an online format. Also, the following periodicals collect and abstract works relating to EDP and telecommunications: *ACM (Association of Computer Machinery) Guide to Computing Literature, Computerworld, International Computer Bibliography, New Literature on Automation,* and the *Quarterly Bibliography of Computers and Data Processing.*

While no single tool can possibly address all of the issues associated with the identification and selection of EDP products, this chapter attempts to provide an overview of options. For the uninitiated, it serves as an introduction, defining the generic categories of hardware and software commonly associated with technology-based MIS systems. For the experienced administrator or MIS professional, it suggests management strategies that recognize and maximize the benefits of existing corporate DP resources. Indeed, it may be argued that few executives fully exploit their in-house capabilities. It is the responsibility of the corporation's information service professionals to search for these untapped capacities and to match them with problems requiring MIS solutions.

By way of introduction, this chapter looks into the various hardware components of typical computer systems, how they are linked together, and their respective roles in providing information services to end users. Similarly, the software section reviews the general categories of computer programs available for off-the-shelf purchase. After summarizing the equipment and programming options available to MIS administrators, I conclude this chapter with a brief consideration of system costs and some of the financial and administrative problems related to obtaining in-house computer services. My approach is management oriented and strategic. I therefore purposely avoid references to specific computer products. The reader will need to modify my recommendations to reflect the unique requirements of his or her organization and its DP environment. The ultimate choice of EDP components will very much depend on the job at hand. All I attempt to provide is assistance with the selection process.

Hardware

At the heart of every computer system is its "brain," commonly referred to as the "central processing unit" (CPU). The CPU is the workhorse that many may associate with the term "computer." However, the CPU does not function alone. Users need to communicate with the CPU and the CPU needs to respond. Though it possesses an enormous electronic "scratch pad" capable of executing numerous mathematical and textual manipulations at high speeds, the CPU needs access to external data storage facilities and other pieces of data processing hardware to produce any useful end product. Together, these electronic devices comprise what is commonly referred to as electronic data processing systems.

For example, most large computer systems communicate with remote user nodes or even other computers located at a distance.

Some type of telecommunications facility is required to accomplish these tasks. Thus, when viewed in its totality, a computer consists of a CPU linked with user communication (input) devices, computer communication (output) devices, external data storage (add-on memory) devices, and remote communication (e.g., modems or microwave antennas) devices. As a group, these machines are described as computer "peripherals," because they allow the CPU to do its job without actually involving themselves directly in the manipulation of data.

The link between a peripheral and a CPU is referred to as an "interface." It usually entails both additional hardware and specialized software. In some instances, an interface includes printed circuit cards in the CPU that are tied through computer cable directly to similar boards in a peripheral. Other circumstances might require the use of an intermediate device, such as a controller unit, that will route traffic to and from various pieces of external equipment to the central processing unit. In addition to the hardware, all system interfaces require computer programs to provide the communications links for interfacing DP products. The number of possible combinations in configuring a given computer system is for all practical purposes unlimited. The challenge for the manager of such facilities is to devise an economical and efficient approach to his or her use of available hardware components.

The CPU

A few remarks about central processing unit operations may help to dispel some of the mysticism surrounding how computers actually work. While industry experts may at times refer to "intelligent machines," computers really understand only two things: on and off. The positive flow of electricity is indicated in EDP terminology by "1," and its absence by "0." The ones and zeros of computer communications are called "bits." The use of these alpha-numeric symbols is also referred to as "digitized" or "binary" communications. Groups of seven or eight ones and zeros together form "bytes," which are in turn the single smallest unit of machine language that conforms with human language.[2] The two universal computer coding struc-

---

2. Computer languages are categorized in terms of their proximity to human language, usually English. Higher-level languages are those approximating English, and of these, BASIC and PASCAL are currently the most widely used. Older languages that fall into this category include FORTRAN, employed primarily for "number crunching" and scientific software, and COBOL, the predominant language used in the design of business software. Assembler languages are more primitive than FORTRAN and the rest, while machine language is the binary form of communication understood by the computer. Since the computer must ultimately convert whatever language is employed to machine language before it can respond, the closer the user is to programming in

tures are the American Standard Code for Information Interchange (ASCII) and the Extended Binary Coded Decimal Interchange Code (EBCDIC). The latter code was pioneered by IBM and runs primarily on IBM machines or the computers of so-called IBM plug-compatible vendors. Figure 6 lists both the ASCII and EBCDIC codes and their alpha-numeric equivalents.

The CPU takes instructions and data entered by the user from some higher-level language and converts it into bits and bytes for machine manipulation.[3] Conversely, once the computer has completed its work, it converts the code from ones and zeros to alpha-numeric characters for communication with the user. A discussion of the capabilities of a computer often refers to the "word size" handled by the CPU. This is the size of the smallest unit managed by the machine during data processing. Thus, an eight-bit processor handles eight bits at a time, a thirty-two-bit machine handles thirty-two bits, and so on. Generally, the larger the word length employed by a computer, the greater its capabilities, computing power, speed, and cost. Most information service professionals need not concern themselves with all this technical detail. On the other hand, they must possess sufficient knowledge to select peripherals and software that are compatible with their computer system's CPU. For example, a program designed for a 32-bit CPU will not run on a 16-bit processor. In this instance, an understanding of hardware allows the user to limit the selection process to equipment that will work with the application.

Any given computer CPU may be categorized as one of three basic types of device, namely, a mainframe, a minicomputer, or a microcomputer. Each is distinguished from the others by its size, cost, computing power, and speed. Prior to the advent of the microprocessor, all computers were large, expensive mainframes that required special energy sources and environmental conditions to operate properly. Currently, these machines are used in institutions that handle many millions of transactions on a daily basis. For example, banks, insurance companies, government agencies, university research centers, and airlines require the services of mainframe com-

---

machine language, the faster programs will run. Unfortunately, it is very easy to make errors when programming in lower-level languages and most difficult to uncover mistakes once they are made. For a thorough introduction of this subject, see Clement L. McGowan and John R. Kelly, *Structural Programming Techniques* (New York: Mason/ Charter, 1975).

3. For a state-of-the-art review of available computer systems, see *ACM Computing Surveys*, which is the Association of Computing Machinery quarterly devoted to industry-wide surveys of CPUs. See also *Business Automation Reference Service: Computer Equipment, Datapro EDP Solutions*, and *The Computer Directory and Buyer's Guide* (Newtonville, Mass.: Berkeley Enterprises, published annually). Another helpful tool in this regard is Darlene Myers, *Computer Science Resources: A Guide to Professional Literature* (White Plains, N.Y.: Knowledge Industry, 1981).

Alpha-Numeric Value	ASCII Equivalent	EBCDIC Equivalent	Alpha-Numeric Value	ASCII Equivalent	EBCDIC Equivalent
A	01000001	11000001	a	01100001	10000001
B	01000010	11000010	b	01100010	10000010
C	01000011	11000011	c	01100011	10000011
D	01000100	11000100	d	01100100	10000100
E	01000101	11000101	e	01100101	10000101
F	01000110	11000110	f	01100110	10000110
G	01000111	11000111	g	01100111	10000111
H	01001000	11001000	h	01101000	10001000
I	01001001	11001001	i	01101001	10001001
J	01001010	11010001	j	01101010	10010001
K	01001011	11010010	k	01101011	10010010
L	01001100	11010011	l	01101100	10010011
M	01001101	11010100	m	01101101	10010100
N	01001110	11010101	n	01101110	10010101
O	01001111	11010110	o	01101111	10010110
P	01010000	11010111	p	01110000	10010111
Q	01010001	11011000	q	01110001	10011000
R	01010010	11011001	r	01110010	10011001
S	01010011	11100010	s	01110011	10100010
T	01010100	11100011	t	01110100	10100011
U	01010101	11100100	u	01110101	10100100
V	01010110	11100101	v	01110110	10100101
W	01010111	11100110	w	01110111	10110110
X	01011000	11100111	x	01111000	10100111
Y	01011001	11101000	y	01111001	10101000
Z	01011010	11101001	z	01111010	10101001
0	00110000	11110000			
1	00110001	11110001			
2	00110010	11110010			
3	00110011	11110011			
4	00110100	11110100			
5	00110101	11110101			
6	00110110	11110110			
7	00110111	11110111			
8	00111000	11111000			
9	00111001	11111001			

Figure 6. Human-Language Alpha-Numeric Symbols and Their ASCII and EBCDIC Equivalents.

puters because they must rapidly process enormous quantities of information and support large networks of users. Even in-house local area networks (LANs) that involve many hundreds or thousands of terminals are not unusual. The processing power of a mainframe computer is essential for these types of applications.

Mini- and microcomputers, by contrast, are generally much smaller and, in most instances, do not require specially maintained environments for operation. They are also slower and can handle fewer users simultaneously.[4] For example, while a mainframe might execute ten million instructions (i.e., transactions) per second (10 MIPS), minicomputer productivity is measured in the thousands and microcomputer output in the hundreds. While a mini might be able to support ten, twenty, or even one hundred workstations, most micros can rarely support more than one user or task at a time. Only recently has this situation changed. The latest generation of micros runs on "32-bit" chips that support a multiple-user operating system.[5] Even so, these LANs are limited to the network of three to twelve personal computers (PCs) at a time.

The reader should bear in mind that the aforementioned situation is by no means static. The distinctions between the processing power of mainframes, minis, and micros are becoming less clear all the time. Today's advanced PCs can perform many of the tasks associated exclusively with large computer systems just a few years ago. For that matter, many of the machines produced under a common label, such as those of IBM or DEC, have the same type of CPU. They are purposely designed in the manner to promote their "integrative" capabilities. Where this characteristic has been successfully implemented, mainframe, mini, and microcomputer CPUs run the same applications programs under similar, if not identical, operating systems environments.

In terms of cost, mainframe CPUs run from one million dollars each to ten or more times that amount. The cost of most minicomputers ranges from thirty to five hundred thousand dollars. Microcomputers can cost as little as one hundred dollars or as much as five or ten thousand dollars. The expense of peripherals, system support, and overall maintenance for each type of CPU more or less corresponds in magnitude to that of the purchase price of the unit. In general, the unit costs for computer hardware have plummeted over the past decade and are likely to continue to decline, although not as dramatically. However, in the future, management will find that the expenses associated with the purchase of EDP systems will

---

4. The technical aspects of microprocessor operations as they influence the evolution of mini- and microcomputer systems are covered in Charles J. Sippl, *Microcomputer Handbook* (New York: Petrocelli, 1977); Robert Allen Bonelli, *The Executive's Handbook of Minicomputers* (New York: Petrocelli, 1978); William Barden, Jr., *Guidebook to Small Computers* (Indianapolis: Howard W. Sams, 1980); and Peter Large, *The Microcomputer Revolution Revisited* (Totowa, N.J.: Rowman & Allanheld, 1984).

5. For an interesting consideration of what new microprocessor applications are in various stages of development, see John G. Posa, "Superchips Face Design Challenge: Computer-based Tools May Help Users Configure Single-Chip Systems," *High Technology* 3,1 (1983): 34–42. See also Stevanne Ruth Lehrman, *Local Area Networks with Microcomputers: A Guide for the Business Decision Maker* (New York: Prentice Hall, 1986); and V. E. Cheong and R. A. Hirshheim, *Local Area Networks: Issues, Products, and Development* (New York: Wiley-Interscience, 1983).

grow because of the number of users who must tie into networks and because of the demands by these users for a broader range of support services and DP capabilities. As a result, MIS will be obliged to purchase more peripherals, PCs and voice/data networking equipment, even as the cost of CPUs drifts downward. The ongoing expense of training will also expand rapidly.

On the other hand, users' dependence on centralized computer facilities for their information management requirements will continue to decline. Just a few years ago, the mainframe computer was the only EDP solution available. The costs of maintaining these facilities and guaranteeing the most efficient use of their resources necessitated the centralization of DP services. As a result, many computer centers dictated their own terms to users, and work schedules did not necessarily correspond with the wishes of those who relied upon the center for their MIS needs. Since records management programs, libraries, and archives have traditionally held positions of low priority within most institutions, it is not surprising that the timely delivery of services to these MIS consumers was more the exception than the rule.

All of this changed, however, with the emergence of small computers. Advances in microprocessor design led to economical and yet powerful machines well suited to "dedicated" functions.[6] Since these new generations of computers did not require special environments to operate properly, and because they were specifically designed with the non-data processing professional in mind, they were appropriate for installation in user locations. As a result, computing experienced and continues to experience a trend toward decentralization, in which a machine is matched with a specific set of tasks. This movement toward "distributed processing," as it is called, has had a profound effect on information service professionals.[7] With

---

6. One may cite any number of examples in which large information service consumers, such as libraries, have moved away from mainframe environments because these services did not respond to their needs. See Association of Research Libraries, Office of Management Studies, *The Use of Small Computers in ARL Libraries* (Washington, D.C.: Association of Research Libraries, 1981); Richard W. Boss, *The Library Manager's Guide to Automation* (White Plains, N.Y.: Knowledge Industry, 1979); and Richard M. Kesner, "The Computer and the Library Environment: The Case for Microcomputers," *Journal of Library Administration* 3,2 (1982): 33–50. See also Tom Fox, "Business Systems for '82," *Interface Age* 7,1 (1982): 74–93; E.J. Kazlauskas and T.D. Holt, "The Application of a Minicomputer to Thesaurus Construction," *Journal of ASIS* 31,5 (1980): 363–68; and Gregory A. Marks, "Implications for Archives of Computer Hardware Advances," *Archives and Machine-Readable Records*, Carolyn L. Geda, et al., eds., (Chicago: Society of American Archivists, 1980): 149–57.

7. For a thorough consideration of the theory and practice of distributed processing, see Judson Breslin and C. Bradley Tashenberg, *Distributed Processing Systems: End of the Mainframe Era?* (New York: AMACOM, 1978); Robert W. Shirey, "Management and Distributed Processing," Parts 1–4, *Computerworld* (In Depth), 14,41–44 (1980): 1–20, 1–8, 1–20, 1–16; Bennet P. Lientz, *An Introduction to Distributed Systems* (Reading,

the advent of minis and micros, such operating units as records centers may now establish their independence from centralized DP facilities and can tailor their equipment and programming acquisitions to more accurately reflect their unique information management requirements.

Nevertheless, there continues to be an important place for mainframe computers in MIS services. In the first place, small computers may not be available to information managers. Instead, they will be obliged to turn to their parent institution's central computer facility for their data processing needs. Furthermore, large operations, such as major libraries, research centers, and records management operations, may need the computing power that only a mainframe can deliver. For that matter, neither micros nor minis are capable of supporting far-flung online user networks. Thus, any type of national or international information system with multiple user nodes will inevitably rely upon mainframe computers to provide network-related services. In point of fact, most MIS programs employ both small and large computer systems as part of their overall information management strategy.

Chapter Five, which deals with needs assessment and the MIS planning process, will suggest a methodology for determining which CPU best fits a particular institutional setting. For the moment, it is only necessary to state that the ultimate selection of a CPU will rest upon a number of different factors considered in combination. For some of my readers, the selection has already been made. They must employ the data processing facilities of the parent institution. Still other corporate users may choose to integrate distributed and mainframe-based data processing. With all of these options at their disposal, the challenge has become one of making the most appropriate choice for a given setting and set of resource limitations.

Computer System Peripherals

To communicate with the CPU, an input device is required. During the mainframe era, computers processed information in a batch mode, whereby tasks are grouped and processed independently of data entry. The user communicated instructions and data to the CPU via punch cards or paper tape and the appropriate input device reader. Both the keypunch (card) and paper tape machines resembled oversized electric typewriters. Almost no systems employing cards and

Mass.: Addison-Wesley Publishing, 1981); C. Bradley Tashenberg, *Design and Implementation of Distributed Processing Systems* (New York: American Management Association, 1984); and James H. Green, *Local Area Networks: A User's Guide for Business Professionals* (Glenview, Ill.: Scott, Foresman, 1985).

paper tapes for input remain in operation today, cathode-ray tube terminals (CRTs) are now the most widely used data entry device. These machines, which include television monitors with attached typewriter-like keyboards, may include tiny CPUs of their own that communicate directly with the computer via some interface, such as a controller unit.[8] So-called standalone systems (i.e., microcomputers) often have a CRT built into the same housing as the CPU itself.

Modern computer facilities tend to maintain a batch operating mode for some information systems and an online interactive environment for others. During batch processing, user tasks are placed in a queue and treated by the computer as part of a continuous job stream, whereas online environments allow the user to interact with the computer more or less conversationally. These interactive operating modes are found in all micro- and most minicomputer systems. Batching, on the other hand, is the almost exclusive reserve of mainframe systems. Whatever the CPU, the selection of input devices and other peripherals must comply with its operating standards. These are usually set by the manufacturer as part of the marketing strategy for that computer configuration. In most instances no problems will arise since this equipment is obtained via the data center, whose personnel will observe all necessary standards. As standalone products, micros and minis do not pose such problems. One normally purchases a compatible configuration all at once, and the choice of input devices is more restricted from the outset.

Most computer applications necessitate large amounts of data entry. For example, a company will load in all of its financial transactions prior to generating an end-of-the-year accounting report. Sales applications require the entry of product and customer information. Libraries and bibliographic services retain vast bodies of data on book and periodical publications. Even utility services must store vast amounts of data so that they may produce accurate and timely bills for their consumers. Since data entry is costly and time consuming, computer systems provide for the mass storage of information. These storage devices include magnetic tape, hard disk and floppy diskette drives, and optical videodiscs.[9] Though these technologies differ from

8. Tony Webster, *Terminals and Printers: Buyers Guide* (New York: McGraw-Hill, 1984).

9. See Richard A. Voltz, "Computer-based Mass Storage Technology," *Archives and Machine-Readable Records*, Carolyn L. Geda et al., eds., (Chicago: Society of American Archivists, 1980), 158–81; and S. Michael Malinconico, "Mass Storage Technology and File Organization," *Journal of Library Automation* 13,2 (1980): 77–87. See also F. E. March, Jr., "Videodisc Technology," *Journal of ASIS* 33,4 (1982): 237–44; Dick Moberg and Ira M. Laefsky, "Videodiscs and Optical Data Storage," *BYTE* 7,6 (1982): 142–68; Gerard O. Walter, "Video Disc for the Storage of Office Documents and Engineering Graphics," *Journal of Micrographics* 15,1 (1982): 12–20; and Coopers & Lybrand, *Information and Image Management: The Industry and the Technologies* (New York: Coopers & Lybrand, 1987).

one another, they operate in the same manner from the user's point of view. Information is loaded into the CPU through an input device. The computer then runs a set of programs that format and manipulate the data, and sends it to designated storage devices. During this process, the data is coded in such a way that the system can, when instructed by the user, return to storage and access it. In this manner automated systems store vast amounts of information, avoiding the expensive process of rekeying data.

Storage in the random access memory (RAM) of the CPU is very expensive, and it is also volatile. If the computer is powered down, its RAM is wiped clean and the information is therefore lost. Thus, less expensive nonvolatile external storage devices are employed instead. Computer facilities that run in an online interactive mode tend to rely almost exclusively upon disk drives for data storage. These drives can hold many billions of bytes of storage that can be accessed at great speeds. Since disk drives are also expensive, most computer facilities employ them only for current information storage. Historical and backup data are stored on magnetic tapes. Tape drives are then used to update and backup disk storage, as well as to restore and load infrequently accessed data to the system. While tape drives are slower than hard disk devices, they are also less expensive.

Most mini- and mainframe computers rely on hard disk storage. Smaller systems use floppy disks (or floppies) of either five-and-a-quarter or three-and-one-half inches in diameter. Older systems employed eight diskettes but these devices are now anomalies in modern data processing environments. Like tapes and certain types of hard disk packs, floppies are removable. The user merely inserts the diskette into the appropriate drive to access the information stored there. When another disk is required, it is simply exchanged in the drive. Floppies hold much less information than hard disks or tape, and are also considerably slower. However, floppy drives and media cost a fraction of what one would pay for hard disk and tape drive devices.

More recently, optical videodiscs have gone from the laboratory into limited commercial competition with other mass storage devices. They are capable of storing fifty-four thousand images and two separate audio channels on each side of a twelve-inch-diameter platter. The disc is made of a multilayered synthetic resin, with a grooveless surface of silvery appearance. Lasers are employed to etch images onto the videodisc and to read it thereafter. While most current applications involve published information (CD-ROMs) and, hence, mass-produced discs, a number of manufacturers, including IBM, DEC, and Phillips, are in the process of releasing "write-once-read-many" (WORM) videodisc systems.[10] The storage capacity of these devices

---

10. For a discussion of recent developments in WORM technology, see *PC Week* 4,25 (1987): 107–20. See also William Saffady, *Optical Disks for Data and Document Storage* (Westport, Conn.: Meckler, 1986), for a nonspecialist technical overview.

is phenomenal. Because they are optical rather than magnetic recordings, they are also much more stable. Once WORM products are perfected, videodiscs will prove more economical and efficient than disk drives, and will come to supplant other storage media, such as micrographics, as well.

The deciding factor in the selection of an optical videodisc system or any other external memory device is its ability to respond to user operating requirements. For example, a system with many users who are simultaneously accessing a common large database may require the speed and capacity of hard disk storage, but a single user will find the response time of a floppy disk system sufficient for many of his or her applications. In most instances, thoughtful needs assessment (as well as budgetary limitations) will dictate the choice of appropriate hardware. In the case of optical discs, the computer industry has yet to fully interface these products with CPUs and appropriate retrieval software for use in information management settings.

The next basic type of computer component one must consider is the output device. Once the CPU has done its job, the data must be communicated back to the user. The CRT, which acts as an input device, may also serve as a vehicle for output. Similarly, a tape-mounted drive, a hard disk pack, or even a floppy diskette may act as the recipient of output from the computer. If a user is looking for a very specific piece of information out of a computer file, the CRT works well. However, if the user plans to analyze, manipulate, or edit the data further, a more flexible approach to the digital storage of output is desirable. For this reason, many MIS shops have developed mainframe to microcomputer "downloads" that take a portion of a large file or database from the main computer and transfer it to a PC's storage device.[11] The growth in this type of activity and its importance to corporate information services is demonstrated by all of the product development currently underway in this area.

In most instances, the user will also want "hard" or printed copy. This may entail paper output via a computer printer, or microfilm via a computer output microfilm system. Unlike other system components, printers are primarily mechanical devices that simply receive digitized instructions from the CPU and convert these into formatted alpha-numeric characters or graphics. These components fall

---

11. *PC Week* publishes a weekly supplement, entitled *Connectivity*, which is devoted entirely to the latest developments in microcomputer networking and LANS. *Computerworld* also runs a weekly section on this subject under "Communications." Both publications include regular product surveys and reviews. See also Udo W. Pooch, *Telecommunications and Networking* (Boston: Little, Brown, 1983); David A. Stamper, *Business Data Communications* (Menlo Park, Calif.: Benjamin Cummings, 1986); and "Critical Connections," *Computerworld* 21,36A (1987): Focus 1–56.

into four general categories: impact, thermal, jet ink, and laser.[12] Furthermore, they may be differentiated in terms of whether they produce full (letter-quality) or dot matrix characters, and whether they work with different type fonts, colors, and graphics. Some printers require specially treated paper while others will print on any kind. As with other computer peripherals, user requirements will dictate the features of printer selection.

For example, service bureaus that generate large quantities of printouts on continuous-form paper would normally employ big chain-driven or laser printers that run in conjunction with mainframes. Smaller production shops that deal with any form of word processing, especially where the preparation of camera-ready copy is involved, will require a printer that can produce letter quality materials. Dot matrix printers will suffice in many applications and are essential for the generation of graphics. Indeed, the quality of recent dot matrix technology has risen to the point where they have supplanted daisy wheel impact printers. Flexibility, lower cost, and a lesser incidence of failure give them a definite edge. If, on the other hand, the output is to be of the highest quality, as would be the case with photocomposition and "desktop publishing" work, laser printer production would be a good choice. Here again costs are declining even as the products are improving.[13]

Unfortunately, no single printer appears to meet all needs. As a result, even the smallest system configurations often include two or more types of printers. (I will return to the subject of selecting and implementing computer hardware in Chapters Five and Six. The reader will also find a discussion of COM services in Chapter Seven, as well as the role of microfilm in MIS activities.) Let it suffice here simply to observe that COM units are quite common in the larger DP shops, where these peripheral devices are attached directly to the CPU from which they receive output. The big advantage of COM end products is that they avoid the costs associated with paper printout production and storage.[14]

---

12. See *Printers: The Next Generation*, supplement to *PC Week* 4,35 (1987); and Hesh Wiener, "The ABC's of Printing," *Datamation* 32,23 (1986): 56–68. The market for PC printers is highly competitive and it is therefore difficult to keep up with product developments. *Infoworld* and *PC Week* do a fairly good job of it. For a useful introduction to the subject, see Stanley S. Veit, "Everything You Want to Know About Printers," *Personal Computing* 5,3 (1981): 58–69.

13. Desktop publishing and laser printers are currently areas of high activity and visibility within the computer software and hardware industries respectively. See John W. Seybold, "The Desk-top Publishing Phenomenon," *BYTE* 12,5 (1987): 149–58; Connie Winkler, "Desktop Publishing," *Datamation* 32,23 (1986): 92–96; Tom Holmes, "Make My Page," *BYTE* 12,5 (1987): 159–70; and Arthur Little, "Four Laser Printers," *BYTE* 12,3 (1987): 217–22.

14. Selection criteria for computer peripherals are addressed in Chapters Five and Six of this book. See also Brian R. Smith, "Questions to Ask About Business Computers," *Small Business Computers Magazine* 4,6 (1981): 6–11.

The final category of hardware components to be considered at this time is remote communications equipment. Some of these devices are little more than circuit boards that allow computer components to interface with one another, while others have the size, complexity, and multiple functionality of many mainframes. For example, within the same facility or building, user CRTs are often linked to the CPU through coaxial cable. The cable runs from individual input/output devices to a controller unit and, eventually, to the central computer. This approach to communications works well when users operate within limited distances of the CPU—usually no more than two thousand feet and often less than six hundred feet. Similarly, in the case of so-called local area networks (LANs), a number of terminals may run off a master micro- or minicomputer. These configurations often include a file server for the common storage of data by LAN users. Coaxial or twisted-pair (i.e., telephone) cable links small groups of users with the local network's primary CPU.

However, when system users are dispersed over great distances, LANs and simple channel to channel connections between computers and their peripherals will not suffice. It should therefore come as no surprise that a burgeoning new industry has emerged to address the need for long-distance data communications networks. Furthermore, the recent deregulation of the telecommunications industry, the breakup of American Telephone and Telegraph (AT&T) into its constituent parts, and the subsequent creation of Bell Data Communications have raised the possibility of an even wider range of product offerings to those building voice/data networks.[15] As new hardware comes to the market and as the common carriers of voice and data traffic, such as AT&T, U.S. Sprint, and MCI Communications, offer more services, MIS managers will need to remain flexible and avoid long-term commitments to what could rapidly become obsolete and overpriced networking solutions.

Regardless of future developments, the most widely used approach to remote data communications currently is via the telephone system. Through the use of modems (devices that permit computers to transmit data over telephone lines) and multiplexors (devices that handle multiple, digitized communications), information travels over telecommunication facilities from one computer node (pathway termination) to another. In effect, an individual with a terminal and a

---

15. One of the primary motives behind AT&T's efforts to separate its long distance systems from its regional networks is Bell's desire to enter the data communications marketplace. After the FCC approved the breakup, AT&T has moved aggressively into the field with new data transmission systems and services, and new networking hardware. See Victor Block, "New Competition in the Marketplace," *Infosystems* 29,3 (1982): 40–46. See also the special report, "IBM-AT&T: The Coming Collision," *Datamation* 28,8 (1982): 1–68; and James H. Green, *The Dow Jones-Irwin Handbook of Telecommunications* (Homewood, Ill.: Dow Jones-Irwin, 1986).

modem may interact with a mainframe, or even a fellow PC user, with no more difficulty than it takes to dial a long distance telephone number. Some networks operate through costly direct digital transmission lines, while others go through Telenet or some other dial-up utility. Surface microwave antennas and even satellite communications are also employed in some networking configurations.[16] Where data communications involves many user nodes and a variety of common carriers, multiplexor hardware and software provide for the efficient management of the system.

Cost is not necessarily the ultimate consideration in configuring a network. In most instances, those paying the bill are more concerned with such factors as speed, transmission quality, backup and dependability, and flexibility. For these corporate leaders, the investment in voice/data communications is a necessary part of doing business. While it should be efficient and economical, the bottom line in networking is availability. Senior management will pay what is necessary to keep information flowing within the organization. Admittedly, for certain applications it may prove just as effective to mail a tape or disk to another user as it would be to "talk" with his or her machine directly. On the other hand, where the system is interactive and time is of the essence, networking may also be the most cost-effective alternative. To be sure, the general direction among large organizations is toward the development of complex, flexible, and expensive communication capabilities as a component of their total EDP strategy.

In the final analysis, institutional needs and financial resources will serve as the basis for the selection of any computer and its peripherals. Since each corporate environment presents MIS administrators with unique EDP requirements, it is difficult to generalize about selection. Furthermore, the choice of hardware may ultimately reside with a higher authority in the parent organization. Under these circumstances, the information services professional is obliged to make the best use of available resources and to lobby for enhancements to existing systems with his or her superiors. On the other hand, the affordability of microcomputers and their growing processing power provide MIS personnel with greater independence of action. Indeed, many of today's most successful information management strategies are built upon the concept of distributed processing and, hence, de-

---

16. For a technology-oriented perspective of the situation, see Stephen Connell and Ian A. Galbraith, *Electronic Mail: A Revolution in Business Communications* (White Plains, N.Y.: Knowledge Industry, 1982); Charlene Lavinger, "How Standards Affect Business: Part III, Communications," *Today's Office* 17,1 (1982): 59–64; Oswald Harold Gonley, *To Inform or to Control: The New Communications Network* (New York: McGraw-Hill, 1982); and Alfred Glossbrenner, *How to Look It Up Online* (New York: St. Martin's, 1987).

livering computer capabilities to the desktop of the end user. At this point in the discussion, it would be premature to ignore any EDP option.

Software

The technological leaps in computer hardware evolution have unfortunately left many software developers very much behind the times in building system capabilities that exploit the latest generation of CPU processing power. Indeed, some industry specialists refer to a critical shortage in state-of-the-art programming. Nevertheless, in selecting operating systems or specialized application programs, there are many fine software packages from which to choose. What is more, fourth generation programming tools have assisted the software industry in closing the gap between computer and system capabilities. In planning MIS services, management must realize the limitations as well as the opportunities afforded by these products and, therefore, how best to deploy them within the workplace.

To begin, this section introduces the reader to generalized software categories and how these computer programs might fulfill specific functions within a larger information management scenario. In dealing with this subject, I exclude from consideration in-house software development. While the power and so-called user friendliness of the latest generation of programming tools lend themselves to this type of creativity, such efforts are costly, time consuming, and largely unnecessary in relation to the MIS needs of most organizations. It is clearly the case that the typical MIS administrator has neither the resources nor the expertise to develop his or her own computer programs for all applications. Indeed, MIS personnel are under constant pressure to provide immediate services through the use of off-the-shelf products. As changes occur in their corporations' requirements or EDP environment, they will be in no position to cope with such challenges exclusively, or even largely, through home-grown solutions.

Furthermore, I would argue that this type of effort is largely unnecessary. At their core, most information management tasks have much in common. Even a cursory study of industry offerings will reveal a wide range of application programs for almost any need. In fact, the demand for such products has contributed to the rapid growth of companies that specialize in generic computer systems, such as those for accounting, manufacturing, human resource management, computer-assisted design, database administration, and voice/data communications. Each of these concerns maintains a critical mass of experts to build and modify software products in relation to the demands of the marketplace and in light of appropriate tax and regulatory legislation. The careful purchaser may therefore select from readily available, commercially produced software that can meet most, if not all, of management's MIS requirements.

Even the modification of so-called canned software programs can lead to problems. For example, it should be noted that the modification of existing software packages requires considerable time, effort, and expertise. Furthermore, these changes often void any warranties that accompany the original product. It is, in my view, better to select general-purpose software carefully and to use these packages to their fullest extent, rather than going through the trouble of modifying them. This may require some compromise on the part of users, but in terms of time savings, efficiency, and better service, the sacrifice is well worthwhile. Given these observations, my discussion of software products will concentrate on off-the-shelf offerings and how these fit into the larger EDP picture for MIS services.

As a starting point, one may categorize computer software any number of ways. For example, in the preceding section of this chapter I refer to machine and high-level programming languages. These are attributes of the software environment, just as accounting and word processing packages represent specific products. More generally, systems may be grouped under two comprehensive headings—operating systems and applications software. Operating systems manage the running of the computer hardware, allow its various components to work in harmony, and produce calculated and predictable responses to the sundry EDP tasks of a computer facility. They also provide the so-called data processing environment in which original programs may be created.

In addition, operating systems run the other general category of programs—applications software. As its name suggests, these latter systems include all those packages designed to perform specific functions, such as word processing, financial/statistical modeling, and database administration. The mix of operating and applications software will determine to a large extent the functionality of the organization's computer hardware in executing information management assignments. While the subject is technical and complex, an introduction to EDP software products may serve as a means of alerting administrators to the options available to them in this area.

Computer Operating System Software

The operating system is a collection of programs that control the CPU and run all of the communication between the main processor and its peripherals. For example, it controls the flow of data between the computer's random access memory (RAM) and its external storage units (e.g., disk drives). It also serves as the internal network for the flow and translation of information between the DP environment's programming languages (such as BASIC or COBOL) and its hardware. In many instances, the operating system is permanently wired into the CPU through storage within the read only memory (ROM) of the machine. When software is installed in this manner, it is referred to as "firmware."[17] For many computers, the operating system is an integral part of the purchase price as well.

From the standpoint of an information services professional, the selection of an operating system (OS) may be a moot point. In large mainframe environments, senior MIS and/or corporate management choose this software without reference to specific user requirements. For that matter, most mainframe manufacturers provide customers with only a limited number of OS options. While in mainframe environments the acquisition of a third-party operating system may occur from time to time, it is not very common. When purchasing a small computer, the OS often comes as a "bundled" part of the machine's purchase price. There are few other options. Whatever the choice of operating system, one must ensure that it will support both the programming language to be employed for in-house development projects and the types of application packages required by the parent organization. Any MIS manager who ignores these simple relationships could do his or her organization a serious disservice. Similarly, when purchasing a personal computer, one should also be cognizant of the OS needed to run popular off-the-shelf microcomputer software.

Though an operating system may come to MIS as an integrated component of the organization's computer configuration and though it may run the desired applications programs, it may nevertheless prove difficult to use. For example, a user may have trouble getting jobs to run, may be disappointed by the system's performance in generating graphics, or may not approve of its ability to handle programming tools or database and query systems. To facilitate these types of EDP activities, the information service professional will turn to utility packages that supplement OS capabilities. These products facilitate many of the routing procedures associated with data processing, such as sorting information, renumbering programming lines, or making backup copies of programs. Furthermore, utilities obviate the need to reinvent the wheel each time a rather routine function

---

17. For further information on operating systems, see Alan Boyd, Philip Good, and Stanley Veit, "A User's Guide to Operating Systems," *Personal Computing* 5,5 (1981): 27–32, 83-108; William C. Davis, *Operating Systems: A Systematic View*, 3rd ed. (Reading, Mass.: Addison-Wesley, 1986); and Andrew S. Tanenbaum, *Operating Systems: Design and Implementation* (Englewood Cliffs, N.J.: Prentice-Hall, 1987).

within a larger, more complex program is required. Some utility packages are designed to run in tandem with applications software. As with systems software, the purpose of these utilities is to facilitate the user's execution of tasks on the system. It is therefore important for MIS managers to identify opportunities where system utilities will foster greater throughput.

Computer Applications Software

In a typical implementation scenario, the OS software is already in place. The information manager's job is to identify those applications packages that address organizational MIS requirements and to install these products within the existing hardware and software environment. While there are thousands of different applications packages available today, those relevant to this discussion may be grouped into five general categories: word processing systems, database management systems, financial/statistical modeling systems, graphics systems, and communications systems. Each of these families of applications has an important role to play within the organization's larger information management strategy. I will therefore review the basic characteristics of each grouping and consider their interrelationships.

Word processing packages provide facilities for the entry and editing to text via computer. The text may be in the form of a letter, a mailing label, a brochure, an article, or even a book. Though they vary widely in quality and ability, most word processors allow for the alteration and reorganization of text interactively and online. They also offer some type of simple indexing and retrieval system to assist the user in storing and recalling text from external storage devices. Many also possess spelling and synonym dictionaries. To get the most out of a word processing package, one's computer system should be able to support both upper- and lower-case characters, text highlighting, special characters, and at least an 80-column screen. With a good system in place, document editing becomes a simple task, dramatically improving the efficiency and productivity of staff writing.[18] Any function that requires written communications would ben-

---

18. See International Micrographics Congress, *Word/Information Processing Concepts: Careers, Technology and Applications* (Bethesda, Md.: International Micrographics Congress, 1981); Richard W. Scamell and Michael W. Winkler, "WP: The Overlooked Dimension of Information Management," *Journal of Information Systems* 30,1 (1979): 36–41; Jeanne W. Halpern, *Computers and Composing* (Carbondale, Ill.: Southern Illinois University Press, 1984); and Jonathan Price, *The Definitive Word-Processing Handbook* (New York: Penguin, 1984).

efit from a computer-based word processing capability. Subsequent chapters develop this theme in more detail.

Database management systems (DBMS) store and manipulate data. Most packages provide the user with a formatting capability to create electronic forms. Highly specialized database systems include pre-formatted fields designed to address the requirements of a particular application, such as real estate management or inventory control. Once the form is established within the system, the user loads the data into formatted screens. Edit features allow for the immediate correction of entry errors and the facility to return and make changes at a later date. As information is entered, the database system assigns "tags" to each datum. Through some type of retrieval system—usually driven by Boolean-qualified search terms, the user may then recall discrete data from memory or generate reports based upon the information stored in electronic files.

Simple databases control one file at a time, but advanced, relational databases are capable of updating, manipulating, and consolidating information stored in different files during the course of a single pass-through of the data. Thus, one set of keystrokes can affect different database files simultaneously (or nearly so). In addition, relational systems can create new files from existing ones and can receive "flat" files (files containing records of only one type), without the restrictive pointer structures associated with less highly developed DMBSs.[19] This characteristic affords MIS personnel the opportunity to migrate software systems without rekeying data. As with word processing products, DBMSs are often employed to support a wide range of functions within the organization. For example, they may serve as the indexing and retrieval device for customer accounts, parts inventories, research files, or microfilmed records. They are also employed to manage performance measurement, telephone usage, quality control systems, and decision support tools for senior management.

Though database management systems can manipulate both numerical and textual data, they are not often designed for use with financial data. Here a financial/statistical applications package is required. Many of the PC-based versions of this product type are popularly known as "electronic spreadsheets" because their electronic format is reminiscent of manually created accounting worksheets. However, the automated form has all the facilities to carry out com-

---

19. Publications on this subject are plentiful and generally quite good. See, for example, E. G. Brooner, *Microcomputer Database Management* (Indianapolis: Howard W. Sams, 1982); V. A. J. Maller, "Retrieving Information," *Datamation* 26,9 (1980): 164–72; James Bradley, *Introduction to Data Base Management in Business* (New York: Holt, Rinehart and Winston, 1983); Mary E. G. Loomis, *The Data Base Book* (New York: Macmillan, 1987); and Mark L. Gillenan, *Database Step-By-Step* (New York: Wiley, 1985).

plex financial analysis. Other financial products include such packages as general ledger, accounts payable, cost accounting, and fixed assets management systems. The most obvious use of these tools is in the areas of budgeting and financial control. When tied together with a complementary statistical and graphics package, the user has a powerful prognosticative tool for the charting and examination of performance data.[20]

Beyond that, information services personnel are increasingly called upon to provide greater functionality in two additional areas. On the one hand, users are now demanding the capability to generate tables, graphs, gant charts, illustrations, and the like. To achieve these ends, MIS managers usually introduce graphics and electronic publishing packages that run off of PCs but may manipulate data drawn from a mainframe host.[21] On the other hand, corporate leaders are looking for ways to improve and economize on their organization's communications network. They are therefore turning to MIS for phone traffic management systems, PC-to-mainframe and mainframe-to-PC links, data communication compaction and encryption products, and the like.[22] Both of these categories of computer software enhance the exchange of information within the organization and between it and the outside world. Graphics systems present data pictorially while communications software maximizes transmission over the network. Increasingly, these types of products have become staples of the MIS operating environment and essential components of user services.

Managing EDP Resource Utilization

Thus far, Chapter Four has dealt with a rather cursory introduction to computer hardware and software. Because the mix of equipment and programming is virtually unlimited in its variations, each MIS manager will need to define his or her system requirements and build a configuration that best addresses these specifications. In the

---

20. For a general discussion of applications, see Irwin M. Jaret, *Computer Graphics and Reporting Financial Data* (New York: Wiley, 1983); and Lawrence N. Nitz, *Business Analysis and Graphics with Lotus 1-2-3* (Englewood Cliffs, N.J.: Prentice-Hall, 1985). For a wide range of specific applications and illustrations, see *Library Hi Tech News* and *Library Software Review*.

21. Donald Hern and M. Pauline Hern, *Computer Graphics* (Englewood Cliffs, N.J.: Prentice-Hall, 1986); Ian O. Angell, *A Practical Introduction to Computer Graphics* (New York: Wiley, 1981); and Edward M. Fisher, "A Graphic Change of PC's," *Datamation* 33,2 (1987): 44–50.

22. See, for example, Myles E. Walsh, *Database and Data Communication Systems: A Guide for Managers* (Reston, Va.: Reston Publishing Company, 1983); Merv Adrian, "Micro-to-Mainframe Links End Drudgery of Data Extraction," *PC Week* 4,36 (1987): c14–c27; Thomas C. Bartee, ed., *Data Communication Networks and Systems* (Indianapolis: Howard W. Sams, 1986); and Dimitri Bertsekas and Robert Gallager, *Data Networks* (New York: Academic Press, 1987).

ideal world, information services personnel begin with no system at all, and may therefore pick and choose from a vast array of hardware and software without any constraints. Unfortunately, few of us will ever find ourselves in such a situation. Typically, information managers are confronted with circumstances that significantly reduce their options. For example, many will be obliged to use existing corporate facilities, while others will be forced to operate on such a limited budget that they must rely on the largess of other in-house corporate entities to make any progress at all toward automation.

Consider, for example, the following scenarios. It is possible to spend a great deal of money in purchasing computer hardware and software to meet system requirements. Costs range from five thousand dollars for a microcomputer system to millions of dollars for a mainframe-driven EDP network. Many discrete applications can now run on powerful standalone PCs or as part of modest LANs. Others will require substantially more hardware and larger, more powerful software systems. Since information management services within most organizations are highly fragmented, the resources required, even for modest configurations, may come from different jurisdictions within the parent company.

In expanding upon this premise, let us assume that the information manager must approach other operating units for his or her EDP services. For instance, the manager can turn to the parent institution's data center, or if in-house resources are in short supply, perhaps to some outside computer service bureau. These outside firms can provide batch or online processing, keypunching, laser or computer output microfilm production, and so on. The user pays for services rendered. However, many applications require more internal control, less computing power, online/interactive capabilities, and greater flexibility than one can usually establish through a relationship with an outside processing house. It is therefore unlikely that a service bureau will meet many MIS needs, except in the case of special projects, such as the massive data entry process associated with automating a manual card file index, or certain applications, such as payroll processing.

Perhaps a centralized in-house EDP facility provides the information service professional with more options, but it may also raise problems of another sort. For example, the work of the records center or library may be given a low priority. The EDP people responsible for seeing these projects to fruition within the data center will, in all likelihood, know nothing about records administration or some other discrete information service. They may not have a strong commitment to these projects. Furthermore, like service bureaus, in-house data centers tend to charge handsomely for their services without at times providing good value to their MIS colleagues. While these circumstances are not insurmountable (nor are they true in all cases!), they raise a number of serious management issues. In moving forward, it is necessary that management buy into each MIS project as part of a larger corporate strategy and that all players agree on resource allocations. Any transfer pricing mechanism put in place should be competitive with services available on the outside. Users as well as the MIS team should have a say in priority setting, work scheduling, and investments in new systems and hardware.

Alternatively, it may make more sense for the project team to approach the realization of its objectives through distributed processing. Indeed, in many instances the current EDP technologies provide users with sufficient computing power to avoid the use of in-house data centers and outside service bureaus, in favor of standalone micro- and minicomputers. If the cost of a mini or micro cannot be justified solely on the basis of a single undertaking, I recommend that MIS seek partners to share the financial burden. There are sure to be enough common needs among the records center, the archives, the corporate library, and various administrative and support services units to adopt a cooperative approach. Similarly, potential users might inquire into the availability of in-house time-sharing on a minicomputer already in place in some other user area. Planning along these lines will lead to a flexible and more responsive solution to corporate information management problems.

In terms of the actual financing of a hardware or software acquisition, there are a number of possible choices. For example, users may lease equipment with an option to buy at some later time, usually two, three, or five years from the initial lease date. While small computers are sometimes available on a rental basis, rates tend to be higher than under lease/purchase arrangements. For those operating in the private sector, tax benefits related to the acquisition of computer software and hardware can offset a portion of the original purchase price. Finally, not-for-profit organizations may apply for grants or solicit community financial support to assist in the purchase, lease, or rental of EDP equipment and services. Once a system is installed for a specific purpose or project, MIS can look for additional ways to maximize its utility to the organization.

If all of these options appear to confuse my readers, I ask that they take heart. Bear in mind that a myriad of choices also means a multitude of opportunities. For your assistance, I have prepared figure 7 which summarizes these choices. This evaluation matrix juxtaposes EDP system options and services, and sources of funding. Use it as a checklist. Needless to say, each institution will need to follow its own course in terms of how it finances hardware and software purchases. More often than not, the entire organization will follow a common policy, driven by its cash flow financing and tax

EDP System Research Option	Funding or Financial Option						
	Payment by Job or per Hour	Intra-Company Charges	Rent	Lease	Purchase as Part of Grant	Outright Purchase	
Service Bureau							
Batch Processing	*						
Online Processing	*						
Data Entry	*						
Print Production	*						
COM Production	*						
Programming & Analysis	*						
In-House DP Facility							

Star (*) = Probable option choice

Figure 7. **Analysis Matrix of EDP Options.**

EDP System Research Option	Funding or Financial Option	Payment by Job or per Hour	Intra-Company Charges	Rent	Lease	Purchase as Part of Grant	Outright Purchase
Batch Processing		*	*				
Online Processing		*	*				
Data Entry		*	*				
Print Production		*	*				
COM Production		*	*				
Programming & Analysis		*	*				
Shared Minicomputer							
CPU			*				
Peripherals				*			

Star (*) = Probable option choice

Figure 7. (Cont.)

EDP System Research Option	Funding or Financial Option	Payment by Job or per Hour	Intra-Company Charges	Rent	Lease	Purchase as Part of Grant	Outright Purchase
Software					*		
Owned Minicomputer							
CPU					*		*
Peripherals					*		*
Software					*		*
Owned Microcomputer							
CPU							*
Peripherals							*
Software							*

Star (*) = Probable option choice

Figure 7. (Cont.)

situation, as it approaches such acquisitions. Figure 7 is structured to show various financing options. The preferability of one over others will vary by institution. However, from a management point of view, the greater the degree of control exercised by the end user over the operation of the EDP environment, the more he or she will benefit from system development and performance. I therefore indicate (where appropriate) the most desirable (or likely) way that an organization can fund its EDP purchases.

For example, if MIS looks to a service bureau to satisfy its data processing needs, it usually pays by the job or by the hour. Even if it turns in-house for DP, it is likely to be charged in a similar manner, unless it also runs the data center itself. Since it is improbable that a records management, archives, or library program is likely to operate its own mainframe shop, figure 7 accurately represents possible options. On the other hand, minicomputer facilities might run under the aegis of MIS, though perhaps on a shared basis with some other user group. A dedicated mini might be leased or purchased outright, while a PC is invariably purchased by the owner. Keep in mind that this simple evaluation tool ignores which system best addresses specific corporate information service requirements. It seeks only to heighten the MIS manager's awareness of the resource options at his or her disposal. It should therefore be employed as a survey tool in developing one's strategic and tactical plans.

CHAPTER
5

The Planning Process

Preliminaries

Chapters One through Three have presented a series of general observations concerning the nature, structure, and function of information management services as these relate to the needs of one's parent organization. In addition, I have summarily described various hardware and software options, and standard EDP terminology. The present chapter focuses on the mechanisms whereby these insights are put to practical use by MIS managers in planning for and selecting new EDP and telecommunication systems. As a first step in this process, the pre-planning procedures discussed in Chapter Two are reviewed here in greater detail. By proceeding in this manner, MIS managers position their efforts in the context of the larger organization's strategic plans. New information systems and services should relate to these constructs and hence foster broader institutional objectives.

My discussion of the aforementioned process therefore begins with a description of how MIS strategies should emerge as a subset of the overall corporate plan. I next proceed with an analysis of the issues associated with creating a project planning team, preparing a request for proposal (RFP), and reviewing vendor responses. All of my remarks emphasize management issues, with a view toward assisting MIS personnel in the selection of appropriate applications for transfer from manual to automated or computer-assisted procedures. **99**

As already indicated, the first step in this process is to establish strategic and tactical MIS plans based upon the more general goals and objectives of the parent organization. In addition, MIS senior management must take into account the immediate demands placed upon existing services by its user constituencies. Indeed, the planning and development of future projects will more readily find the necessary institutional support if they are built upon the successful delivery of established functions.

Figures 3, 4, 5, and 7 will assist the information manager or records administrator in focusing upon those institutional issues that will affect the direction of MIS efforts and the consumption of their resources. These tools will also encourage information managers to raise certain fundamental questions about their responsibilities, including: What type of organization do I work for and therefore what general types of information services are required? How does the general structure of the MIS area fit into the larger information services matrix of the parent corporation? What is my personal role? What types of records (informational content and format) do I manage and how will problems inherent in these media affect the delivery of services? What kinds of MIS products do my users currently require and how will changes in our business environment or advances in EDP and telecommunications technologies influence these requirements, going forward?

Wherever possible, the answers to these questions should be prioritized according to the human, physical, and financial resources of the MIS unit or units, without losing sight of the larger corporate plan. To a considerable extent, information services personnel may find that the parent organization has already answered some of these questions or at the very least has limited the options open to MIS personnel. For example, as part of a more extensive MIS infrastructure, a corporate records management program may already be charged with scheduling and eliminating all company files that are no longer necessary for day-to-day operations. Surviving materials are housed in inactive storage or preserved in an archival repository where access is restricted to the office of origin and certain corporate officers. Records of long-term research value to the organization might be preserved for future reference, but the remainder of the records would be discarded as soon as the law or reasonable business practices allow.[1] In this case, the institutional objectives of the records management program, as well as its user constituency, are easily

---

1. In recent years, the private sector has become increasingly aggressive in its destruction of old records so as to avoid the potential liability of what these files might contain about past corporate practices. See Michael Allen, "U.S. Companies Pay Increasing Attention to Destroying Files," *Wall Street Journal* 210,46 (September 2, 1987): 1, 10.

definable. The astute administrator would set his or her management priorities to reflect these institutional needs, protecting the organization from unnecessary expense and unwarranted disclosure.

A public institution, such as a Federal archives program, has a more difficult job defining its mission and operational objectives. In all likelihood, the organization will function under rigorous legal restrictions which limit the options of the leadership in directing the actions of its records management personnel. On the other hand, these same institutions face outside pressures from Congress, the judiciary, sister institutions with overlapping jurisdictions, and so forth. The need for greater accountability than that required of private sector organizations also clouds the picture.

Thus, whereas the files and information services of a given business corporation tend to be managed in a uniform and highly restricted manner, the same is not always true for the public sector. In the latter case, the user population ranges more widely and may, in addition to government officials, include congressional and court personnel, scholarly researchers, school children, and the general public. The chief administrators of such programs must exercise discretion in catering to the needs of any particular group. Furthermore, as a program designated to serve the public interest, government MIS operations face a complicated process of identifying objectives and setting information service priorities.

As difficult as this task of defining a focus might appear at first, it is essential to the process of establishing automated systems and, more generally, efficient MIS services.[2] For those institutions with a formal strategic planning process in place, MIS personnel need only refer to the published documentation for direction. Unfortunately, not all organizations embrace such practices. In those instances where plans are not in place, the MIS team must take a more proactive role, seeking out key users and soliciting from them their short- and long-term objectives. Together, operations and information services personnel should be able to develop a common list of priorities for the coming twelve to eighteen months, and a longer-range, five-year document. This data will prove invaluable to MIS in completing an internal appraisal of their resource allocations.

Figure 5, or something very much like it, will assist these information service professionals in identifying constituent needs as they work through this process of self-analysis. In addition, by employing figure 5 as a checklist, senior MIS personnel will have created a

---

2. The definition of institutional objectives is essential to the healthy development of information and records center services—whether manual or automated. I have previously presented the reasons for this in some detail; see Richard M. Kesner, "Archival Collection Development: Building a Successful Acquisitions Program," *The Midwestern Archivist* 5,2 (1981): 101–12.

comprehensive description of ongoing services, staff functions, and in-house information systems. The data collected in the course of completing figure 5 will not only indicate the direction and commitment of program resources, but also potential opportunities for the development or enhancement of services. Once identified, these opportunities could lead to new MIS products or, at the very least, to the introduction of more up-to-date EDP technologies.

During analysis, the question will invariably arise: To what degree does the program's allocation of resources correspond with its corporate mission? In response, management might find it necessary to poll its information service staff and the wider user constituency. In so doing, the MIS leadership will want to ask what tasks are neglected or given short shrift due to the program's current allocation of resources. Furthermore, it is quite common to find institutions that have upgraded their information systems without addressing the user side of the equation. As a result, new MIS products and services are underutilized, and even misused, by operating personnel. Not surprising, when bypassed during the planning process, users are less than enthusiastic in their support of system implementation. A disproportionate amount of resources must then be consumed to win them over to the new product or service offering. To identify these types of inefficiencies, management should also critique ongoing procedures and techniques. Similarly, those who are served can comment on the quality of existing services and on those that need to be added. With this information, the MIS unit will be in a better position to appraise their operations and to determine how specific functions might be realigned to better fit corporate objectives, user specifications, and resource limitations.

However, to be truly responsive to the needs of the organization, MIS management must not only raise questions about current needs, but they should also expand system specification definitions as far into the future as possible. For example, they must consider information exchange requirements. Even if no immediate need manifests itself, it is highly probable that, in an increasingly networked information environment, organizations will want to share data. To achieve this objective, they will be obliged to agree upon bibliographic, data description, and at times data storage standards. When considering new hardware and software configurations in this scenario, the MIS team must insure that vendors can provide products that support these standards. In the case of most libraries and many of our larger archives programs, the ability to read Machine Readable Catalog (MARC) record formats and to produce MARC-formatted output is fast becoming an essential system attribute.[3] This severely limits one's

---

3. For more on the MARC format and description/retrieval standards, see David

choice of EDP options. On the other hand, if information exchange is a strategic requirement, this type of investment will prove justifiable if not necessary.

Once these facts and impressions are known, program administrators may focus upon the issue of automation. First, the leadership must identify those systems that will lend themselves to computerization. They should then view their EDP options in light of agency priorities. The pre-planning analysis process will also assist MIS in restructuring and rendering more efficient those elements in the program that will remain manual operations. With this accomplished, management is in a position to establish a task force composed of those who will participate in the design, acquisition, and implementation of specific, automated information systems and services.

The Planning Team

The introduction of new MIS products into any type of organization is by no means a simple task. It would be quite unusual to find an individual who possesses both the knowledge and expertise required to see such a project to fruition. Therefore, a team approach is preferable. In many instances, the size of the parent company and the MIS unit will serve as limiting factors on the size of this group. Obviously, smaller agencies will have fewer professionals to draw upon for participation in the planning process than larger institutions. At the very least, one information service professional should serve on the team, and perhaps act as the task force chair, since he or she will best understand the MIS unit's internal priorities, operations, and limitations. For the same reason, one ought to include the person responsible for all of the unit's pre-planning analysis. (In many instances this person will be one and the same.) An outside professional colleague might join this group to supplement in-house expertise with his or her work experience in a similar institution. Finally, an EDP specialist, as well as one or more user group representatives, should join the team.

Such a task force for a small organization might have as few as three participants: an in-house professional, a technical (EDP) specialist, and a user. Each person brings a distinctly different perspective and set of skills to the process. At times, MIS will serve as the project sponsor and should therefore retain control by providing the

Bearman, *Towards National Information Systems for Archives and Manuscripts* (Chicago: Society of American Archivists, 1987); Harriet Ostroff, "From Clay Tablets to MARC AMC," *Provenance* 4,1 (1986): 1–11; and David Weinberg, "Automation in Archives: RLIN and the Archives and Manuscripts Control Format," *Provenance* 4,1 (1986): 12–31. See also Henrietta D. Arram, *MARC: Its History and Implications* (Washington, D.C.: Library of Congress, 1975).

group with leadership. However, from time to time it may prove expedient (if not beneficial) to have a knowledgeable user at the helm. MIS management must be sensitive to the political dynamics of the situation and respond accordingly. Bear in mind that it is the end product of the task force assignment that is of utmost importance. The path to its realization should be as direct, painless, and economical as possible. Team staffing and leadership selection should aim at results, and not serve as an extension of corporate turf battles.

Whoever represents MIS must have the ability and knowledge to articulate the needs of potential system users to the technical expert. This person will also serve as the liaison between the operational world of the users—who will have task force representation—and team technologists. For his or her part, the EDP specialist will provide guidance in the design and selection of computer and telecommunication system hardware and software. This player should also have sufficient vision to recognize problems that may arise from the introduction of advanced information technologies into new operational settings. Finally, the user will round out the team as the advocate for those served, to ensure that the course of action chosen by the group corresponds with current services and user expectations. In this regard, the broader the base of user participation the better. Whatever work comes out of task force deliberations should have their full support, which may prove essential if the automated system is to win acceptance on the shop floor.

The individual influence of planning-team members will vary with the type of project and the prevailing corporate culture. It is the project leader's responsibility to make certain that the team observes its mandate in developing a plan compatible with the requirements of key users. In many matrixed management settings, the leader will out of necessity act more as a coordinator and facilitator than as a direct participant in this process. When in-house resources do not in and of themselves suffice, either the leader or senior corporate management may also seek outside assistance. As long as MIS retains control over the direction of deliberations, this external source of expertise will broaden the team's perspective and strengthen its ability to deal with the difficult intellectual challenges facing its members without dissipating its drive or focus. To ensure that this occurs, senior management must provide the project leader with sufficient authority and ongoing support to see the undertaking to its desired conclusion.

Large organizations may find themselves with too many (rather than too few) players on their MIS planning and development teams. For example, the project leader may be obligated to appoint a representative from each operating department or functional area affected by the proposed change in information services. Corporate management may insist upon the inclusion of outside consultants who are specialists in some subfield, such as microwave communications or distributed processing, which will swell the ranks of the team and add to project costs. In my view, it is essential that the working group be kept to a minimum, and certainly no more than seven. If necessary, sub–task forces may be established to deal with particular project components. When this is done, a single core member should chair the subgroup and report on its accomplishments to the team. In this manner, MIS management can coordinate major project components while freeing small groups of specialists to focus on technical details.

Ideally, the task force's leadership will retain control of the planning efforts and, therefore, the ability to direct the work of team and subteam members into areas that are most productive from the parent organization's point of view. This is particularly important in the majority of those instances where the ultimate objectives of the task force are not commensurate with the resources allocated. When the time comes to choose among options, MIS and operations management together should know best which activities warrant attention over others. At the same time, some team players may have a vested interest in the status quo and are therefore unable to envision alternative, automated approaches to long-established tasks and procedures. Line managers also tend to get bogged down in operational details which may impede the task force's planning process. Team leadership must be strong and well focused if these types of pitfalls are to be avoided. In the final analysis, the inclusion of action-oriented and well informed players ought to provide satisfactory results.

Outsiders as MIS Task Force Players

As knowledgeable as the planning team's information management professionals may be, they will often require the assistance of one or more outside technical experts. These outsiders may have little or no understanding of the problems associated with the delivery of a specific organization's information services. However, they bring to the table a certain conversance with the latest trends in technology. If, for example, the preliminary findings of the in-house group suggest a solution based upon a standalone microcomputer, a local area network, or an electronic mail system, technical advisors with germane work experience should, if possible, join team deliberations when these products are discussed.

Preferably, the team should draw upon the human resources of its parent institution for these technical advisors. The organization's network center, data processing operations, microcomputer user's group, finance division, or research and development unit are likely to have individuals with the credentials for participation on the planning team. The task then becomes a matter of identifying the appropriate individuals and obtaining their services. If the project is vested with sufficient importance from higher authorities within the parent institution, it should not prove difficult to obtain the necessary cooperation. At times, personal diplomacy and interdepartment negotiations will be necessary before the team wins the assistance of technologists working in other cost centers. Even then, care must be taken to ensure the effective integration of the EDP specialist as a team member, especially if he or she lacks an appreciation for the special information management problems to be addressed by the team.

When in-house expertise is not available, MIS management must then go outside the parent institution for this resource. Rarely will one find an expert who is willing to donate time to the effort. Instead, one must find an appropriate technical expert at the most reasonable cost. For example, if the in-house team is focusing upon various microcomputer options, a local computer club or user group might serve as a useful and economical source of technical advice. Similarly, the planning team might seek the assistance of vendor representatives who already sell computer hardware and software to the parent organization. However, these vendors have an obvious vested interest in helping the project along, because it may lead to further purchases from his or her company. When exploiting this type of resource, one must therefore recognize the prejudices that a vendor, serving in a consulting capacity, will bring to the table. On the other hand, if properly managed, these people can provide useful information and sound advice without adding consulting dollars to project costs.

In some instances, the planning team could also turn to the staff of a reputable nearby computer store. These professionals tend to be extremely knowledgeable about small computer systems and their applications. Indeed, the "hobbyist" tradition within the microcomputer-user community lends itself to this approach. If these people cannot help directly, they usually provide an introduction to a colleague who can be of assistance. Some agencies may also have the option of turning to a trade or professional association for guidance. Many of these bodies maintain information clearing houses that retain the names of other members who have mounted similar information system projects. They may also offer consulting and training services of their own or references for third-party offerings. Finally, one might turn to a local users group some of whose members have no doubt faced similar hardware and software problems and are usually glad to assist newcomers.

Though many of the sources of technical assistance mentioned here are free or nearly so, they are also limited. It is unlikely that any of these persons, with the possible exception of a systems vendor, will have the time or the interest to review the planning team's work in considerable detail. A more likely arrangement would involve team members asking a cooperative outsider specific questions. To take advantage of this source of technical expertise, the team should do its homework in advance. Specifically, task force members should read through the literature—both popular and trade—and identify hardware and software products that appear to fit well with the project's objectives.[4] Once the team has trimmed its options to a reasonable list, it will be less difficult to approach a sympathetic technologist for advice.

Employing Consultants

As a last resort, the team may turn to outside consultants for guidance in hardware and software selection. Be forewarned! People who earn their living by advising others in the areas of electronic data processing and telecommunications charge handsomely for their services. Indeed, the field of EDP consulting is currently in a period of booming activity and profits. Standard fees range from four to sixteen hundred dollars a day, plus expenses. When consultants are used properly, they earn every penny they are paid. However, to ensure a good return on the investment, the project team must select the right consultant and be fully prepared before his or her arrival.

Not all EDP consultants are similar in background, training, or interests. For instance, an individual may have all the necessary credentials to design a mainframe system (with its accompanying software environment) but may, at the same time, know nothing about microcomputers. Similarly, he or she may have expertise in application areas, such as financial and accounting systems, but may be totally unacquainted with text-handling and electronic mail products. Before hiring a consultant, ask for a resume and references. Review these with care. If the consultant's experience appears to reflect those areas of concern to the planning team, proceed by contacting him or her for an in-house review of the project and a determination of how the consultant might contribute to the process. This initial visit will not require any fee payments. But it will give the team a sense

---

4. Richard M. Kesner, *Information Management, Machine-Readable Records and Administration: An Annotated Bibliography* (Chicago: Society of American Archivists, 1983), is particularly helpful in this regard. The chapter dealing with periodicals and reference tools (pp. 17–30) provides general guidance as to which journals, magazines, and loose-leaf information services regularly publish hardware and software product reviews.

of this outsider's potential worth, and may assist in identifying further options and fresh approaches. Never hesitate to ask for references and always check at least three of them, especially those that may have called upon the consultant to perform tasks similar to those envisioned in your plan.[5]

Even after a suitable consultant has been hired, much needs to be done before that person participates in the deliberations of the planning team. Bear in mind that the longer the consultant is on the job, the more it will cost your organization. Thus, complete as much of the work as possible before the consultant arrives. Map out the plan and all its details. Make the best estimate possible pertaining to the selection of equipment and systems. Calculate what the package will cost and how it will be implemented. In short, present a complete scenario to the consultant, stating explicitly what the team would like this person to accomplish. If your task force lacks the expertise to prepare this level of detail for the consultant, you may wish to have this outsider assist in getting the team started. However, avoid assigning the preliminary work to a consultant. He or she will require a great deal of time (at your expense!) to learn about your organization. It is better to have the outsider sketch various options that the team will in turn research for their applicability to your MIS requirements.

This approach makes the best use of the consultant's time and your program's limited resources. The consultant can then quickly appraise your position, point out what is and what is not feasible in the team's proposals, and make further specific recommendations for the project staff's consideration. The consultant should then provide the team with a written report of findings and recommendations. Be sure to specify firm dates for the completion of all work by the outside specialist. The project staff should also reserve the right to submit a revised proposal to the consultant for review. This additional step should not entail an on-site visit (and its associated costs) by the consultant, and might be included as part of the original fee.

The role of the consultant or any other source of technical support engaged by the planning team is to advise. Direction of these outside experts must come from within. In-house MIS professionals

---

5. For planning teams seeking expert advice in the areas of electronic data processing and telecommunications, the American Federation of Information Processing Societies (AFIPS), the American Society for Information Science (ASIS), the Institute of Electrical and Electronic Engineers (IEEE), and the Association for Computing Machinery (ACM) all provide guidelines and recommendations pertaining to consultant selection. See also Kevin Hegarty, *More Joy of Contracts: An Epicurean Approach to Negotiation* (Tacoma: Tacoma Public Library, 1981); Susan Blumenthal, *Understanding and Buying a Small-Business Computer* (Indianapolis: Howard W. Sams, 1982), 151–52; and Robert J. Kalthoff and Leonard S. Lee, *Productivity and Records Automation* (Englewood Cliffs, N.J.: Prentice-Hall, 1981), 63–65, 81–82, 233.

or key users should therefore establish the development guidelines for the project and coordinate the activities of everyone else within the process. Concomitantly, these same information managers will present in-house technical personnel with implementation scenarios and system options. The latter will then evaluate the feasibility of these proposals. This process implies that all team players must develop and maintain a certain level of technical competence so that they can intelligently evaluate the recommendations of their EDP specialists and outside consultants. By reading widely, visiting organizations where automated systems are already in place, and attending professional meetings where colleagues discuss EDP applications, team members can better prepare themselves for this task. Even if these types of activities are not always open to them, team members will become more familiar with the technical aspects of the assignment simply through working on it.

The Role of Systems Users in the Planning Process

Users should play a prominent role in the development of any new MIS product or service. In industries such as banking, utilities, education, and health care, where the importance of MIS services is paramount, the planning process may very well benefit from their leadership. Similarly, members of the legal, advertising, and research and development divisions of an organization might insist upon having representatives on the planning team, since any alteration in the way company records are administered directly affects the successful execution of their work. In a university, one or more researchers might join the team, thus providing an additional perspective and a voice for those who rely most heavily upon library and archives services. Furthermore, it might be useful to include representatives from operating units, such as the network center or the telecommunications department, where automated information management tools may already be in place. The latter approach affords the task force the benefits of previous experience at tackling similar MIS assignments.

With the inclusion of users, the planning team is complete. A fully staffed team should include the MIS officer who conducted the pre-planning process. This person should also serve as the project leader. He or she may be assisted in turn by one or more colleagues and perhaps a fellow information professional from outside the organization. To support this core of experts, technical specialists whose areas of expertise correspond roughly to those areas under consideration by the team are required. If, for example, the project involves integrating microcomputer operations with the corporation's in-house mainframe-based systems, the establishment of an automated records management system, or the expansion of a series of online information services to other offices within the institution through networking, the team's technical members would be expected to be proficient in one or more of these areas. Ideally, these individuals would be drawn from internal resources such as the parent institution's data center. However, outside consultants might also serve as alternative resources. The inclusion of user group representatives would then round out the staffing of the planning team.

For the best possible results, the task force should remain small, without sacrificing the breadth of technical expertise required for successful completion of the project. The team may get unmanageable if it has more than five or seven members. Similarly, teams with less than three members will probably suffer from overwork and will not possess the necessary depth to cover all aspects of an information management problem. If nothing else, the project will certainly benefit from a healthy mix of viewpoints. Since each automation effort has its own special requirements, project staffing will usually differ from one application to the next. The MIS manager should therefore strive for the proper balance between corporate strategic knowledge, operational experience, and technical competence among team players. The team leader should also encourage a willingness on the part of all participants to view their task with a fresh, unprejudiced perspective and with a modicum of entrepreneurial zeal.

The Planning Matrix

With the completion of preliminary research and the establishment of the project team, formal planning may begin. First, it is advisable to expand upon the work conducted in the preparation of the MIS resource allocation matrix (figure 5). During the aforementioned process, the information service professional or records administrator responsible for the pre-planning effort itemized and prioritized the information systems currently maintained by the MIS unit. As the next step, it is now necessary to break down these procedures into their constituent parts or functional elements. For example, the action steps in preparing an agency's newsletter for publication might include word processing, layout and design, mailing list maintenance, scheduling, printing and production, mailing, and financial management. Similarly, the physical control of files would involve accessioning, retention and disposition scheduling, storage, and so on.

In conducting this analysis, MIS management will note that each service component encompasses its own unique array of operating procedures and responsibilities. No two MIS units are likely to be identical in the way they function, are staffed, and report to the larger parent organization. The model presented in figure 8 is therefore meant only as an illustration of how one might conceptualize discrete MIS functions. Individual managers will need to draw from their experiences and modify my list for use in their own information service environments. Nevertheless, one may observe certain common threads that run through the findings of any such evaluative process.

In the first place, the reader should realize that automated or manual information systems cannot be viewed in isolation. They are part of a larger corporate fabric that encompasses the full lifecycle of records, from original design and creation through use to final disposition. While a given user group may value a particular MIS service or function over that of another, this sense of priority may not be shared by all. In the absence of clearly defined priorities, MIS personnel must make their own judgments, based upon their sense of institutional requirements and clearly expressed user needs. More proactive or "intrapreneurial" information managers often take these deliberations one step further by advocating systems and services that, in their view, provide the organization with a competitive advantage, reduce expenses, improve customer service or in some other manner address more global institutional objectives.

Second, the reader should not assume that high-priority items are those most likely to benefit from automation. Fund raising, for instance, may be of top importance to a not-for-profit organization's management team. If the team is to prove successful, however, many aspects of this function require a human and not a computer "interface." Alternatively, the introduction of an automated system for library reference services or for the record center's accessioning process might, in turn, free staff members so they can devote more effort to fund raising or some other people-intensive activity.

Thus, it may be argued that the service priorities of MIS need not lead to the automation of those particular functions. Instead, the planning team should look for those areas of activity that will return the most to MIS or the larger organization, once computerized. These need not be important in and of themselves, as long as their automation frees staff time for more significant assignments or value-added services elsewhere. In presenting such an approach to senior management for approval, the task force should avoid references to "cost savings through automation" unless it is quite certain of the correctness of its findings. It has been my experience that while one may earn an excellent return for each dollar spent on an automated information system, the total number of these dollars will invariably equal (or exceed) the cost of manual systems that they replace. If there is a "savings" to be found, it usually results from the avoidance

Systems and Subsystems	Resource Allocations	Priority Rank	Manual Functions	WP Application	DBMS Application	FIN/STAT Application	Graphics Application	Comm Application
Information Resource Gathering								
Record Surveys			0	2	3	2		
Forms Design				3			2	
Distribution			0					
Analysis					3	3		
Lead File Maintenance								
Correspondence				3				
Analysis					3	3		
Follow-Up			0					

3 = high correlation of applicability; 2 = moderate; 1 = low; 0 = manual or n/a

Figure 8. The Planning Matrix: Systems versus EDP Options.

Systems and Subsystems	Resource Allocations	Priority Rank	Manual Functions	WP Application	DBMS Application	FIN/STAT Application	Graphics Application	Comm Application
Case File Maintenance								
Correspondence				3				
Analysis					3	3		
Legal Documentation				1				
Follow-Up			0					
Physical Control								
Accessioning					2	1		1
File/DOC Receipt					2			1
Processing			0					

3 = high correlation of applicability; 2 = moderate; 1 = low; 0 = manual or n/a

Figure 8 (Cont.)

Systems and Subsystems	Resource Allocations	Priority Rank	Manual Functions	WP Application	DBMS Application	FIN/STAT Application	Graphics Application	Comm Application
R & D Scheduling				2	2	2		
Forms Design				2			2	
Survey			0		2	1		
Analysis					3	3		
Item Retention			0		3	1		
Item Destruction			0		3	1		
Microfilming			0					
Document Encoding					3			

3 = high correlation of applicability; 2 = moderate; 1 = low; 0 = manual or n/a

Figure 8 (Cont.)

Systems and Subsystems	Resource Allocations	Priority Rank	Manual Functions	WP Application	DBMS Application	FIN/STAT Application	Graphics Application	Comm Application
Intellectual Control								
Information Reorganization			0					
Appraisal			0					
File/DOC Processing			0					
Description				3	3			3
User/Reference Services								
Circulation					3			3
Reference Tools				3	3			3
Online Retrieval				3	3			3
Publications					2	1	1	
Research			0	3	2			2

3=high correlation of applicability; 2=moderate; 1=low; 0=manual or n/a

Figure 8 (Cont.)

Systems and Subsystems	Resource Allocations	Priority Rank	Manual Functions	WP Application	DBMS Application	FIN/STAT Application	Graphics Application	Comm Application
Access Control								
Physical Security			0		2			
Facility Planning			0		1	1	1	
Data Security					2			2
General Administration								
Word Processing				3				
Correspondence				3				
Management Reports				3	3	3	3	
Grants Administration				3	3	3		

3=high correlation of applicability; 2=moderate; 1=low; 0=manual or n/a

Figure 8   (Cont.)

Systems and Subsystems	Resource Allocations	Priority Rank	Manual Functions	WP Application	DBMS Application	FIN/STAT Application	Graphics Application	Comm Application
Financial Control								
General Accounting						3	2	
Budgeting						3	2	
Grants Administration					3	3	2	
Publication Planning					2	2		
Publication Production				3			3	

3 = high correlation of applicability; 2 = moderate; 1 = low; 0 = manual or n/a

Figure 8. (Cont.)

of future expenditure. Consequently, a system justification based on the principle of cost avoidance may appear perfectly reasonable to you, but will prove a "hard sell" before your organization's controller. It is therefore necessary to take these distinctions into account when lobbying for a new automated information systems.[6] Where possible demonstrate the time saved and the value of the information generated by the new MIS product.

It ought to be clear by now that the priority rankings of MIS tasks may not, in and of themselves, indicate the appropriate direction for the planning of automation projects. Instead, the team should focus its analysis upon the flow of work and document life cycles within its organization when plotting its list of assignments. Such a study will no doubt encompass an overview of all those systems and services involved with data collection, physical and then intellectual control over files, reference services and, finally, more general administrative tasks.

Figure 8 illustrates this approach toward the categorization of MIS functions. It should be obvious to the reader that my list is incomplete and that my subcategory breakdowns are not sufficiently detailed. They are offered only as an example for review, adaptation, and elaboration. Your organization may in fact view its operations quite differently. It is therefore essential that your activity lists be prepared by someone thoroughly acquainted with all aspects of your institution's existing programs and information needs. Furthermore, it should be set forth in considerable detail, and may even benefit from the flow-charting of more complex MIS services and their accompanying procedures.

For the purposes of my example in figure 8, I have elaborated on the functional areas listed in figure 5. My categories attempt to serve as generic references to many of the services found within typical records management and related MIS programs. In most organizations, these responsibilities are shared among various operating units, such as the library, the archives, the records center, EDP operations, and administrative services. They include information resource gathering, physical control over files, intellectual control over data, user services, and access controls. Still others are aspects of work found throughout the parent organization under the heading

---

6. For examples of cost-benefit analysis as it relates to information and records management, see Herbert S. White, "Cost Effectiveness and Cost-Benefit Determinations in Special Libraries," *Special Libraries* 70,4 (1979): 163–60; Charles R. McClure, *Information for Academic Library Decision Making: The Case for Organizational Information Management* (Westport, Conn.: Greenwood Press, 1980); Robert S. Runyon, "Towards the Development of a Library Management Information System," *College and Research Libraries* 42,4 (1981): 539–48; and Michael R. W. Bommer and Ronald W. Chorba, *Decision Making for Library Management* (White Plains, N.Y.: Knowledge Industry, 1982).

of "general administration." It is now our task to transform this listing into an agenda of EDP options through which the reader may assess opportunities for the introduction of new information technologies into his or her workplace.

Before proceeding, however, I would like to add one last caveat about priority setting. For the purposes of analysis and planning, it is useful to subdivide information delivery systems and services into their constituent parts. On the other hand, as I indicate in my references to the record life cycle, all of these components are conceptually interrelated. In many instances, it is desirable to track a document or publication throughout its useful life—from acquisition to cataloging and description, to final disposition and storage. When moving from planning to implementation, it may prove difficult for the end user to follow this evolution unless he or she foresees the desirability of compatibility among system modules. For example, if the planning team identifies document tracking as a system requirement in the initial design phase of the project, subsequent decisions should address this need. In general, the organization will benefit from a high level of connectivity and communication among its various information service products. When employing my planning matrices, the reader should, therefore, identify project objecitves within their broader operational contexts.

Matrix Design and Implementation

Now that we have concluded our listings of departmental functions, the task force may develop its planning matrix. This analytical tool serves as the most important guide for the team. It will identify all systems requirements and suggest where the staff might look for EDP solutions to its information management problems. In addition, the planning matrix performs a vital task by focusing attention upon those procedures in greatest need of change—automated or otherwise. Through the careful use of this tool, information managers may also identify redundancies and waste in their ongoing operations. Thus, even those systems left unaffected by the unit's automation program may nevertheless benefit from a rationalization of their manual functions.

The planning matrix (figure 8) lists typical records and information management functions along its vertical axis. The horizontal axis includes columns for the entry of resource allocations, priority rankings, and correlation rankings for both manual functions and several EDP-based applications. The EDP categories include word processing, database management systems, financial and statistical modeling, graphics, and communications (i.e., networking). The appropriateness of a particular EDP application to a given task will vary from institution to institution. In the planning matrix example provided here, I have indicated by way of illustration the potential relationships between specific information service functions and the aforementioned group of EDP applications. Figure 8 employs a three (3) to indicate a high level of correlation between the MIS activity and an EDP function, a two (2) signifies a moderate level of correlation, and a one (1) indicates a low, but nevertheless relevant, level of correlation. Those boxes with a zero (0) represent areas of activity that must remain manual. I emphasize this point by providing manual functions with their own column for data entry.

The costs of any particular activity and its priority ranking may be drawn from the figure 5 analysis matrix. For a given service component it may be preferable, and certainly easier, to concentrate only on labor and materials expenses, factoring out overhead and intercompany transfer charges. In other instances, it may be appropriate to develop a formula for the allocation of facility costs, insurance, staff training, parent company fees, and so forth. The project team should determine which method best reflects the fiscal realities of its program's operations. From my point of view, it is important to determine the unit costs for all services so as to ascertain their "value" to the greater organization. Cost accounting, especially in a service area, is a difficult assignment in and of itself. Fortunately, there is a great deal of guidance available.[7] On the other hand, nothing can avoid the considerable mental effort associated with setting accurate unit prices. This step is necessary if one is to present the rigorous type of cost/benefit analysis advocated at the close of this chapter to justify new MIS projects.

Once the planning team has finished its list of activities, assigned them priority statuses, determined their resource consumption levels, and correlated them against various EDP applications, the finished matrix may serve any number of purposes. First, it assists in focusing team attention on all of those variables to be considered during the process of transforming manual functions into EDP operations. Furthermore, it indicates which office practices have similar attributes from an information (and EDP) processing point of view. These observations will then suggest strategies for the rationalization and the combination of information systems to best exploit the data processing capabilities of particular hardware and software configurations.

For example, the planning matrix might indicate the need for the introduction of word processing capabilities into a records center

---

7. For an introduction to the complex field of transfer pricing and cost accounting, see Robert G. Eccles, *The Transfer Pricing Problem* (Lexington, Mass.: Lexington Books, 1985) and Robert S. Kaplan, *Advanced Management Accounting* (Englewood Cliffs, N.J.: Prentice-Hall, 1982).

environment. While the machine(s) may be located in the collection processing area to facilitate accession list generation, other work, such as finding aids, general correspondence, and office publications, could be routed to these same workstations for production purposes. In brief, then, the planning matrix not only suggests where automated systems may be installed for greatest effect, it also indicates how the institution should organize itself internally to best exploit these new resources.

The correlations provided in figure 8 are subjective and serve only as a general guide. For instance, the use of word processing as part of the collection development process is obvious in the preparation of lead letters, follow-up correspondence, and legal agreements. A database management system may also be employed to track lead and case file activity, to manage the circulation of documents to users, and to control physical access and data security. However, each of these components in turn might also benefit from the incorporation of statistical and financial capabilities to track worker productivity and customer usage. Such a system could automatically bill users for services rendered.

Similarly, communications systems and local area networking may be exploited to enhance the reference services provided by the MIS unit to its users. In preparing a work for publication, the program might employ a database management system to generate mailing labels, a financial package to bill subscribers, and a word processor to develop and print the camera-ready copy. In certain instances, hardcopy distribution might be supplemented by online transmission of the work over the network. Whatever the application, system limitations and institutional requirements will determine the extent to which EDP options are exercised. My planning matrix is designed to promote flexibility in the thinking of MIS management so that its efforts in turn will accommodate (and exploit!) the particular circumstances of its own information management capabilities.

Preparing a Request for Proposal (RFP)

The planning matrix helps the MIS team identify its priorities as well as its current modes of operations. In addition, it will assist the team in noting any imbalances between its program's objectives and its allocation of resources. Most of all, it is expected that, through the planning matrix, the team will have singled out those services or operational procedures ripe for conversion from manual functions to fully automated or computer-based applications. The team's next step is to put this assessment of needs into greater focus. To achieve this end, it should prepare a request for proposal (RFP) which communicates its analysis in terms that both senior management and EDP software, hardware, and service vendors will understand.

Ostensibly, the purpose of a request for proposal is to control the bidding process so that competing vendors quote prices on a common basis to the purchaser.[8] If the RFP is prepared properly, its authors will receive proposals that respond to specific selection criteria in a manner that facilitates comparison. In addition, the task force may (and should) employ the RFP process to acquire greater familiarity with the subject under consideration. Indeed, it is quite possible to obtain a first-rate education and some high-quality, yet inexpensive, consulting through working with vendors as they prepare their responses to your RFP. As discussions mature, these exchanges will assist the team in refining its project objectives and the EDP solutions for which it must ultimately receive senior management approval.

As a methodology for RFP preparation, I would recommend that the team begin with some general inquiries based upon the directions set out by the planning matrix. For example, if the matrix identifies a need for word processing, electronic mail, or a distributed information indexing and retrieval system, the team should invite recognized vendors in these areas for discussions. In many instances, it might make sense to include your mainframe or minicomputer sales representative as well as the software or peripheral dealer in question to such review meetings. These outsiders have tackled information management problems similar to yours many times. They will know what questions to raise about your MIS environment and will also provide you with valuable background information. Much of this data will prove useful when preparing your RFP. You may go so far as to ask the assistance of a vendor in the drafting of your request, but make it clear from the outset that while such help is very much appreciated, it will not predispose your team to purchase that particular vendor's products or services. For his or her part, the vendor will gladly assist you, if for no other reason than to build rapport and get a jump on the competition. All the same, be sure to place this person's recommendations in the proper perspective and recognize from the outset his or her biases.

If the planning team follows the approach outlined above, its RFP may go through a number of preliminary stages before it is officially issued. All of the time consumed on the development process is well

---

8. For an excellent study of procurement techniques, especially as they apply to the creation of RFPs and contract negotiations, see Joseph Auer and Charles Edison Harris, *Major Equipment Procurement* (New York: Van Nostrand Reinhold, 1983). See also Edwin M. Cortez, *Proposals and Contracts for Library Automation: Guidelines for Preparing RFP's* (Studio City, Calif.: Pacific Information, 1987); and Roger Fisher and William Ury, *Getting to Yes* (Harmondsworth, U.K.: Penguin, 1983).

spent in that it will save the team effort later on, ensure the best bidding results, facilitate effective decision making by task force members, and ultimately assist the team in winning senior management support. To realize these goals, the team must do its homework—an effort that will include the interrogation of vendors and the thorough preparation of a final request for proposal document. Remember, if the team is lax when drafting its RFP, the resulting vendor responses will in all likelihood fail to meet your requirements. Even worse, MIS might in the end purchase an EDP solution that does not meet its needs.

While each RFP will address its own project requirements, all requests for proposal seek to control the format of vendor responses, force them to quote competitive prices, and commit them to deliver services and products in keeping with the timetable of the planning group. As such, the RFP must be a fairly rigorous document. In my experience, it must in one form or another include the following components:

introduction
general project description
description of project components
for which a vendor response is requested
general bid instructions
bid response requirements
vendor responsibilities
vendor site requirements
cutover (from the old to the new system) and post-
cutover requirements
vendor services and warranties
pricing
appendixes (e.g., organizational charts, glossaries,
floor plans, equipment lists)

The introductory section of the RFP provides potential bidders with summary background information about one's parent company and the MIS unit or service affected by the proposed project. It should include a statement pertaining to the business objectives of this particular undertaking, such as cost reductions, the avoidance of obsolescence, customer service enhancements, and so forth. The introduction may also include as appropriate such documents as organizational charts and annual reports. The objective of this data is to give the vendor a sense of his or her audience and their needs. Following from these opening statements, the RFP should become more detailed and focused. The next section should briefly outline the planning team's strategy for dealing with specific MIS issues, including immediate and long-term needs, project phases (as appropriate), and anticipated vendor recommendations. Always leave yourself open for a change in course. Encourage the vendor to come back with an alternative if he or she disagrees with your initial approach.

The next two sections of the RFP set out the ground rules for a vendor response. Under "description of project components," spell out in narrative form the types of software, hardware, and service solutions that you desire. If cost is an issue, set limits; if maintenance is important, make this clear; and if the backup and redundancy of systems is essential, make this a response requirement. This section should conclude with some fairly unambiguous statements, reinforcing the fact that the bidder *must* conform to your RFP format, that he or she must deliver the response to you by the day and time indicated, and that your organization reserves the right to reject any and all bids. Finally, this section should provide a delivery address for vendor responses, and a contact person and telephone number in case problems arise.

The "general bid instructions" section that follows provides more specific directions and guidelines. For example, you may wish to deal with only one contractor, and you should therefore indicate that vendors must manage all of their own subcontractors. You should make it clear that vendors respond to the RFP at their own expense but that their proposals become your property upon submittal. Insist that all products be quoted on both a purchase and a lease basis. Also ask for both single unit and bulk purchase prices. If service, migratability, obsolescence, performance reliability, and vendor stability are concerns, state your expectations in detail. Be blunt and do not compromise. Your bidders will either respond as you request or drop out. In all likelihood, those that remain and comply with your RFP will prove to be the types of suppliers with which your organization would wish to do business.

Since many MIS projects encompass areas of considerable complexity, their RFPs often contain a request for detailed system specifications. For example, in sizing a multiplexor for a data communications network or a central phone exchange (CBX) for a telephone network, the request document will need to indicate the size of the existing network, growth projections, the number of devices (i.e., phones, terminals, printers, controllers, etc.) tied into the network, and activity rates (usually expressed as kilo- or mega-bits per second flowing through the system). The vendor would be asked to recommend equipment, carrier services, and the like, based upon the data provided. Similarly, the team may want to evaluate specific product features in terms of their financial and operational impact on the EDP solution under consideration. You may therefore wish to ask the vendor which features, in his or her view, are necessary for the success of the project and which are merely added to your costs.

The remainder of the RFP identifies vendor responsibilities. The purpose of these sections is to solicit commitments from bidders that, if chosen, they have the ability to deliver according to the specifications of the RFP. In the area of implementation, for example, insist that the vendor coordinate all services and subcontractors associated with the project, and that he or she is responsible for any equipment or labor problems that may arise. At the same time, it should be the vendor's responsibility to keep you informed of any issues that may impede the timely and successful conclusion of all work. In terms of site requirements, make the vendor liable for any damages to your property or injuries to your people in conjunction with his or her assignment. Your expectations concerning rubbish removal, the safekeeping of tools and supplies, and postimplementation cleanup should also find mention in the RFP.

Since service is such an important aspect of most MIS conversions, the RFP should set forth clearly worded guidelines governing cutover procedures. Whether the organization is moving from a manual to an automated system or from an old EDP technology to a state-of-the-art system, the vendor should be on hand (in force) at the time of conversion. If something should go wrong, technicians will therefore be in place to either abort the cutover or correct all problems without adversely affecting ongoing operations. Similar commitments need to be made for the immediate post-cutover period and for ongoing servicing. Since most computer and telecommunications vendors make as much money on the maintenance of systems as they do on their initial sale, these conditions will not appear unreasonable to bidders. Unless, of course, you expect them for free! Finally, the RFP should request copies of all warranties that would accompany the equipment under consideration if purchased.

Last, but certainly not least, the RFP should specify how the team wishes project bidders to state their prices. It is very easy for a vendor to disguise his or her lack of competitiveness by quoting an "unbundled" price for what appears to be a bundled package, only to come back later saying that the "total system" costs more. Insist on unbundled, unit pricing and detailed descriptions of what one is purchasing at the unit price. Depending upon the product, ask for various leasing and maintenance contract options. Do not settle for the "standard product," which invariably favors the vendor. Furthermore, do not assume that because the vendor presents you with a printed contract, it cannot be altered. If the vendor wants your business, he or she will modify the final document in response to your specifications. When negotiating terms, also work for an up-front commitment from the vendor on the cost of upgrading, modifying, and/or expanding the system at a later date.

The secret to a successful RFP is hard work and thoroughness. Vendors have a vested interest in meeting your needs; you are in control. Use your advantage to its full and you will get quality proposals and, ultimately, workable EDP solutions to your information management needs. Admittedly, some projects will not require as detailed an RFP as others. In some instances, only one vendor has what you are looking for. Even so, the RFP will serve your team well in that it will encourage you to focus upon the essential elements of your plan and to raise all of the salient issues associated with its satisfactory implementation. The educational process of RFP preparation is in and of itself a bonus because it will better prepare the team to evaluate EDP options and to bring its final choices before corporate senior management for approval.

Hardware/Software Selection

With the culmination of the request for proposal process, the MIS task force has completed its needs assessments and its data collection. The next step becomes one of selecting the appropriate automated information systems that fulfill these specific requirements. The pre- and early planning processes (including the planning matrix and the RFP) provide the tools and information gathering to accomplish this set of tasks. While project participants will define those areas of their work that will potentially benefit from the introduction or enhancement of EDP capabilities, they will also discover the limitations placed upon their choices by their resources. For example, very few MIS units enjoy the luxury of choice in the selection of EDP hardware. If the parent institution operates an IBM shop, or if a sister unit has available space on its DEC mini, these are the only choices open for consideration. Moreover, most large computer centers and minicomputer configurations will already possess established software environments that other information services personnel may be free to use but not to alter. Thus, applications packages must be able to run on existing in-house hardware and operating software if they are to be of any use. Even though personal computers afford an economical alternative and, certainly, greater flexibility to some, these machines are not always available and may not satisfy all needs.

In a sense, well-established EDP facilities within the parent institution make the selection process simpler for the planning team. However, this narrowing of options, though perhaps unavoidable, is not always desirable. I have already discussed some of the problems arising from a reliance on centralized DP facilities. Here I would only add that microprocessor technology provides an alternative through a vast array of software within the reach of even the smallest information service and records management programs.[9] Furthermore, the choice of a distributed approach to information processing does not preclude the use of a mainframe system for certain applications. Those who enjoy access to small computers and large centralized facilities might very well choose to use both. However, microcomputers should be included in any consideration of automated solutions to MIS problems.[10]

The Evaluation Matrix

Even if the EDP options are not as varied in practice as they are in theory, the selection of equipment and systems remains important to the planning process. In institutional settings where hardware and software already exist, application software and perhaps system peripherals for on-site data input and output must still be selected. Other instances may call for the establishment of complete stand-alone systems or EDP configurations that are compatible with information nodes in other parts of a far-flung corporate network. With this in mind, I have adapted a flexible tool, originally developed by Deloitte, Haskins, and Sells, to assist in the comparison of vendor responses to the RFP. As with any of my other models, this management tool is generic and yet comprehensive. Admittedly, it raises more questions than most product comparisons will require. The reader should therefore feel free to drop certain components and modify others to meet immediate needs. However, for the purposes of this discussion, I will review the entire hardware/software evaluation matrix, as presented in figure 9 so as to familiarize the reader with my methodology.[11]

---

9. Many tools are now available to assist the information manager in locating appropriate software. McGraw-Hill's Datapro Research Division, for example, publishes a two volume loose-leaf service devoted entirely to microcomputer software. Both Service Development Corporation and Lockheed DIALOG offer online versions of this product. At a less expensive level, detailed information pertaining to the software for a given small computer can be obtained through reference tools such as *The Blue Book for the Apple Computer* (Gurnee, Ill.: Visual Materials, 1981) and *PC Magazine's IBM Personal Computer Product Guide* 1/5 (1982).

10. I have advocated this approach in any number of previous publications. See, for example, Richard M. Kesner, "Computers, Archival Administration, and the Challenge of the 1980's," *Georgia Archive* 9,2 (1981): 1–18; "Microcomputer Applications in Archives: A Study in Progress," *Archivaria* 12 (1981): 3–20; and "Microcomputer Archives and Records Management Systems: Guidelines for Future Development," *American Archivist* 45,3 (1982): 299–311.

11. This matrix is based upon a model developed by Earl Jones and his colleagues at Deloitte, Haskins, and Sells (Boston). It is similar in both design and function to models found elsewhere in the literature.

The evaluation matrix provides for the comparison of EDP vendors, products, or services. If, at the conclusion of one's solicitation and review of the prosposal, the planning team has identified more than three candidates for each of these categories, the tool may be adapted accordingly. The reader will note that each element within the evaluation matrix is weighted in terms of its overall significance to the configuration of an EDP system. By rating each evaluation criterion from zero (0) to ten (10), then multiplying this figure by its weighting factor, a score for each comparison component can be obtained. In theory, the alternative with the highest total number of points should be selected. However, it may come to pass that a crucial criterion, such as availability or compatibility, could otherwise exclude the highest scorer from further consideration.

The evaluation matrix proceeds through six areas of analysis: vendor proposal response, vendor firm evaluation, hardware, system software, application software, and miscellaneous factors. For those operating under certain constraints, such as fixed hardware and/or software, the planning team need only enter under "Alternative 1" the specifications for those established elements that will influence project implementation. The matrix may then help identify the best choice among remaining options. Also note that each area of analysis is accompanied by a percentage notation which indicates its share of total potential points. If a particular component is dropped, the remainder of the matrix may be completed without compromising the outcome of the comparison. Though somewhat qualitative in its scoring methodology, the matrix nevertheless provides a quantifiable and easily documented evaluation of EDP alternatives. At the very least, it is a comprehensive listing of all those factors that ought to be considered in the selection of automated systems.

The matrix itself is organized in a rational order. However, the user need not proceed with selection as the matrix indicates. Indeed, since the greatest variable in any automated system is in the identification of applications software, it might prove most effective to begin with this aspect of bid comparisons. Once one has identified desirable software, it is a much simpler task to limit the field to the operating software and computer hardware required to run that particular application. It would be a mistake, in my view, to proceed with the choice of computer hardware until it is certain that the software meets the information management requirements of the project team. On the other hand, if the corporate EDP environment is a fixed entity, with established hardware and operating systems, the team should recognize these limitations and narrow its selection of application software accordingly.

Putting the Evaluation Matrix to Work

The planning team will need to contact systems vendors and share with them the findings of the pre-planning process, as well as the action plan that has emerged from these deliberations. As I have indicated, the best vehicle for the communication of this information is a formal request for proposal, possibly preceded by informal discussions. The vendors themselves may be the sales representatives of computer equipment manufacturers or software houses, or they may be third-party sellers, such as the proprietors of local computer stores. In any case, the team should relate its needs and expectations to each prospective provider of systems hardware and software in a fair and evenhanded manner. Vendors' responses will be your first indication of their ability to satisfy the needs of your organization. As such, these documents and the data they contain should be rated against one another through the evaluation matrix (figure 9A).

To supplement these impressions, the team should investigate vendor services by asking pointed questions and checking with cus-

Evaluation Category	Alternative 1 Weight × Score = Rating	Alternative 2 Score Rating	Alternative 3 Score Rating	Remarks
1. Proposal (5%)				
1.1 Understanding of requirements	2			
1.2 Project plan & implementation schedule	2			
1.3 Response to all areas as requested	1			
Subtotal (1)	5			

Project Name: _____

Prepared by: _____

Date of Analysis Submission: _____

(scoring: 10=outstanding; 7.5=good; 5=average; 2.5=poor; 0=unacceptable)

Figure 9A. The Evaluation Matrix: Vendor Proposal Response.

tomers. When checking such references, raise questions concerning service, dependability, and continuing vendor support. Bear in mind that the organization is purchasing more than a computer configuration. The team will want to be fairly confident that the selected vendor not only meets the institution's immediate needs but is also in a position to deal with system enhancements as they are required. (See figure 9B.) This approach is particularly important in a period when the marketplace is overrun with unauthorized dealers and mail order companies that lack the stability, resources, and expertise to offer ongoing product support. Do not neglect geographical considerations. If a vendor has no presence in your locale, it is unlikely that he or she will be in a position to provide your project team with the required support during and after implementation.

Once the team completes its review of prospective vendors, the next phase of the evaluation encompasses an analysis of each vendor's hardware (figure 9C), operating systems software (figure 9D), and applications software (figure 9E) proposals. In each of these instances, the matrix draws the planning team's attention to the appropriateness or "fit" of the proposed system. The concerns here include: the match of the product with current and expected system demands, reliability, ease of use, quality of documentation, and product "upgradeability" (i.e., the facility to enhance system capabilities in conjunction with the release of new or more advanced technologies). Users intending to modify an applications software package (refer to figure 9E, points 5.7 and 5.9) will need the original programming or "source" code for the package. Some vendors will provide it, others will not. Even with the source code, changes will be expensive and difficult if the design of the package is not modular, thus allowing portions to be altered rather than the entire system. Do not hesitate to ask the vendor for the names and phone numbers of customers who have purchased the products under discussion. Check with a few of them to ensure that the vendor's claims are justified. Where possible, consult a user whose system specifications are similar to your own, and actually visit that facility to observe the system in operation.

For those contemplating the purchase of microcomputer systems, access to demonstration models can be obtained at any authorized sales outlet. Vendors of larger systems may allow potential customers to test their products on-site for a thirty- to ninety-day period at a reasonable rental rate. Those MIS units that are obliged to use their parent institution's equipment will often have free access for testing purposes and subsequent use.

When examining the choices for the acquisition of small computer systems, project members may be attracted to the advertisements of mail order vendors. In many instances, these catalog prices

Evaluation Category	Alternative 1 Weight × Score = Rating	Alternative 2 Score	Rating	Alternative 3 Score	Rating	Remarks
2. Vendor firm evaluation (25%)						
2.1 Staffing level and caliber of profess. staff	4					
2.2 Client refers.	4					
2.3 Support & services	3					
2.4 Firm's financial stability	3					
2.5 Firm's organization stability	3					
2.6 Flexibility of contract	2					
2.7 Experience with similar industry	2					
2.8 Experience with similar hardware and operating system	2					
2.9 Experience with similar applications	2					
Subtotal (2)	25					

Project Name: _____

Prepared by: _____

Date of Analysis Submission: _____

(scoring: 10=outstanding; 7.5=good; 5=average; 2.5=poor; 0=unacceptable)

Figure 9B. The Evaluation Matrix: Vendor Firm Evaluation.

are considerably lower than those obtained directly from manufacturers or through computer stores. Despite the potential savings offered by this approach, I strongly recommend dealing directly with a reputable manufacturer's representative or a local computer store. Even if the wholesale house will honor a return of defective merchandise, the distance and time delays involved will prove more

Evaluation Category	Alternative 1 Weight × Score = Rating	Alternative 2 Score	Rating	Alternative 3 Score	Rating	Remarks
3. Hardware proposed (15%)						
3.1 Capacity for current and projected vols.	3					
3.2 Expandability of computer and peripherals	2					
3.3 Reliability	2					
3.4 Ease of use	2					
3.5 Maintenance and service support	2					
3.6 Suitability for the application	2					
3.7 Availability	1					
3.8 State-of-the-art technology	1					
Subtotal (3)	15					

Project Name: _____

Prepared by: _____

Date of Analysis Submission: _____

(scoring: 10=outstanding; 7.5=good; 5=average; 2.5=poor; 0=unacceptable)

Figure 9C. The Evaluation Matrix: Hardware.

costly than the initial savings at the time of purchase. Furthermore, few mail order operations provide repair services or customer assistance. A local computer store offers all of these things—and convenience. Certain items, such as standard software application packages, can be obtained through the mail with little risk. However, the team should reserve its major purchases for local vendors.

The final section of the evaluation matrix (figure 9F) groups together a number of miscellaneous elements. Beyond the mechanics of implementation and maintenance, this portion of the tool considers user training, report generation, disaster preparedness, in-house technical requirements, and the ability of the system to move into

Evaluation Category	Alternative 1 Weight × Score = Rating	Alternative 2 Score Rating	Alternative 3 Score Rating	Remarks
4. Systems software proposal (10%)				
4.1 Ability to meet requirements	3			
4.2 Reliability	2			

4.3 Capacity for
    current and
    projected
    volumes
	2			

4.4 Suitability for
    the hardware
    and applications
	1			

4.5 Availability	1			
4.6 State-of-the-art technology	1			
Subtotal (4)	10			

Project Name: _____

Prepared by: _____

Date of Analysis Submission: _____

(scoring: 10=outstanding; 7.5=good; 5=average; 2.5=poor; 0=unacceptable)

Figure 9D.   The Evaluation Matrix: Systems Software.

service immediately upon installation. Having addressed these questions, the planning team is then prepared to make a formal recommendation of the EDP options which best comply with its system requirements. In preparing comments for senior management review, the evaluation matrix provides both answers and supporting arguments. By employing this document in conjunction with the planning matrix reviewed previously in this chapter, the team should have all that it requires to win the support of superiors.

However, before you proceed with the management approval process, the costs of your MIS proposal must also be placed in a comparative context. All too often, an otherwise worthy, and indeed necessary, project has failed to win the approval of senior management because the planning team neglected an evaluation of the true costs and benefits of procuring and maintaining the new MIS product.

Evaluation Category	Alternative 1 Weight × Score = Rating	Alternative 2 Score	Rating	Alternative 3 Score	Rating	Remarks
5. Application software (25%)						
5.1 Ability to meet application requirements	4					
5.2 Extent of modifications needed	3					
5.3 Maintenance & service support	3					
5.4 Quality and completeness of documentation	3					
5.5 Capacity for current and projected needs	3					
5.6 Ease of use	2					
5.7 Availability of source-code	2					
5.8 Availability of softwr. packages	1					
5.9 Design & modularity of software	1					
5.10 Number of installations	1					
5.11 Programming language	1					
5.12 Availability of other future application packages	1					
Subtotal (5)	25					

Project Name: _____

Prepared by: _____

Date of Analysis Submission: _____

(scoring: 10=outstanding; 7.5=good; 5=average; 2.5=poor; 0=unacceptable)

Figure 9E.   The Evaluation Matrix: Applications Software.

	Alternative 1	Alternative 2		Alternative 3		
	Weight × Score					
Evaluation Category	**= Rating**	*Score*	*Rating*	*Score*	*Rating*	*Remarks*
6. Miscellaneous factors (20%)						
6.1 Ease of conversion and installation	4					
6.2 Quality and thoroughness of acceptance test procedures	3					
6.3 Extent of training needed	3					
6.4 Report generator capabilities	3					
6.5 Treatment of backup, recovery and disaster	2					
6.6 Necessity for in-house technical expertise	2					
6.7 Compatibility with current operating procedures	2					
6.8 Level of turnkey approach	1					
Subtotal (6)	20					

Project Name: _____

Prepared by: _____

Date of Analysis Submission: _____

(scoring: 10=outstanding; 7.5=good; 5=average; 2.5=poor; 0=unacceptable)

Figure 9F.   The Evaluation Matrix: Miscellaneous Factors.

Quite naturally, enthusiasm for an EDP solution on purely operational grounds at times obscures its fiscal soundness in the minds of its recommenders. On the other hand, some have also been blinded by the technology, to the extent that they have ignored sound business reasons for the project's rejection. Thus, no thorough and successful evaluation of system options can be concluded without a financial analysis in keeping with the accounting standards of the parent organization.

The reader may recall that in Chapter Four I briefly survey the various options for financing the acquisition of computers and their peripherals (see figure 7). To supplement these previous observations and the findings of the evaluation matrix, I have developed figure 10. This worksheet brings together all factors involved in setting a full and accurate price for any given EDP configuration. In analyzing costs, the initial purchase price of hardware and software, installation, technical support, system modifications, system updates, maintenance, and supplies must be included. Both hardware and software may be purchased, leased, or rented—with the exception of the microcomputer end of the range, where products are most often available for purchase only. With large systems, a maintenance contract, though expensive, is essential. Remember that maintenance expenses may come to play an increasingly substantial role in budgeting for ongoing automated systems support. If software modifications are required, programming costs may also prove to be a significant factor in overall system expenses.

Finally, the possibility exists that incidental costs may force the price of an automated system above initial projections. Special staff training (if not provided as part of the equipment or software purchase price) will add to costs. Similarly, the need for facility remodeling, cabling, additional power sources, phone lines for networking, or changing environmental (heating and air conditioning) systems may run into significant dollars. Accessories, such as cooling fans for the CPU, storage containers for system disks and appropriate furniture for the equipment, must also be considered in calculating the cost of the new system. Furthermore, relatively expensive supplies, including disks, printer ribbons, printer paper, forms, and letterhead, will be required once the system is operational. The cost evaluation worksheet provides the team with a convenient tool for the calculation and comparison of these expenses and for estimating the ongoing cost of each project alternative.

While determining the true cost of an EDP conversion is an important step in the planning process, it is by no means the final one in justifying the expense to senior management. They will want to know how these MIS enhancements will benefit the larger organization. If one can simply demonstrate that the new systems will reduce operating costs, this in and of itself may suffice. However, as I have suggested, few projects enjoy this type of transparent justification. Instead, one must often build a case around cost avoidance. (Here, detailed unit-cost information, derived from figure 5 may prove invaluable.) The planning team may, alternatively, take the approach

Cost Elements	Alternative 1	Alternative 2	Alternative 3

1. Hardware
  a. purchase
  b. monthly lease
  c. monthly rental
  d. monthly maint.
  Total hardware cost
    lease (b + d)
    rental (c + d)			

2. Software
  a. basic package
  b. modifications
  c. total (a + b)
  d. monthly lease
  e. monthly rental
  f. monthly maint.
  Total software cost
    lease (d + f)
    rental (e + f)			

3. Other
  a. training
  b. phone lines
  c. added personnel
  d. vendor assist.
  e. taxes, freight, furniture
    & accessories
  f. remodeling
  g. supplies
  Total other costs
    Monthly
    One-time costs			

Total Purchase (Capital)			

Total Monthly Costs
  Lease/purchase
  Rental			

Project Name: _____

Prepared by: _____

Date of Analysis Submission: _____

Figure 10. Cost Evaluation Worksheet.

Study Components	Alternative 1	Alternative 2	Alternative 3	Remarks

A. Evaluation Matrix
  1. Proposal response (max. 50 points)
  2. Vendor firm evaluation (max. 250 points)
  3. Hardware (max. 150 points)
  4. System software (max. 100 points)
  5. Application software (max. 250 points)
  6. Miscellaneous factors (max. 200 points)				

Grand Total (max. 1,000 points)				

B. Cost Evaluation
  1. Hardware
  2. Software
  3. Other				

Cost Grand Total				

Project Name: _____

Prepared by: _____

Date of Analysis Submission: _____

Figure 11. Evaluation Summary Worksheet.

that an upgrade of information systems as proposed is in keeping with corporate strategies, and is in fact a business necessity. Even this type of qualitative argument will require an underlying financial justification if it is to win support. In the end, the team's method of presentation must address larger organizational concerns as seen through the eyes of senior management. The planning process creates the database from which MIS personnel may build such a case.

With the completion of the evaluation matrix and its related cost study, the planning team may summarize its findings (see figure 11). This form takes the ranking totals from the six sections of the selection matrix (figures 9A-F) and matches them with the hardware, software, and miscellaneous expenditures as itemized in the cost survey (figure 10). Through this process the planning team will not only have documented each aspect of system performance and cost but will have also checked vendor and product references. Ultimately, this thorough analysis of alternatives should point the team in a single, clearly identifiable direction. With this data in hand, the team may now approach senior management for approval. If it has done its homework and has made every effort to respond to the parent institution's strategic plans and user needs, the task force should now be in a position to win plan acceptance and subsequently to move from the project planning stage toward system implementation.

CHAPTER
6

Implementation

The Action Plan

The preceding chapter examined four of the essential elements of
any planning process. The first of these and the most important component for the success of an automation effort is needs assessment.
Through this activity, the MIS unit determines its institutional objectives, defines ongoing manual services and procedures, and identifies
service priorities in light of available resources. Next, the project staff
needs to survey in-house electronic data processing options with a
view toward limiting the choices to those that best complement the
information management problem under consideration. In particular, it is useful to match generic EDP applications such as word processing, database management, and telecommunications networking,
with specific MIS operations such as records retrieval, archival and
library services, and publications production.

Through the use of the matrixes and worksheets provided in
Chapters Three and Four, the team may then proceed with the creation of a request for proposal (RFP). This document will guide potential vendors in their structuring of EDP product, systems, and
service recommendations to address the organization's project requirements. As the next and final planning step, MIS task force members will involve themselves in actual hardware and software selection. Typically, the information services team will focus primarily
140 upon appropriate applications software packages. In so doing, it will

take the existing DP environment into account. Where the purchase of computer hardware is also involved, the choice of software will often dictate a course of action in the identification of compatible hardware.

As straightforward as these steps may appear, they are neither simple nor easily achieved in real life situations. Considerable research and self-appraisal is required in both the pre-planning and planning stages to ensure that judgements based upon data in the evaluation (figure 9), cost analysis (figure 10), and summary (figure 11) matrices are sound ones. Even when accomplished successfully, these activities do not conclude the process but merely move it on to the next sequence of tasks. These include: the purchase of equipment and its installation; the integration of automated systems into the organization's workflow; and the development of data input procedures, forms, system products, staff and user training programs, and system followup procedures. Together, these activities comprise the implementation process.

As with planning procedures, there is no single "right" way to implement MIS solutions. The development of each newly automated information service will invariably take a new course from those of its predecessors. Thus, the methodology presented here demonstrates one person's approach to automation project management. While I have enjoyed a considerable degree of success with these techniques, my readers will need to refine them in light of their individual and organizational requirements. At the very least, Chapter Five offers information service professionals a comprehensive checklist and a number of practical tools to assist in the complex processes of converting manual to automated systems, of modify existing MIS products, and of establishing an in-house service bureau.

Developing an Action Plan

At the heart of any implementation process is an action plan. This plan specifies the steps to be taken by the team in bringing its efforts to fruition. It may be as general or as detailed as the participants care to make it. As with the planning process, the reader should consider the action plan in terms of differing levels of activity, each requiring its own management approach. At the most general level, the MIS team should create an action plan that provides an overview of the entire process from pre-planning through final implementation. Each part of this task outline may, in turn, encompass a multitude of activities that are summarized in more detailed implementation documents of their own. In so doing, the team places individual assignments, such as hardware evaluation, system documentation, and staff training, within a larger, logical framework.

For the purposes of this presentation, I have developed a hypothetical, macro-level action plan in figure 12. In this particular MIS scenario, a team of information service professionals from the XYZ Corporation has been asked to automate document retrieval for the records management unit of their organization. The key players include "Burns," as the project director and the agency's chief information officer; "Jones," as the director of the Records Management unit; and "Smith," as the project technologist. Other corporate players are also involved, including the staff of the records management unit, data processing operations personnel, and key users of the records management service.

At the macro level, figure 12 itemizes clusters or sets of activities. Each large project component is given its own identification number, from RM1.0 to RM13.0. The action-plan matrix next includes task descriptions, followed by the name of the person responsible for each of these activities and the date of the assignment. The primary resources required to complete that particular job are listed in the column so indicated. In this regard, the reader will note that figure 12 cites the management matrices described previously in Chapters Three, Four, and Five as "Required Resources." My model assumes that senior MIS management has already conducted these "context" and resource studies, and has kept them current in anticipation of new projects.

Other resources may be drawn upon by the team as well. In particular, the team will from time to time require the participation of a wide range of corporate players. For example, MIS may need to involve the operational area—in this case Records Management—affected by the proposed program. Similarly, the users of the services to be automated must be involved throughout the period of system design and implementation. Since the project will draw upon data processing resources, DP personnel also have a role. Finally, vendors and other outsiders will in all likelihood play an important part in supplying the team with information, recommendations, consulting, and cost estimates.

Since figure 12 is designed to serve as a practical management tool, it also provides space for comments on the status of individual task steps, projected and actual assignment completion dates, and expense updates. As the implementation process gets underway, all participants should agree to the action plan steps, timetables, and budgets as indicated on the project's figure 12 document. To emphasize the importance of this "buy-in" process, the evaluation of individual player performance should be based upon the overall success of the team in realizing project objectives. Team members should report on a weekly or monthly basis (as appropriate), so that the

Project ID. No.	Objective/ Task Description	Task Leader	Date Assigned	Required Resources	Task Status	Planned Dates Start – End		Actual Dates Start – End		Costs Budget – Actual	
RM1.0	Analyze institutional basis of MIS units within corp.	Burns	1/2/87	Data from Fig. 1, p. 29		1/2/87	1/9/87				
RM2.0	Survey documentation handled by records management program	Burns	1/2/87	Data from Figs. 3 & 4, pp. 53 & 58		1/2/87	1/9/87				
RM3.0	Review MIS services in light of resource allocations	Burns	1/2/87	Data from Fig. 5, p. 67		1/12/87	1/16/87				
RM4.0	Review DP resources for opportunities in RM services	Burns	1/2/87	Data from Fig. 7 p. 95		1/19/87	1/30/87				
RM5.0	Perform detailed needs assessment for doc. retrieval	Jones	2/2/87	RM Staff Key Users Auditors		2/2/87	3/27/87				

Figure 12. Macro-Level Action Plan Matrix.

Project ID. No.	Objective/ Task Description	Task Leader	Date Assigned	Required Resources	Task Status	Planned Dates Start – End	Actual Dates Start – End	Costs Budget – Actual
RM6.0	Review information technologies for doc. retrieval	Smith	2/2/87	Jones Key Users Vendors		2/2/87 3/27/87		
RM7.0	Develop project specifications doc. and RFP	Burns	3/30/87	Jones Smith Vendors		3/30/87 5/1/87		
RM8.0	Receive and evaluate vendor responses involve consultant??	Burns	5/4/87	Data from Fig. 9, pp. 129, 131–135		5/4/87 5/15/87		
RM9.0	Revise plan and formalize proposals for senior management	Burns	5/4/87	Data from Figs. 10 & 11, pp. 137 & 138		5/18/87 5/29/87		
RM10.0	Purchase and install hardware & software; redo forms, workflow	Smith	6/1/87	RM Staff Key Users Vendors		6/1/87 8/28/87		

Figure 12 (Cont.)

Project ID. No.	Objective/ Task Description	Task Leader	Date Assigned	Required Resources	Task Status	Planned Dates Start – End		Actual Dates Start – End		Costs Budget – Actual	
RM11.0	Implement data entry procedures & train staff	Jones	6/1/87	RM Staff Key Users Vendors		6/29/87	8/28/87				
RM12.0	Phase in new service user training, output products	Jones	8/17/87	Smith RM Staff Users		8/17/87	9/30/87				
RM13.0	Periodic system review and modification	Jones	After Cut Over	Burns, Smith Key Users Vendors		As Needed	As Needed				

Figure 12 (Cont.)

matrix's information represents the current status of all activities as measured against the original plan.

To a certain extent, one's corporate culture and traditional modes of operation will influence the MIS manager's approach to action-plan development. Nevertheless, most of these processes have certain elements in common. First, each plan must recognize and work within some type of organizational context. For this reason, figure 12 includes research steps that analyze agency structure, the use of documents and the flow of information within the corporation, available MIS resources, and the institution's EDP capabilities and limitations. Since many of these characteristics will remain fairly constant from one project to the next, the team may choose to rely upon studies done in conjunction with previous projects. However, I would recommend that a team member validate these findings before their introduction into the current assignment's analytical tools.

With this "pre-planning" work in hand, the team must next conduct an objective assessment of user needs as these relate to the specific objectives of the new project. Nothing is more important to the success of the whole process. In the case of my example, the task force would need to assess the document retrieval requirements of the organization. Such an effort will undoubtedly raise a number of key questions, including: How do we do things now? Why is change necessary? What are the business goals of the proposed change? How will it impact current operations, procedures, and practices? Who will be affected as a result? What are the costs and benefits of the status quo and of the action-plan proposal? Bear in mind that without sufficient attention to these and related issues during the assessment process, the team will never deliver a satisfactory answer to the organization's information management problems. For that matter, they are likely to fail when initially presenting their ideas to senior management.

As a complement to needs analysis, staff technologists should scan the industry for appropriate EDP solutions. The objective of this exercise is not to come up with specific answers, but to develop a list of possible options. The project team must then refine this data and relate it to expressed user needs in developing well-focused project specifications and a clearly worded request for proposal. From this point forward, the dynamics of the implementation process are more predictable, involving bid analysis, procurement, forms and work-flow analysis and design, staff training, documentation preparation, user training, system implementation, and system maintenance.

For the purposes of effective management, each individual grouping of action-plan assignments will require a matrix of its own. Indeed, depending upon the complexity and scope of a given project, the division of tasks into various levels of subtasks could get quite involved. Figure 13 demonstrates how one goes about adding detail to the group's macro-level plan. For the purpose of this illustration, I have chosen to elaborate on step RM10 of the more general workplan. A complete action planning matrix would include similar sheets for each task component. Collectively, these sheets provide the team with a means of initially identifying all relevant tasks and of ultimately measuring project progress in relation to key milestones.

In my illustration, Smith, XYZ Corporation's technologist, is responsible for RM10—the purchase and installation of an automated document retrieval system for the Records Management Unit. To accomplish this task, he must involve records management and data processing personnel as well as vendors. He will also require the services of the company's Facilities and Telecommunications departments, and the advice and support of his bosses, Burns and Jones. To appreciate the need for expanding participation in this manner, all one has to do is to examine the task steps within RM10. For example, steps RM10.2 and RM10.3 recognize the need for building modifications and added phone lines as prerequisite to the installation of the new system. When new procedures come under scrutiny (steps RM10.4 through RM10.7), senior MIS management support—and at times direct participation—may be necessary to win user support. Throughout the figure 13 scenario, deliverables must be coordinated, expenses monitored, and people trained. Each of these points is in turn accounted for in the matrix.

In this regard, action planning tools, such as those employed above, serve a dual purpose. First, they communicate the work to be done and, second, they commit specific players to deliver on clearly defined project components within explicit timeframes and budgets. It is in fact the case that the approach suggested by figures 12 and 13 also affords team leaders (and in turn their superiors) enhanced project and staff management capabilities. Thus, it may be argued that the time spent on the development and refinement of the action plan will provide many benefits to MIS, beyond those of keeping the project personnel focused on the work at hand.

Enhancing Project Management

The action-plan matrix indicates who is responsible, what is to be done, when it is scheduled for completion, and how much it is to cost. There is also space to indicate whether or not that particular component is coming in on or over budget. This latter point is particularly important because senior corporate managers often approve a MIS project for one of two reasons: either the task is a necessary part of doing business or it is a money saver. In either case, the timing

Project ID. No.	Objective/ Task Description	Task Leader	Date Assigned	Required Resources	Task Status	Planned Dates Start – End		Actual Dates Start – End		Costs Budget – Actual	
RM10.0	Purchase and install hardware & software, redo forms, workflow	Smith	6/1/87	RM Staff Key Users Vendors		6/1/87	8/28/87				
RM10.1	Place orders with hardware & software vendors		6/1/87	Purchasing DP Ops. Vendors		6/1/87	6/8/87				
RM10.2	Establish & develop facilities to accommodate new systems		6/15/87	Facilities DP Ops. Vendors		6/15/87	8/14/87				
RM10.3	Order telecom. links for remote retrieval devices		6/15/87	Facilities Telecom. Vendors		7/13/87	8/14/87				
RM10.4	Develop budget doc.; evaluate existing forms & procedures		6/15/87	Burns Jones Key Users		6/15/87	7/3/87				

Figure 13. Detailed Action Plan Matrix.

Project ID. No.	Objective/ Task Description	Task Leader	Date Assigned	Required Resources	Task Status	Planned Dates Start – End		Actual Dates Start – End		Costs Budget – Actual	
RM10.5	Draft revised forms and procedures		6/15/87	Burns Jones Key Users		7/3/87	7/31/87				
RM10.6	Review proposed forms & procedures with key users		7/31/87	Burns Jones Key Users		8/3/87	8/14/87				
RM10.7	Revise and finalize forms & procedures with key users		8/14/87	Burns Jones Key Users		8/14/87	8/28/87				
RM10.8	Complete facilities & telecommunications work for hardware		6/15/87	Facilities Telecom. Vendors		6/15/87	8/14/87				
RM10.9	Receive and install hardware; review budget DOC.		6/1/87	RM Staff DP Staff Vendors		7/28/87	8/14/87				

Figure 13 (Cont.)

Project ID. No.	Objective/ Task Description	Task Leader	Date Assigned	Required Resources	Task Status	Planned Dates Start – End		Actual Dates Start – End		Costs Budget – Actual	
RM10.10	Load and test software; review budget doc.		6/1/87	RM Staff DP Staff Vendors		8/17/87	8/21/87				
RM10.11	Test run of new RM system; revise forms & proceds. as neces.		6/1/87	RM Staff DP Staff Key Users		8/24/87	8/28/87				
RM10.12	Assist in staff/user training; cutover; review budget doc.		8/17/87	RM Staff DP Staff Key Users		8/17/87	9/30/87				

Figure 13 (Cont.)

and cost of deliverables are foremost among their concerns. It is the organization's information services professionals who, in cooperation with key users, bring these projects to the company's leadership for approval, and it is therefore incumbent upon them to ensure that, once raised, these expectations are satisfied. Conversely, if things start to go wrong, it is best that this news come from a well-informed project manager rather than later on in the process, from an unhappy controller or a disgruntled user.

This approach to management is particularly imperative when implementing MIS projects because of their complexity and, hence, the greater opportunity for things to go wrong. Indeed, it has been my experience that something unexpected always emerges during the course of planning and implementing automated systems which will, in turn, delay, complicate, or redirect a particular assignment. Thus, it is almost axiomatic in these types of undertakings that "No major project was ever developed on time and within budget; yours will not be the first."[1] Furthermore, it is often the case that your users will come back to you with changes to the project's specifications, adding cost and time to your team's efforts.

In anticipation of these types of problems, I have developed a set of simple management tools to assist MIS personnel monitoring changes in the delivery and cost of project components. The first of these, figure 14, graphs each of the task steps, identified in figure 12, against a time line. The duration of each activity is measured in weeks, and is marked with a star (*) for an independent step, a minus (−) for a dependent action, and a plus (+) for a concomitant activity. In this manner, figure 14 provides a visual representation of the project schedule and the relationships between the various tasks.

For example, the figure indicates that steps RM1 through RM4 may be accomplished independently of one another but must precede action point RM5. While RM6 may be tackled at the same time as RM5, both assignments must be complete before the team moves on to RM7. Thus, figure 14 captures the "critical path" of project activities. If delays occur during implementation, these should be graphed against the original time line so as to determine their impact. When changes occur in the schedule due to product delivery delays, a redefinition of the project's scope, or any other problem, the model can then be readjusted to reflect these alterations. For this reason, it is best to construct a dynamic model so that scheduling changes are easily accomplished. Both magnetic programming boards and PC-

1. See William R. Synnott and William H. Grube, *Information Resource Management: Opportunities and Strategies for the 1980's* (New York: Wiley, 1981): 273. See also Synnott and Grube, Chapter 11, "Project Selection and Management," 273–312.

PROJECT: RM/1, AUTOMATION OF DOCUMENT RETRIEVAL
WORK SCHEDULE FOR PERIOD: JANUARY 2, 1987 TO SEPTEMBER 30, 1987

1987

Activity	January 5 12 19 26	February 2 9 16 23	March 2 9 16 23 30	April 6 13 20 27	May 4 11 18 25
Project process					
RM1. MIS org. analysis	***********				
RM2. RM survey & doc. study	***********				
RM3. MIS resource allocations	***********				
RM4. Review of DP resources	***********				
RM5. Detailed needs assessment			- - - - - - - - - - -		
RM6. Technology scan: doc. retrieval		+ +			

Figure 14. Project Schedule.

Activity	January 5 12 19 26	February 2 9 16 23	March 2 9 16 23 30	April 6 13 20 27	May 4 11 18 25
RM7. Project secs & RF					
RM8. Evaluate vendor responses					
RM9. Revise plans; get sen. manag. okay					
RM10. Purchase & install systems					
RM11. Implement data entry & train					
RM12. Phase in new sys. applications					
RM13. Period reviews & modifications					

Activity	January 5 12 19 26	February 2 9 16 23	March 2 9 16 23 30	April 6 13 20 27	May 4 11 18 25

KEY: "*" = INDEPENDENT ACTIVITY
"-" = DEPENDENT ACTIVITY
"+" = CONCOMITANT ACTIVITY

Figure 14. (Cont.)

1987

Activity	June 1	8	15	22	29	July 6	13	20	27	August 3	10	17	24	31	September 7	14	21	28
Project process																		
RM1. MIS org. analysis																		
RM2. RM survey & doc. study																		
RM3. MIS resource allocations																		
RM4. Review of DP resources																		
RM5. Detailed needs assessment																		
RM6. Technology scan: doc. retrieval																		
RM7. Project specs & RFP																		
RM8. Evaluate vendor responses																		

Activity	June 1	8	15	22	29	July 6	13	20	27	August 3	10	17	24	31	September 7	14	21	28

Figure 14 (Cont.)

Activity	1	8	June 15	22	29	6	July 13	20	27	3	August 10	17	24	31	7	September 14	21	28
RM9. Revise plans; get sen. manag. okay																		
RM10. Purchase & install systems			- - - - - - - - - - - - - - -														
RM11. Implement data entry & train					***												
RM12. Phase in new sys. applications											+ +							
RM13. Period reviews & modifications																	ONGOING	

Activity	1	8	June 15	22	29	6	July 13	20	27	3	August 10	17	24	31	7	September 14	21	28

KEY: "....." = INDEPENDENT ACTIVITY
"- -" = DEPENDENT ACTIVITY
"+" = CONCOMITANT ACTIVITY

Figure 14 (Cont.)

based project planning software afford such flexibility.[2] Finally, the team may decide to prepare similar documents as necessary for each set of subtasks (e.g., for the activities listed in figure 13).

Financial control in project management calls for additional tools as well. The budget and expense information provided in the far-right columns of figures 12 and 13 are summary in nature and are meant only to highlight problem areas. By contrast, figure 15 indicates the detailed total amount of anticipated cost in each expense category. The table also provides space to the right for the indication of the amount and the month in which funds will be required. Since in major projects cash flow issues could be significant, MIS managers will find that this document or something similar will be very much appreciated by those managing the organization's finances. It will also prove useful in plotting a tax strategy for dealing with project expenses. Furthermore, the table forces the team to scrutinize costs more rigorously as part of initial proposal preparation.

For example, hardware and software could be purchased or leased. If the system is purchased, the project manager will need to account for the amortization of the equipment and/or software, as well as the associated costs of financing the acquisition (i.e., cost of funds). If the system is leased, the arrangement includes regular monthly and possibly final byout or balloon payments. From a business perspective, there may be advantages to either approach. No doubt, your Accounting Department will assist you in making this determination. No matter the option of choice, there will be related maintenance costs and perhaps customized programming modifications. Facilities improvements may also be amortized, but for lesser items, you may choose simply to expense them.

If training is not included as part of the purchase or lease price of the hardware and software, project management should anticipate added expense in this area. Similarly, new information systems may require additions to staff or the upgrading of personnel to reflect changes in job responsibilities. Supplies, furniture, freight, taxes, and so forth will also contribute to the total cost of the undertaking. I doubt that figure 15 identifies all of the possibilities, but it demonstrates the list of expense categories to be drawn up by the project team at the outset of an assignment.

---

2. Magnetic planning boards have been with us for some time. They provide a grid upon which magnetized chips of varying shapes and colors can be placed to track projects over a period of time. While useful in identifying and monitoring the progress of the various stages of a project, they are not particularly flexible or easily updated. More recently, many software vendors have developed a wide range of management tools that perform the same tasks in an online, interactive mode on small computers. The Harvard Project Manager and Diagram Master are two excellent examples of this type of product, in which the user can enter scheduling, financial, and workforce data; easily alter them at will; and generate reports, tables, and graphs.

PROJECT NUMBER: RM/1
NAME OF PROJECT: AUTOMATION OF DOCUMENT RETRIEVAL

Project Activity	Total	1987 Cash Flow Jan Costs / Feb Costs		1987 Cash Flow Mar Costs / Apr Costs		1987 Cash Flow May Costs / Jun Costs	
Hardware							
Item-1 (Purchase)	$0						
Amortization	$0						
Cost of funds	$0						
Lease	$0						
Maintenance	$0						
Item-2 (Purchase)	$0						
Amortization	$0						
Cost of funds	$0						
Lease	$0						
Maintenance	$0						
Item-N (purchase)	$0						
Amortization	$0						
Cost of funds	$0						
Lease	$0						
Maintenance	$0						
Software							
Item-1 (purchase)	$0						
Amortization	$0						
Cost of funds	$0						
Lease	$0						
Modification	$0						
Maintenance	$0						
Item-2 (purchase)	$0						
Amortization	$0						
Cost of funds	$0						
Lease	$0						
Modification	$0						
Maintenance	$0						
Item-N (purchase)	$0						
Amortization	$0						
Cost of funds	$0						
Lease	$0						
Modification	$0						
Maintenance	$0						
Other							
Facilities							
Construction	$0						
HVAC	$0						
Electrical	$0						
Telecom connects	$0						
Training	$0						
Added personnel	$0						
Furniture	$0						
Supplies	$0						
Freight, tax, misc.	$0						
Totals	$0	$0	$0	$0	$0	$0	$0

Figure 15. Budget Control Sheet Showing Cash Flows.

Project Activity	Total	1987 Cash Flow Jul Costs	Aug Costs	1987 Cash Flow Sep Costs	Oct Costs	Total
Hardware						
Item-1 (Purchase)						$0
Amortization						$0
Cost of funds						$0
Lease						$0
Maintenance						$0
Item-2 (Purchase)						$0
Amortization						$0
Cost of funds						$0
Lease						$0
Maintenance						$0
Item-N (purchase)						$0
Amortization						$0
Cost of funds						$0
Lease						$0
Maintenance						$0
Software						
Item-1 (purchase)						$0
Amortization						$0
Cost of funds						$0
Lease						$0
Modification						$0
Maintenance						$0
Item-2 (purchase)						$0
Amortization						$0
Cost of funds						$0
Lease						$0
Modification						$0
Maintenance						$0
Item-N (purchase)						$0
Amortization						$0
Cost of funds						$0
Lease						$0
Modification						$0
Maintenance						$0
Other						
Facilities						
Construction						$0
HVAC						$0
Electrical						$0
Telecom connects						$0
Training						$0
Added personnel						$0
Furniture						$0
Supplies						$0
Freight, tax, misc.						$0
Totals	$0	$0	$0	$0	$0	$0

Figure 15   (Cont.)

The limitations of figure 15 should be clear to anyone who has managed a project of any complexity. While budgets are a fine starting point for financial control, they cannot reflect the dynamics of the implementation process. As specifications and the scope of work change, so do costs. Similarly, the introduction of new technologies and the discovery of unanticipated problems may add to or reduce expense at any time during the project's life cycle. With these management issues in mind, I have devised a cost analysis worksheet, depicted in figure 16. This table provides a column for the budget, subsequent vendor quotes, the cost of change orders, and the projected actual cost. Figure 16 will also show dollar and percentage variances between budgeted amounts and anticipated actuals. There is a column for the total number of dollars paid to date, the amount in dispute (if any), and the percentage paid.

It is usually the responsibility of the project manager to keep this type of report current. As his or her team members report any changes in cost estimates, these would be entered into the vendor quote or change order columns. As bills are paid, the manager would enter the revised totals in the appropriate places. If a disagreement arises between the team and one of its contractors or suppliers, the table accommodates sums in dispute. For the team leader, the value of figure 16 is in its ability to point out problems. Any category that is running over budget will be immediately evident. Similarly, project components that are far from completion but for which the organization has already paid a substantial amount will become obvious. By alerting themselves to these issues, task force players can more readily address them prior to their coming to the attention of key users or corporate senior management.

Indeed, if employed effectively, figure 16 should lead to an avoidance of many of the messy problems often associated with the financial side of MIS project management. While all of this may appear trivial to the information services professional concerned with bringing new EDP technologies to his or her organization, it is extremely important to deliver projects in time and on budget. Corporate management may not recognize the importance of your contribution but it will remember your failure to control costs. MIS personnel who neglect these "details" will find that their supporters among the organization's leadership will diminish over time. Furthermore, even the perception of poor MIS management through inadequate controls will hurt team credibility, while a proactive approach will help in winning support for subsequent undertakings.

Sequencing Project Activities

Returning once again to the action plan matrix (figure 12), let us consider the actual sequence of project activities. First of all, note

PROJECT NUMBER:
NAME OF PROJECT: AUTOMATION OF DOCUMENT RETRIEVAL

RM/1 STARTING DATE: JANUARY 2, 1987
PROJECTED END DATE: SEPTEMBER 30, 1987

Project Activity	Budgeted Expense	Vendor Quote	Change Orders	Projcted Actual Cost	$ Budget Variance	% Budget Variance	Tot $ Paid to Date	Total $ Currently Disputed	% Paid to Date	Comments
Hardware										
Item-1 (purchase)					$0	0.00%	$0		0.00%	
Amortization					$0	0.00%	$0		0.00%	
Cost of funds					$0	0.00%	$0		0.00%	
Lease					$0	0.00%	$0		0.00%	
Maintenance					$0	0.00%	$0		0.00%	
Item-2 (purchase)					$0	0.00%	$0		0.00%	
Amortization					$0	0.00%	$0		0.00%	
Cost of funds					$0	0.00%	$0		0.00%	
Lease					$0	0.00%	$0		0.00%	
Maintenance					$0	0.00%	$0		0.00%	
Item-N (purchase)					$0	0.00%	$0		0.00%	
Amortization					$0	0.00%	$0		0.00%	
Cost of funds					$0	0.00%	$0		0.00%	
Lease					$0	0.00%	$0		0.00%	
Maintenance					$0	0.00%	$0		0.00%	
Software										
Item-1 (purchase)					$0	0.00%	$0		0.00%	
Amortization					$0	0.00%	$0		0.00%	
Cost of funds					$0	0.00%	$0		0.00%	
Lease					$0	0.00%	$0		0.00%	
Modification					$0	0.00%	$0		0.00%	
Maintenance					$0	0.00%	$0		0.00%	

Figure 16. Cost Analysis Project Status Report.

Project Activity	Budgeted Expense	Vendor Quote	Change Orders	Projcted Actual Cost	$ Budget Variance	% Budget Variance	Tot $ Paid to Date	Total $ Currently Disputed	% Paid to Date	Comments
Item-2 (purchase)					$0	0.00%	$0		0.00%	
Amortization					$0	0.00%	$0		0.00%	
Cost of funds					$0	0.00%	$0		0.00%	
Lease					$0	0.00%	$0		0.00%	
Modification					$0	0.00%	$0		0.00%	
Maintenance					$0	0.00%	$0		0.00%	
Item-N (purchase)					$0	0.00%	$0		0.00%	
Amortization					$0	0.00%	$0		0.00%	
Cost of funds					$0	0.00%	$0		0.00%	
Lease					$0	0.00%	$0		0.00%	
Modification					$0	0.00%	$0		0.00%	
Maintenance					$0	0.00%	$0		0.00%	
Other Facilities										
Construction					$0	0.00%	$0		0.00%	
HVAC					$0	0.00%	$0		0.00%	
Electrical					$0	0.00%	$0		0.00%	
Telecom connects					$0	0.00%	$0		0.00%	
Training					$0	0.00%	$0		0.00%	
Added personnel					$0	0.00%	$0		0.00%	
Furniture					$0	0.00%	$0		0.00%	
Supplies					$0	0.00%	$0		0.00%	
Freight, tax, misc.					$0	0.00%	$0		0.00%	
Totals	$0	$0	$0	$0	$0	0.00%	$0	$0	0.00%	

Figure 16. (Cont.)

that nearly three-quarters of the matrix is composed of steps outlined in the discussion of the planning process in Chapter Five. This should come as no surprise, since the successful completion of planning activities must precede actual system implementation. For that matter, the number of functions in the planning process serves to emphasize its importance to the overall project framework.

Having completed the analysis stage, the project staff is now in a position to proceed with formal implementation. Step 1 is systems procurement. If the team has done its homework, it will have a clear understanding of its information management needs, as well as which configuration best addresses these requirements. Assuming that the staff has agreed upon the choice of a particular product line, it is then necessary to establish the vendor(s) who can offer the best prices and servicing for specific system components. As alluded to earlier, the staff has a number of options regarding the actual purchasing of the system. One may rent, lease, or purchase, depending on one's financial constraints and operational objectives.

However, cost is not the only factor to consider. It is, in my view, a mistake to accept the lowest bid and, in so doing, sacrifice quality customer service. Vendors such as IBM, which are known for their servicing, realize this and therefore tend not to reduce prices during negotiations.[3] Remember that an automated system is no use to anyone if it is not functioning properly. If necessary, it is far better to trade a higher purchase price for written assurances of ongoing vendor support, as substantiated by the successful support of similar configurations elsewhere. Furthermore, it is not uncommon to require noncompliance clauses in contracts, in which monetary penalties are invoked as a consequence of the vendor's failure to deliver product services within a specified time.

Depending upon one's location and the market's demand for the EDP products in question, it will take some time to identify hardware and software options and to negotiate a final purchase price. With the possible exception of microcomputer configurations, anticipate delays between vendor commitment and delivery. For example, delivery of "off the shelf" equipment, such as IBM 3178 terminals with standard keyboards, will take much less time to deliver and install than customized products. In some of these latter situations, six months to a year may be needed. Whatever the case, delivery dates should

---

3. IBM policies in this area are perhaps the strictest in the industry. While IBM does grant discounts to volume purchasers, it usually requires the customer to commit to the purchase of a specific number of units over a specified range of delivery dates. Other vendors are less stringent in their demands. Nevertheless, many cost-conscious purchasers of EDP equipment continue to deal with IBM because they know that they can rely on the quality of IBM products and the subsequent support of the equipment, once purchased.

be part of the terms of any final sales agreement. Here again, if the situation is critical to your operations, insist on some type of penalty clause if your vendor lets you down. Once the order is signed, there will be little recourse to a prolonged delay unless delivery, installation, and testing schedules are part of the contract. When preparing the action plan, the project staff should allow for these issues.

To be honest, no matter how prolonged it may at first appear, the time between system selection and installation is a vital period in the project's life cycle. This is because the team will employ these weeks or months to train staff and users, and to prepare the environment for the new hardware and software. For instance, as soon as the system specifications have been established, the staff must begin the process of readying data for input. If manual procedures are in place, these must be adapted for conversion to a set of automated services. In addition, activities that are currently unstructured must be rationalized so as to make the best use of resources within the new operations scenario. Generally, the team will find the routinization of established functions the most demanding and time consuming of all implementation process assignments. It may, for example, entail the creation and enforcement of new procedures for the capturing and gathering of vital data, the designing of data screens and new input forms, and the establishment of quality control systems.

The task of preparing data will also prove formidable to those institutions with a substantial backlog of paper records for entry into the automated system. This work will undoubtedly place a strain on user departments already under stress over the introduction of new technologies. To facilitate the conversion process, it may prove beneficial to establish a data dictionary that defines all relevant descriptive terms employed by the department, thus providing a common language and controlling mechanism for all of those employed in data entry.[4] Unfortunately, few activities are as divisive and time consuming as establishing controlled descriptors. Therefore, the data dictionary should be developed with care, but with limited in-house debate. Ultimately, the quality of the new information system or service will be only as good as the data entered into it. Resources al-

4. See, for example, Richard H. Lytle, "A National Information System for Archives and Manuscript Collections," *American Archivist* 43,3 (1980): 423–26 and David Bearman, *Towards National Information Systems for Archives and Manuscript Repositories* (Chicago: Society of American Archivists, 1987). Forms standardization is also essential for the successful implementation of an input process. For those programs with few standardized forms, see College and University Archives Committee of the Society of American Archivists, *Forms Manual* (Chicago: Society of American Archivists, 1982); and William Benedon, *Records Management* (Englewood Cliffs, N.J.: Prentice-Hall, 1969). Some of the forms presented in these volumes lend themselves more readily to conversion to a machine-readable form than others.

located to this project component are therefore easily justified. However, because of its political overtones, such an approach is unlikely to succeed without leadership and direction from senior management. In the final analysis, consistency in database design and data entry will foster the standardization of information collection and dissemination. These developments in turn will facilitate the exchange of data between organizations.

From the user's standpoint, data integrity and security are essential to the success of any input process. The MIS team must share this perspective and take the necessary steps to ensure that automated information delivery systems do not compromise the quality of original data sources and that they protect corporate information from inappropriate disclosure.[5] It is therefore best to prepare for these requirements even before commencing the process of data entry. When a transfer is made from a manual to a computerized system for information storage, everything should appear in its most definitive state. Thus, the date of an accession to the records center should appear as "March 20, 1982," not as "1982." The latter lacks all the specificity of the former. As a result, it limits the possibilities of the end user who goes into the database for some expressed research purpose. Once it is abbreviated as indicated above, it can never be reconstructed. Be as specific and as comprehensive as possible during data entry. Once the information is keyed into the system, it may be accessed, manipulated, and truncated to suit any user requirement.

To further protect the integrity of data during the input process, the implementation team must establish adequate quality control procedures and make certain that these are enforced by line management. In addition, the organization as a whole should observe standard data security practices. Once entered in the system for administrative purposes, all information of a confidential or vital nature ought to be restricted from general access. To prevent individual employees from roaming through databases unencumbered, most automated systems provide varying degrees of security controlled through passwords. Thus, a clerical employee may have access only to file identification numbers, locations, and retention dates on a records management DBMS, but that person's supervisor may have ad-

---

5. Database security is always a hot topic in the trade literature. Industry specialists have identified the problems and are struggling to find the answers. See Randy J. Goldfield, "Records Automation," *Administrative Management* 43,2 (1982): 84–85; Eduardo B. Fernandez, Rita C. Summers, and Christopher Wood, *Database Security and Integrity* (Reading: Mass.: Addison-Wesley, 1981); Donn B. Parker, *Computer Security Management* (Reston, Va.: Reston Publishing Co., 1981); and James A. Schweitzer, *Managing Information Security: A Program for the Electronic Information Age* (Woburn, Mass.: Butterworth, 1981).

mittance to precise documents which indicate the importance of the file to the organization. In this scenario, each has the information required to do his or her job without compromising the security of the database. Similarly, the ability to alter records entered into the system should be restricted to users with the correct clearance.[6] In so doing, the institution is protected and the integrity of the data entry process is maintained.

The EDP system should be scheduled for delivery some time prior to the completion of the input procedures and forms design phase. When the system is installed and tested, staff training should commence at once. Special preference should be given to those who will be involved with the input process. Many times, hands-on experience will point out errors or misconceptions in procedures and forms design that are not apparent during the course of manual operations or the new system's pre-planning stage. With a modicum of experience on the system, those assigned to data input will be in a better position to adjust their procedures before the team proceeds to full implementation. Indeed, it is strongly recommended that the staff experiment with various approaches before making a commitment to a particular data entry methodology. Changes in midstream will prove costly, and may in fact derail the larger effort. Therefore, invest the effort at the front end of the project; you will never regret it.

The Final Stages of Implementation

With a final agreement on input procedures and formats, data preparation may begin in earnest. Depending upon the number of employees involved, different workers may be assigned to the completion of input forms and the entry of data into the new computer system. In settings where input is handled by a single person, it is best to interrupt the process occasionally so that the staff may execute test runs of the data on the new system. This approach ensures that if problems still exist in either data entry formats or in the system's treatment of processed information, these issues will be caught before too many resources have been invested. Once all the kinks have been worked out, information may be entered as quickly as the operating unit's staff resources and computer equipment will allow. At the same time, a member of the project team should be assigned to document the newly established input procedures and the machine-readable

---

6. For a detailed survey of data security products, their varying levels of protection, system costs, and operational considerations, see McGraw-Hill's Datapro *Data Security* and Auerbach's *Data Security* loose-leaf services.

files so created. Staff training materials, and even computer-based instruction (CBI), may supplement these documentation efforts.[7]

With data entry well underway, the team can turn to the identification of products and services based upon the newly automated system. Commonly referred to as "output," these products will range widely. Depending upon the EDP equipment and software environment employed, either batch (hardcopy) or online services may be considered. Some offerings will require staff assistance while others will depend upon users accessing the data themselves. For example, an automated records management system might have the capability to generate retention and disposition schedules for user departments in a batch mode. At the same time, it may allow individuals to search the database online for specific file locations within the organization's storage facility. Whatever products ultimately emerge, the MIS team will need to provide comprehensive training for its own people, as well as users, if the new system is to be fully exploited.

System review and follow-up therefore becomes the final and ongoing aspect of any implementation plan. Certain questions in this context must continue to be raised: Does the system address current in-house and user needs? Are system enhancements (either hardware or software) now available that would make the EDP environment more responsive, flexible, or cost effective? Finally, what can the organization do to expand system capabilities in light of anticipated user demands, future projects, or additional funding? These are not easy questions to answer, but they raise vital issues concerning the long-term viability of any information management system. Keeping them at the forefront of the team's strategic planning is important to the implementation and ongoing success of any MIS project.

To summarize, the development of a MIS action plan and its implementation call upon the information services professional to exercise a great deal of discipline and intellectual rigor. In the first place, the planning process demands thoroughness. To be successful, it requires those tools and techniques designed to identify the information requirements of the organization. By contrast, once the crucial assessment phase has unearthed all of the organization's systems needs, the evaluation of appropriate EDP options is a relatively simple matter. Similarly, procurement, though at times troublesome, is not

---

7. Microcomputers, in particular, are currently touted as ideal vehicles for both CBI and computer-assisted instruction (CAI). Many of the newest software packages include online tutorials that assist users in learning the product. MIS personnel might easily develop training modules of their own in order to free staff from repetitive educational responsibilities. The journals *Educational Technology, Computers and People,* and *Computers and Society* regularly contain articles pertaining to CBI and CAI.

necessarily difficult. All one need do is follow the sensible practices, recommended here and elsewhere, during negotiations.[8]

The second major hurdle in the implementation plan is the complex process of data entry. For operations with long-standing, standardized procedures, inputting merely becomes a process of converting information into a machine-readable form. In other instances, however, the move to automation may necessitate new procedures, new forms, and data collection and conversion. Staff training on the new equipment must precede or coincide with this process, and thorough systems documentation must follow it. The third major area encompasses all those activities related to system output, including report design, batch and online services, user training, and support documentation. Finally, a review and enhancement methodology must be devised for the continuing evaluation of system performance and services.

The Output Process and User Services

The real return on the investment in an automated system comes from its ability to allow the user to enter data once and then apply that same body of information in any number of contexts. For example, the name, address, and telephone number of a vendor with whom one's organization conducts business might be entered into a database management system (DBMS) or a more specialized accounts payable software package. The system would automatically supply the user with standard information for invoices, purchase orders, mailings, and correspondence without requiring the repeated rekeying of data. Thus, the effort originally expended in establishing a record within a computerized application is mitigated by the fact that the information is thereafter available for a wide variety of other and perhaps unrelated uses.

By avoiding redundancy in data entry and storage, such systems save their owners money and time. Most of these information management products also afford extensive report writing and analysis capabilities. For example, while it is necessary that an accounts payable package generate payments, the DBMS which drives this process can, in addition, produce vendor performance reports, monthly and

---

8. For a highly readable discussion of this subject, see Kevin Hegarty, *More Joy of Contracts: An Epicurean Approach to Negotiation* (Tacoma: Tacoma Public Library, 1981); Joseph Auer and Charles Edison Harris, *Major Equipment Procurement* (New York: Van Nostrand Reinhold, 1983) and Edwin M. Cortez, *Proposals and Contracts for Library Automation: Guidelines for Preparing RFP's* (Studio, Calif.: Pacific Information, 1987). See also Michael C. Gemignani, *Law and the Computer* (Boston, Mass.: CBP, 1982); and Stephen A. Becker, "Legal Protection for Computer Hardware and Software," *BYTE* 6,5 (1981): 140–46.

annual summaries of transactions, and even comparative analyses of unit prices. Similarly, a circulation management system might be employed by the Records Management unit to promote collection development, solicit financial support, and enforce retention/disposition schedules. In short, modern MIS systems can and should allow those who employ them to manage and control their operations with greater efficiency and economy. Together, these various products and benefits may be referred to as the output of the system. Like the input process, the successful management of output requires a thorough understanding of existing manual procedures, and systematic planning, and a fairly rigorous implementation process. On the other hand, the payoffs of this effort for both end users and the MIS unit will more than justify the investment of corporate resources.

Before delving into these matters in greater detail, I would like to share a personal experience. As part of a workshop pertaining to the new EDP and telecommunications technologies and their potential influence on records administration, a colleague asked which DBMS could best produce hardcopy indexes. My response to this inquiry was to suggest that the wrong question was being raised. Just as in the selection of computer hardware and software, an organization's output specifications ought to be dictated by its information needs. Thus, one cannot possibly identify particular computer products without first placing the entire MIS undertaking in the appropriate corporate context. I, therefore, asked how these indexes would be used if available, and if my seminar participant's constituents actually required this particular type of information retrieval tool, as opposed to something that would be online and interactive with the user.

The lesson to be gained from this example is twofold. First, do not restrict EDP applications to the approaches traditionally associated with older manual (and for that matter automated) systems. Second, conduct a careful appraisal of information needs and develop those tools that best meet these requirements. The only limitations in this process are the constraints imposed by one's hardware and software environment. Do not restrict yourself to a historical mindset. Break with office traditions and look for new ways—both manually and through automation—to accomplish your organization's operational requirements. Finally, try to address each information service issue with an open mind and no predispositions—except those resource limitations placed upon your team's effort by your parent institution. You will find that this approach will serve you well as you search for the EDP option that best fits your present situation.

Output Options

System output is anything and everything derived from the data inputted into it. Either raw or processed information may be requested. For example, records center personnel may require the location of a particular file, the destruction date for a series of documents, or the text of a service contract that was issued by a vendor. In each of these instances, the staff member asks the system to provide very specific ("raw") information. The data are stored on some magnetic media device, such as a disk or a tape drive, and are accessed through a series of search commands typically driven by Boolean descriptors.[9] The user states the search criteria and the computer looks for all data that match those requirements. No processing of the information is needed; only its retrieval from storage is required.

An online, interactive system would then retrieve these records to a CRT screen, while a batch system would generate a hardcopy printout of its findings. Generally speaking, the latter will not prove satisfactory in the fulfillment of the aforementioned types of requests because users require immediate access to discrete data, and a batch system cannot provide a prompt response. For that matter, printed indexes are not satisfactory because they tend to go out of date very soon after they are produced. Nonetheless, any of these approaches is considerably more efficient than a manual search of the same files. In planning such a system, the MIS team will need to consider the placement of information retrieval terminals, the design and delivery of data extracts and reports, and procedures whereby the user community can conveniently access these services.

The primary factor in the preference of automated information management over manual operations is not, however, in the former's ability to retrieve discrete bits of data, but rather in its capacity to manipulate and "process" large bodies of information at tremendous speeds. Today's supercomputers can conduct as many as ten or twenty million instructions per second. Thus, in a few seconds, one of these machines can execute as many tasks as one might expect out of a human worker in an entire lifetime. Information from different files may be merged, comparisons drawn, and summary documents generated as part of an automated analysis routine. As a result, the user receives refined data and more focused answers to his or her inquiries.

Through advanced word processing systems, for example, it is a relatively simple matter to merge a mailing list with a personalized letter so that each letter appears to have been prepared individually.

---

9. Boolean search techniques involve the logical linkage of search terms with the use of "and," "or," "not." Through the careful use of these qualifiers, the nature of online inquiries can be pinpointed. See Gerald Salton and Michael J. McGill, *Introduction to Modern Information Retrieval* (New York: McGraw-Hill, 1982); Duncan A. Buell, "A General Model of Query Processing in Information Retrieval Systems," *Information Processing and Management* 17,5 (1981): 249–62; and F. Wilfrid Lancaster, *Information Retrieval Systems: Characteristics, Testing and Evaluation*, 2nd ed. (New York: Wiley, 1979).

Yet, each document is in fact the product of a one-time entry of information. Similarly, there are now a number of executive management tools on the market that combine text, graphics, and electronic spreadsheet applications in a single package.[10] These products draw upon both numerical and textual data to provide their users with prepared documents, integrating textual and financial data. For that matter, any adequate database management system has its own report generator that will allow the user to draw down and manipulate information stored within that system for analytical and presentation purposes. In a records management setting, these reports could no doubt replace various manually produced information tools, such as collection guides and inventories, bibliographies, summary accession lists, shelving inventories and repository maps, circulation statistics, and reports.

More sophisticated software products go beyond the mere aggregation of information. They provide analytical tools with which the user may probe for patterns or inconsistencies in their data. For example, an automated file circulation system might include data pertaining to document usage over a ten-year period. After compiling these figures by year and file series, such a system could produce trend analysis data for the service's administrators. It may even have the capability of visually representing these statistical findings through an adjunct graphics model. With such a tool in hand, MIS personnel can better identify the nature and direction of constituency requirements and perhaps anticipate user needs. Prognosticative tools along these lines are in wide use throughout the business community. Inexpensive microcomputer versions are easily within the reach of even the smallest information services program.[11] When employed imaginatively, they offer information service professionals the opportunity to enhance the performance level of their MIS programs.

Prioritizing System Output Production

The output options open to information managers and records administrators are considerable. The question remains: How does one make the best of the situation? First, one must prioritize user needs.

---

10. Multiplan, Jazz, Lotus 1,2,3 and the Professional File Series are all exemplary microcomputer applications packages with these capabilities. While Multiplan and Lotus 1,2,3 integrate their facilities, the PFS packages, though functioning separately, allow the user to manipulate a common body of data through DIF (data information format) files.

11. Of the packages cited in note 10, none costs more than $800, and some are priced under $200. If they are purchased through a mail order house, these products cost even less. Magazines such as *Infoworld, PC World, PC Week, Creative Computing*, and *Personal Computing* are full of review articles and advertisements for products along these lines.

For example, which division—research, marketing, customer services, administration and finance—takes precedence in system use? Is it more important to process retrieval tools or management reports? Is it more important to document the status of lead files, case files, accession lists, or retention disposition schedules? Each of these sample questions looks at the issue of output production in a slightly different manner. They are by no means mutually exclusive and, indeed, the MIS system under consideration may be capable of satisfying any and all of them. However, in responding to user output requirements, information services personnel must identify production options. As a rule of thumb, it is best to generate useful if not high-priority output as soon as possible after the system is operational. This will demonstrate the worth of the initial investment to doubting users and win the MIS team time to implement more complex applications in response to constituent needs.

Once activities are prioritized, the staff must devise appropriate output formats. These decisions will in turn dictate the types of hardware to be employed in the process. If, for example, a particular application requires the timely location and delivery of storage containers from a records facility to departmental users, the records center staff responsible for that function would benefit greatly from access to a local area network running some type of document retrieval system. By contrast, auditing or marketing may require hardcopy, summary descriptions of information holdings pertaining to their respective areas of research. These people would probably prefer to have the results of their reference inquiries printed offline so that they may refer to the printouts as needed. In yet another instance, those assigned to prepare annual reports, research studies, or the corporation's newsletters may desire camera-ready output appropriate for mass duplication and distribution. Each of these options calls for different hardware configurations to service end user requirements. As I have indicated in Chapter Three, the marketplace offers a wide variety of output devices to satisfy almost every conceivable need.[12] Your planning process will identify specific user requirements and system options.

The choice of delivery vehicle is not therefore an issue. However, before this hardware may be brought into play, the project team must face up to the task of developing both report formats and ongoing production procedures. Some computerized reports will come as standard issue within the applications software package selected by the team, while others will need to be designed through the use of the system's report writer. Project members involved in the latter process should work hand in hand with end users and, in so doing,

---

12. See *Printers: The Next Generation, Supplement to PC Week* 4,35 (1987).

establish a clear understanding of the report's purpose prior to project implementation. This needs assessment step will lead to a consensus on document design and content. Once this is done, the team may proceed with the confidence that the end product of their efforts is desired and will be put to good use once generated.

The team will next need to determine who is to generate the output, who should have access to it, and the frequency of issue. In most instances, the MIS unit may establish these processes, guidelines, and procedures and then remove itself from day-to-day involvement. Thereafter, users will produce output from the newly automated systems as they see fit. Online tools would be available whenever the DP environment is operational and batch reports would be issued on request. In other instances, corporate management will dictate these standards. However, the trend is increasingly toward distributed processing and end user discretion (and indeed control). Even if the team does not play a direct role in day-to-day information services, the MIS staff will want to assign a systems administrator to perform quality control, ensuring that reports are run when needed and revised to satisfy the evolving requirements of the organization.

Where MIS is responsible for the scheduling of both online information retrieval and batch report production, the unit's management must integrate these functions with the corporation's larger workflow patterns. In this fashion, new systems will have the most favorable impact on overall institutional performance. For example, online operations are typically run during the day, when the largest number of potential users requiring these services are present. Batch processing often takes place in the late evening and early morning hours, when computer resources are free from supporting online functions. Since, in most instances, online and batch processing cannot operate simultaneously on the same CPU, this arrangement inconveniences the fewest number of users. In smaller EDP environments, where online service demands are limited or irregular, the staff might set aside a block of time during daytime hours for batch processing. Furthermore, local area networks afford users the flexibility of downloading large files to PCs for processing within user areas. It is this latter scenario which offers the greatest flexibility and economy in the use of DP resources.

While all of this local control of information systems is laudable from an operations perspective, it does raise a number of difficult issues concerning data integrity and security. The question of access has been touched upon briefly in the input section of this chapter. Nevertheless, it is worth repeating that sensitive data should be protected from unauthorized eyes. Just as data integrity is essential to the success of the input process, data security is a necessary attribute of any well-run output operation.[13] This means that the staff must restrict the viewing of online files to those with appropriate clearance and circulate hardcopy reports according to rigidly audited procedures.

In brief, if the input process is the investment component of an EDP system, then output is surely its payoff. Interestingly, the full implementation of the output process follows the pattern already established during input; namely: needs assessment, report design, procedure preparation, and finally, resource allocation. Fortunately, the flexibility of automated information management systems affords considerable latitude in the creation of output. As long as the team accurately accesses user needs, maintains data integrity and security, and directs a sound set of data input practices, the staff may be secure in its expectations for overall quality of project output. Though the work may fall to a great extent to clerical people, professional involvement in supervision and quality control is essential. Furthermore, for the sake of system support and continuity all procedures, data files, and reports must be thoroughly documented. In addition, the staff needs to remain abreast of vendor enhancements that will allow system hardware and software to expand and operate more efficiently. These latter matters serve as the focus for the concluding section of this chapter.

System Documentation and Support

Printed information is seen by the human eye. As long as one can read, one has access to data presented in this medium. By contrast, computer systems store information in the form of digitized images. Even at the first level of translation, all that may be obtained from an electronically stored record is binary code—a series of ones and zeros. When generating output, EDP systems reorganize these electrical impulses to produce a report in human-readable form. System documentation serves as a key element in understanding and managing this process. Its purpose is to act as the ultimate authority in hardware and software operations, functionality, and performance.

Systems documentation spans three categories of management tools pertaining to hardware, software, and in-house projects (i.e., specific applications). The first of these types usually accompanies EDP equipment purchased from outside sources. These materials describe the installation and basic operating features of system components. Hardware documents may include schematic drawings of circuit designs, default settings, and error statement definitions. In

---

13. See notes 5 and 6 above.

the case of some microcomputers, the documentation may also include the instruction set for the CPU. Unless the information services professional plans to build, service, or modify the system in-house, the only practical use of these highly technical materials is to direct installation efforts and to assist in the resolution of problems that may manifest themselves during the initial stages of implementation. Subsequent work on the system is often covered through a maintenance agreement with the vendor, who in turn provides updates to his or her printed materials.

Unlike hardware documentation, software documentation will play a central and ongoing role in system maintenance. These materials explain how a given computer operating system, utility, or application package functions. Depending upon the nature of the product, software documents can be voluminous. They fall into two categories: (1) programming documentation which is utilized by programmers and DP operators when dealing with system problems, and (2) systems documentation which is employed primarily by end users and those who service the operations side of the product. From the user's point of view, software documentation may very well determine the relative success of that package in a particular information management setting. Instruction manuals should explain the product's full potential so that the MIS team can exploit its capabilities to the greatest extent possible. Good documentation will also assist in staff and end user training, error detection, problem resolution, and the development of output products. Indeed, without it, the team cannot expect to get the most out of its software selections.

To assist MIS management in this process, I recommend the use of the following eight-point evaluation tool for software documentation.[14] These criteria are, in my view, as important when personal computer products are reviewed as they are when systems that run on mainframes are considered. My checklist includes: appearance, organization, readability, grammar and punctuation, content, visual aids, appendix materials, cross-referencing and indexing. Well-developed materials will score high marks in each of these categories.

For instance, the introduction should include statements concerning the system's purpose and use, a function summary, a listing of interface capabilities with other programs, the purpose of the documentation itself, a table of contents, and comments on product limitations. Next, look for a thorough discussion of installation procedures presented in non-technical terms. The organization and quality of the instructions should then be considered. For example, Does the documentation author provide an overview of each section before

---

14. For a more comprehensive discussion of this evaluation tool, see the article on Victor in *Datapro Small Computer Monitor* 1,2 (December, 1982): 2–4.

delving into details? Are there a sufficient number of examples and illustrations to cover a particular function? Are these examples germane to those employing the application in your organization? Does the text use abbreviations, acronyms, or terminology without satisfactorily defining them? Finally, can the reader move from one section to another with ease, and is the index sufficiently thorough to facilitate the review of particulars at a later date?

The text's physical appearance is also important. The print should be legible and the paper should be of high quality. These points may appear trivial, but keep in mind that once the system is operative, the documentation will receive heavy use. Can it bear the test? Furthermore, the writing should be simple and lucid. Screen formats must be explained in sufficient detail. The manual should (where appropriate) include separate pull-out reference cards for those who generally know the system but need to refresh their memories on a few key technical points. It is a mistake to think that because a reputable company has designed an excellent software package, its documentation is equally good. Often the reverse is true, and this situation may prevent the user from taking full advantage of an otherwise quality product. Admittedly, no software package will satisfy all of the aforementioned criteria, but the more features it possesses, the greater its usefulness during project implementation.

By contrast, the purpose of in-house project documentation is to provide more specific information on how a particular application system is actually employed by the MIS unit or a user department. Figure 17 illustrates a simple prototype for an in-house documentation product.[15] My readers may wish to elaborate on this model to suit their own needs, but even in its pristine state, this example contains all the necessary elements for documentation preparation. For example, a records center may wish to run a number of functional areas off a common PC, employing the DBMS dBase III. In this scenario, each application would have its own set of forms. These would indicate the application's name, its storage location (or diskette identification number, in the case of PC-based products), the storage medium, and any relevant machine-readable record specifications.

Since the creator of any MIS product may not be its sole user, it is advisable to indicate author and date of creation so that the staff will know whom to contact for enhancements, and so on. For security purposes, it is absolutely essential that the user create backup files for the system. At least one set of duplicates, stored separately from the originals, provides a safety net. The file name, backup location, and disk number (as appropriate) will also serve to remind all system

---

15. This form was adapted from one that appears in Donald H. Beil, *The VisiCalc Book: Apple Edition* (Reston, Va.: Reston Publishing Co., 1982): 227–36.

XYZ Corporation: Application Documentation Form

Application Name:

Storage Location: _____ Diskette ID #:

Software Package: _____ Version #:

Author: _____ Date Written:

Backup Location: _____ File Name: _____ Diskette ID #:

Contact Person: _____ Phone Number:

Contact Person: _____ Phone Number:

Passwork Levels and Descriptors:

Function Description of Application:

Figure 17. Sample In-House Application Documentation Form.

RECORD FORMAT DESCRIPTION (GENERAL):

Record Format Description

Page	Field Label	Field Type	Field Size	Comments

Figure 17. (Cont.)

Usage Record:

Date	User	New Field Name	Field Size/Type	Comments

Figure 17. (Cont.)

users to update the backup file once work on the original has been completed. Finally, one might wish to include one or more contact persons, usually from the MIS unit, who are familiar with the software package upon which the application runs. When problems or questions arise, the user will know whom to approach for assistance.

The next section of figure 17 relates to system passwords. Depending upon the application package, the user may have access to as many as eight or more levels of security, each requiring its own password. Though it would be pointless to establish password protection and then provide public access to these keys through written documentation, it is nevertheless advisable to set down password structures somewhere so that they may be accessed if forgotten. The organization's data security officer is usually assigned the task of issuing user access codes and monitoring worker adherence to security procedures. As part of this arrangement, system administrators might provide documentation that includes low level passwords for staff activities while retaining a complete set of security system datasets, accessible only to senior staff.

The next three sections of the form describe the actual structure and function of the automated application. "Functional Description" explains the intended purpose of this particular MIS product. "Record Format Description" lists the specific data frame field structure by type, size, and location. Since no automated file remains stagnant, the final section of the figure 17 documentation form provides space for recording usage activities. If changes are made in the file structure of the application, the information is indicated here. Thus, when a staff member is assigned to update a file, he or she first turns to the documentation governing that activity, becoming familiar with all the necessary details. As staff changes and institutional reorganizations alter responsibilities within an operational or information services area, this body of information also serves as a standardized reference source for those who inherit new responsibilities.

As an added benefit, the type of documentation illustrated in figure 17 will also work in the administration of system output. To adapt the document for this purpose, simply replace those sections that discuss data elements and file structures with output parameters. The introductory information concerning the location and function of application files, as well as password data, is essential in obtaining access for output production. The final documentation form should also include instructions regarding the formatting of printer, storage, and/or telecommunications devices, as appropriate. Where hardcopy generation is involved, it is probably best to attach a sample and to store these materials separately from other systems-related paperwork. Thereafter, when an updated version of a particular report is desired, the MIS team need only consult the file devoted to that application's output for product history and current specifications. A DBMS or even a word processing package might serve as the electronic warehouse for this documentation, facilitating file upkeep.

Staff and User Training

The establishment of an effective and comprehensive program of systems documentation is a major milestone in project management and MIS end product maintenance. However, to ensure that the organization enjoys the full benefits of any automated system, implementation must include staff and user training—both at the outset and as an ongoing activity. As a practical matter, most computer products today are designed for their "ergonomics" and "user-friendliness." Some even come with online tutorials to get users started. Many system developers and third-party organization's offer on or offsite classroom instruction to supplement these products.

Beyond these, the best training comes from hands-on experience with the system. Thus, the more hours that information services personnel can spend working with new MIS products, during and immediately following implementation, the more proficient they will become in the use of those systems. It therefore makes sense to structure work assignments so as to distribute computer time widely while maximizing machine use. Furthermore, workers who fear computers will lose their inhibitions only through hands-on exposure. Be certain that these employees receive a sufficiently thorough orientation to the system to make the most of their initial encounters with it. Management must also recognize the fact that training takes time and the expenditure of resources. At the outset, productivity will undoubtedly drop below levels achieved through the replaced manual systems. This is to be expected. Proficiency will come with time and proper training, and so will higher levels of throughput.

In all likelihood, staff training will come from a combination of three sources: product and systems documentation, computer-based tutorials, and hands-on experience. These may be supplemented by outside instruction through university courses or professional seminars. Further assistance may come from the parent agency's data center, other MIS units, or a local not-for-profit computer users group. The adequacy of this training is an important element in any implementation plan. Even workers who do not use the new automated system on a regular basis should at least have a rudimentary understanding of how it operates, as well as its role within the larger service function. As a practical matter, training will involve most (if not all) MIS personnel affected by the new information system. New hires will require instruction as part of their orientation. Senior management might also consider adding "computer literacy" or some practical hands-on computer experience to the basic recruiting requirements associated with staffing one of the institution's automated MIS operations.

Once the members of the MIS team have prepared themselves for full system implementation, they must consider end user training. As the system moves from a test to an operational mode for the first time, access should be restricted to MIS personnel and key users. It is better to delay the introduction of the product rather than have it fail because its broad constituency of users is unprepared. Training should be tailored to the individual requirements of user areas. Such instruction need not be as detailed and as comprehensive as that undergone by the MIS staff. Instead, operations personnel should get the level of instruction commensurate with their responsibilities in using the new system. In my view, this makes the best use of limited MIS resources and affords the opportunity to train a large group of users quickly. Bear in mind that this is not a one-time event but an ongoing process, as employees "turn over" and as the system is enhanced.

Once the team has identified its end user training objectives, the task should become more manageable. At the outset, MIS personnel may wish to produce a user's manual to instruct their constituents on the nature and scope of this particular information service and its potential advantages to the user. The balance of the manual ought to contain brief, clearly written instructions and germane examples. The criteria applied previously in the evaluation of software documentation will also work well in this context. Keep the manual simple and involve cooperative users in its preparation.

The logistics of training will depend upon the overall EDP environment of the parent institution. Some organizations may provide in-house seminars or institutes. Others will offer video or computer-based training packages that employees may use on their own. Those corporations with local area networks (LANs) for data and voice transmission may issue distributed online tutorials integrated with the very products that they seek to explain. Other settings will make it necessary to provide terminals in the reference room or some other public place. All these matters will probably require the attention of the implementation task force before the terminals function as an integral part of the training program. The effort is a necessary and ongoing component of any successful MIS effort.

Good documentation will help place any training program on a sound footing. It will also contribute to the uniformity and the quality of input and output processes. In addition, staff refresher courses and periodic procedure audits will help to ensure the best use of the system and the success of its various information management applications. Beyond these evaluations, it is important that the program's chief administrators keep abreast of the availability of new or enhanced hardware and software products as these may influence the performance of the application. Bear in mind that remaining current in the technology is not as daunting a task as it might at first appear. Once vendors know that you own or lease their products, they will provide information about the latest in new offerings, upgrades, and enhancements.

Furthermore, the trade literature is always brimming with product announcements. System administrators should regularly peruse these periodicals. Together, these recommendations will allow information service professionals to take advantage of product improvements that address new or previously unrealized system potential. In closing, this chapter has presented a brief discussion of the formulation and implementation of an action plan, the input process, the output process, system documentation, and user training and support. Out of necessity, treatment of these important subjects has been brief. The reader will find additional guidance in this chapter's footnotes.[16]

The tools presented here may appear overburdensome to some of my readers, who would prefer a less rigorous and detailed planning methodology. While I freely admit that my models must be modified to complement the resources and requirements of the reader's institution, I do not accept the argument that an approach along the lines outlined above is unnecessary. Orderly control over the diverse activities associated with automated systems design and implementation requires disciplined management practices. Through the use of modeling techniques, such as those provided in this chapter, the MIS professional can exercise the control required in establishing new computer-based information services while avoiding waste and confusion. However, if it is to be successful, someone must hold responsibility for the entire process. This project leader might ultimately serve as the system administrator but initially he or she would act as the accountable party, insuring that all resources are properly allocated and directed.

---

16. See also Richard M. Kesner, *Information Management, Machine-Readable Records, and Administration: An Annotated Bibliography* (Chicago: Society of American Archivists, 1983); 106–12, 115–22, in which the author reviews the literature pertaining to computer hardware and software and the many applications of information systems development.

CHAPTER
7

Developing Information Management Systems in the Workplace: Paper- and Computer-based Scenarios

By now the reader should be cognizant of the strategic and analytical framework that serves as the basis of this volume's opening chapters. It has been my objective to stress the importance of redefining the role of the records manager, the archivist, the librarian, and the data processing professional in a broad context that encompasses environmental considerations, organizational structure, business planning, and end user or service requirements. Admittedly, the corporate players mentioned above may have no direct influence over the development of their parent institution's overall goals. Indeed, in the case of such bodies as universities, government agencies, and public libraries, these mission statements may even fall beyond the aegis of senior management and may, in fact, emerge out of legislation, established corporate traditions, or community imperatives.

On the other hand, it would be naive to assume that one's institution—no matter how small or parochial—labors without some type of directing plan. For a local library or museum, the mission may be to serve the community, while for the small entrepreneur it may be name recognition and market share. Even these vague statements carry with them certain operational imperatives. Furthermore, the well-managed organization converts its goals into more concrete, measurable tasks. In this manner, a broad mission is rearticulated as a set of overlapping assignments. For example, a community arts center's mission may be to bring "culture" to its locale, but to convert **183** this understanding into a series of programs, the institution must define its constituency, examine its resources, and work toward realizable deliverables.

Whatever its origins, the organization's strategic plan orders its priorities. It is these priorities, in turn, that, at least in part, dictate the activities of the institution's information services professionals and the resources that they will allocate to specific assignments. To remain responsive to these corporate needs, MIS personnel must adapt their skill base and restructure their own organization and services as suggested in Chapter One. They must also become more proactive, sales oriented, and customer-service driven. The challenge posed by this approach demands special analytical skills and management tools. While Chapters Two through Five have illustrated a number of useful techniques in developing this type of focus, they are only elements in an evolving process resulting from the ongoing interaction between information specialists and their constituents. As I have repeatedly indicated, my examples should be redrawn to fit the context of the reader's work environment. My examples, nevertheless, provide the basis for a comprehensive approach to MIS project planning and implementation.

The remaining two chapters and postscript of this volume enlarge upon the aforementioned themes by raising issues of particular relevance to the responsibilities of an organization's information services team. In the first of these sections, Developing Information Management Systems in the Workplace: Paper- and Computer-based Scenarios (Chapter Seven), I concentrate on problems associated with the administration of modern paper and micrographic records. To achieve this end, I examine various scenarios, ranging from traditional records management issues to those involving integrated image/data distribution systems.

While one end product of these discussions is to suggest automated MIS solutions, I must from the outset emphasize the importance of addressing information management issues from an operational perspective. This vantage point requires that the consideration of EDP options take second place to service delivery. If a manual process successfully addresses corporate objectives, one need go no further. The automation of information processing operations for the sake of merely exploiting new technologies will more often than not lead to unnecessary complexity and greater expense. Furthermore, it has been my experience that the introduction of computers into poorly organized and unresponsive paper-based operations will only result in greater confusion. Thus, as a working maxim of this presentation, I would prefer to say: First put your shop in order, and then automate—but only when the financial and operational benefits are demonstrable.

Having warned the reader against the uncritical use of EDP hardware and software to solve information management problems, I am still obliged to observe that computers will find an increasingly important role in the workplace. However, wherever one observes EDP and telecommunication systems, one will also find problems associated with the administration and management of records created by these mechanisms. The final chapter of this volume, Machine-Readable Records: Management Issues in an Evolving Office Environment (Chapter Eight), therefore examines the implications of the modern office's growing reliance on digitized machine-readable records. In particular, this section will focus upon the challenges of appraising, preserving, and documenting both archived computer-based files and constantly changing online, interactive, database systems.

Together, Chapters Seven and Eight take the reader out of the classroom and put him or her onto the firing line. These sections raise the questions What do I do now? and How do I begin? They by no means provide all the answers. Instead, their objective is to direct the reader's attention toward rigorous self-examination. At the outset, each MIS professional must place his or her operation in the context of the larger organization, identify corporate priorities, and shape appropriate responses to these commonly shared objectives. Next, at the tactical level, the information services team will need to scrutinize their specific offerings to ensure that they are efficient, effective, and economical. Finally, these players should work hand in hand with their constituents to develop ways whereby management information systems may better serve the whole.

Paper-based Information Systems

Since the invention of the printing press and inexpensive paper production, the manually written and printed word has served as the preferred medium of information storage. To this day, government agencies, private businesses, universities, libraries, charitable institutions, and almost any other organization that one could mention are clogged with paper records and filing cabinets. The photocopier and the computer have only exacerbated this problem by making it easy and relatively inexpensive to copy documents and to generate reams of printouts. The multiply form and other pernicious bureaucratic tools have added further to this sea of paper. While most organizations recognize the operational and financial liabilities associated with managing this morass of information, few have successfully rooted out all waste and redundancy.

Given the profusion and variety of paper-based systems within even the smallest of organizations, the information services professional faces many opportunities to reduce operating costs and improve corporate performance. To begin, the MIS unit should focus its attention on the primary business of their parent institution and the documents generated as a consequence of these activities. For the records manager or archivist, this could involve filing systems and forms; for the librarian, this could mean a review of acquisitions paperwork and cataloging output; and for the DP professional, this could include an analysis of system documentation and reports generation. While the data gathered during the preparation MIS survey forms (figures 3 and 4) will assist in this regard, these studies need to be expanded to include the location, nature, span dates, and volume of records stored throughout the parent institution.

These types of activities are at the heart of traditional records management programs and should therefore be familiar to at least some of my readers. The techniques involved are well documented elsewhere, and are in any event simple to grasp and execute.[1] Beyond a survey of office files, the MIS team should study reports, printouts, and mass-produced memoranda with a view toward identifying methods of production, quantities produced, and distribution patterns. Last, the team might choose to examine the institution's printed forms to determine how they are employed by users, why they are required for operations, their method of production, and (if they are multiple) the location and disposition of the various copies. In each of the aforementioned areas of inquiry, information services personnel should examine both current records and those placed in semiactive and archival storage.

To assist in this process, I offer figure 18, which prototypes three survey documents. The format labeled "Part I" is intended for the review of traditional office files. Here the analyst is asked to indicate the location of the record, its type or format (e.g. accounting journals, blue prints, correspondence, minutes, project documentation, and so forth), and span dates (usually the date of document creation). The matrix next calls for the volume of records expressed in linear feet. The reader may find it more convenient to use some other standard of measure, such as number of file drawers, storage cabinets, or transit boxes. Finally, space is provided for a summary file description and a retention/disposition (R&D) recommendation. The surveyor would use this field to indicate the frequency with which users access that particular set of files, whether they are originals or duplicates of records housed elsewhere, their arrangement (e.g., "organized

---

1. For a discussion of record survey methodologies, I still recommend William Benedon, *Records Management* (New York: Prentice-Hall, 1969); and John Fleckner, *Archives and Manuscripts: Surveys* (Chicago: Society of American Archivists, 1977). See also Society of American Archivists, *Inventories and Registers: A Handbook of Techniques and Examples* (Chicago: Society of American Archivists, 1976).

SAMPLE SURVEY FORM

PART I: FILE SURVEY

Location	Record Type	Span Dates	Volume Lin. Feet	Frequency of Use/Orig. vs. Dup. Arrangement/R&D Recommendation

Figure 18. Paper-based Systems Survey.

PART II: REPORT PRODUCT SURVEY

Name of Report	Mode of Production	Frequency of Prod.	Quantity Produced	Distribution Pattern and Reason for Production

Figure 18 (Cont.)

PART III: FORMS SURVEY

Name of Form	Mode of Production	Frequency of Prod.	Number of Plys	Distribution Pattern and Reason for Use

Figure 18. (Cont.)

alphabetically," "organized by account number," and so forth), and standard retention dates, such as "destroy after six years," "permanent—retain indefinitely," or "active—keep in user area." In addition, the analyst should describe the relative importance to specific user groups of each record type.

The R&D field will in all likelihood require additional research to ensure that comments are in compliance with government regulations and the organization's operational requirements. In making this observation, I assume that a set of records retention standards are already in place. If this is not the case, the project team has a substantial task on its hands. Fortunately, most businesses, and educational institutions, and governmental bodies may readily obtain standard R&D schedules from either their respective trade associations or state and federal agencies. They must then tailor these guidelines to reflect their unique operational, legal, and fiduciary requirements. MIS personnel would be wise to involve users at various levels of the organization when modifying schedules. Senior management should formally approve the final draft. Once completed, this revised document would in turn serve as a key reference tool during the file survey process.

The typical office manager would employ Part I of figure 18 to survey filing cabinet contents. Organizations with large records storage requirements, such as financial and government institutions, could just as easily use Part I when reviewing vault, storage center, and archival holdings. Agencies with unconventional retention requirements, including architectural firms, museums, libraries, and historical societies, might adapt the records survey format to catalog holdings and the resources required for their support and maintenance. In all likelihood, however, the largest single application for this particular tool will be to facilitate the analysis of paper-based files throughout the organization.

The example labeled Part II is to be used in conjunction with report production. While the file survey in Part I may reveal the location of publications within departmental filing systems, the report product survey examines the generation of this printed matter at its source. Part II therefore calls for the name of each report, the method of production (e.g., computer printer, photocopier, printing press), its frequency, and the number of copies generated. The last column asks the surveyor to inquire into the reasons behind a report's production and to whom the report is distributed. Here again, research—not to mention thoughtful diplomacy—is required to get at the history and justification for each organizational report.

When completed, Part II will identify those internal publications and distribution patterns that no longer serve a useful purpose. By sifting through all of the details, MIS personnel will also root out redundancy and opportunities for the routing and, hence, the sharing of published materials around the organization. In the long run, the rigor of this approach will lead to less time and money spent on reports, printouts, and memoranda. The resultant savings to the organization could be considerable.

Figure 18 concludes with a prototype for the forms analysis section of the survey (Part III). As with Part II, we are concerned here with each form's mode and frequency of production. In many instances, the number of form plys is also relevant to the inquiry. Finally, the survey team must identify those departments that employ a given form and the justifications for its use. These inquiries will reveal the existence of the unnecessary production and storage of separate form plies. When compiling this data, MIS personnel will find that a microcomputer-based tool, such as a spreadsheet or database software package, is most useful in standardizing and summarizing their survey findings.

The assignment envisaged above is considerable. It will prove time consuming and even painfully complex in its execution. One need not therefore consider concurrently surveying the entire organization. Instead, the team might begin by focusing upon a key operational unit or user group. Alternatively, one might first approach a department that openly supports the enterprise. Bear in mind that few line managers appreciate "outsiders" scrutinizing their operations and past recordkeeping practices. A success in one area will breed confidence and break down walls that the team might otherwise encounter. Furthermore, make certain from the outset that senior management supports the survey process and that it communicates this "sponsorship" to all operating units affected by the undertaking.

If the MIS team is successful in its survey and analysis efforts, it will have established a significant body of data pertaining to record creation and retention practices within the parent organization. For example, the survey may reveal that files are being retained for too long a period, that the number of plies on widely used forms is a waste, or that certain reports may be reduced or even eliminated entirely from distribution. With this data in hand, information services can turn to the development of action plans for dealing with the opportunities that will emerge from their analysis.

In structuring a response, MIS management should prioritize assignments in light of the parent organization's larger objectives. The methodology described previously in relation to setting MIS priorities (see figures 5 and 8) may prove useful here. Alternatively, information services personnel may focus in on those projects that will yield an immediate savings to the organization, improve customer service, or streamline operations and production throughput. Given the political situation within the parent institution, it may prove necessary to start small and build on one's initial successes. Whatever the strategy, it is essential that MIS management proceed with positive action steps as soon as possible after the survey's completion.

Failure to do so will diminish the team effort in three respects. In the first place, inaction will dampen the enthusiasm of those involved, reducing their willingness to take on subsequent survey work. Second, the appearance of a lack of responsiveness will lose the MIS unit credibility in the eyes of its user constituency. Third and perhaps most important, any inability to deliver on survey findings will lessen the contribution by information services personnel to the success and continuing prosperity of their parent organization. If survey results are properly packaged, MIS management should have no trouble in making its cases before the corporate leadership. Action should follow closely upon approval. Well publicized successes will convert uncommitted users.

In terms of specific programs, I would envision two different avenues of activity. The first of these may be described as the "low-tech" road to better information management. This set of scenarios involves the development and rigorous enforcement of manual records management and archival practices. For example, the survey may reveal significant savings to the organization if it promptly disposes of dead records that have long passed their legal retention dates, and if it shifts inactive files from storage in user areas to the less expensive environment of a records center. Forms and reports of questionable value could be dropped from production or, at the very least, streamlined to reduce the labor costs associated with their production and use. The MIS team should also be in a position to root out unnecessary records duplication, curtail and centralize retrieval services, and convert important paper files to more economical storage media, such as microfilm. Finally, and perhaps most important, office procedures should be redesigned to make the best use of worker time and the information sources that they handle. This last set of activities may be the most difficult to achieve, but holds the greatest potential rewards for the organization as a whole.

None of these MIS solutions require automation, but they all serve to reduce cost and improve worker efficiency. Some will win the prompt approval of corporate senior management. Other recommendations, on the other hand, will require a concerted marketing effort if they are to be implemented. Be forewarned. Any proposal that calls for a change to standard operating procedures or office traditions will meet with considerable resistance. To earn the support of the rank-and-file, it may prove necessary to establish an educational campaign, stressing both the immediate and long term benefits of the proffered changes. Do not view this endeavor as a waste of

MIS staff time. In the first place, without the support of the workforce, the information services team will not possess the resources and backing to implement the "low-tech" opportunities identified in its surveys. Second, a studied approach to the selling of new manual methods and procedures will make it that much easier to win support for computer-based systems at a later date.

An organizational culture that resists the revision of paper forms, and records retention and disposition schedules, is not likely to be openminded about my second avenue of development—the more dramatic changes wrought by automation. The MIS team should be sensitive to this challenge as it reads through its analysis. Be prepared for an uphill battle in those areas where survey results suggest a strategy that might involve the total elimination of paper in a particular application and its replacement by EDP and telecommunication technologies. As a case in point, consider what libraries have done to their acquisitions and cataloging practices to move away from paper and toward micrographic and machine-readable media,[2] and think back as to how this was first received by senior staff. One might also proceed with the replacement of mass-produced and distributed paper memoranda with an electronic mail system for routine inter-office communications, or the elimination of forms and mailing costs with the installation of networked terminals in cutomer offices. Each of these scenarios would further diminish the flow of paper around the office, but would not reach fruition without a thorough selling job on the part of MIS.

Automated applications along related lines may be found in libraries, hospitals, government agencies, factories, and universities. They are complex and expensive undertakings with potential long-term benefits. As components of an organization's strategic plans, they may be the right moves but they carry with them uncertainties that make the typical senior manager most uncomfortable. Unlike a decision to streamline paper records storage, the installation of a computerized information delivery system requires a considerable investment in capital, time, and effort. Chapters Five and Six of this volume indicate the level of commitment required to successfully implement such a program. Even if survey findings identify an opportunity for an EDP-based service, the timing, the cost, or the lack of commitment on the part of senior management may prevent MIS from going forward with the venture.

To win support, the MIS team must demonstrate that the benefits of its proposals outweigh their costs. These presentations should also

---

2. For background information, see Richard M. Kesner, "The Computer and the Library Environment: The Case for Microcomputers," *Journal of Library Administration* 3,2 (1982): 33–50; and Richard M. Kesner and Clifton H. Jones, *Microcomputer Applications in Libraries* (Westport, Conn.: Greenwood, 1984), 129–62.

tie into the parent's strategic plan. Thus, even if there is no immediate payback from the projects, the fact that they move the organization closer to its long-term objectives will help win support for the propositions. As a beginning, start small and simple. Do not, for example, propose a large microcomputer network for a work environment that has yet to graduate from index cards and manual typewriters. By moving in incremental steps, the team will build a following. In addition, it will gradually raise the skill level of those affected by the automation program, which in turn is essential for the success of the undertaking. The organization's senior managers will also appreciate this approach to "high-tech" MIS services, because it remains innovative while limiting risk. In making this recommendation, I again caution my readers to avoid compartmentalized information systems planning. When building discrete pieces always keep the broader MIS plan in focus.

Specific EDP solutions to office management problems may be as varied as the environments into which they are deployed. This single volume does not allow for the examination of all possibilities. Instead, the remainder of this chapter will focus upon three groupings of general examples. First of all, I will briefly review the current uses of micrographic technologies in the workplace. In so doing, I will mention both the benefits and limitations of this established medium for information storage. Second, I will consider the use of computers in the administration and management of traditional filing and information retrieval systems. Finally, I will examine how the fields of image and data processing are at present moving toward a common technological base in the form of optical videodisc systems. This last set of examples affords the opportunity to consider emerging office technologies.

Micrographic Systems and EDP Applications

In most modern information management settings, micrographics abound. Many organizations have replaced printed records with microfilmed equivalents, reference tools and phone directories now appear on microfiche, and even small public libraries have moved from index cards to book catalogs on film. The purpose of this section is to review the operating principles and respective roles of computer output microfilm (COM), computer-assisted retrieval of micrographics (CAR) and computer input microfilm (CIM), and how these processes contribute to the overall needs of an information management program. The deployment and integration of these technologies, rather than their current availability, are my first concern. With this as a base, I will consider how automated systems can further enhance micrographic system capabilities. Finally, I will summarize key management issues raised by the introduction of this medium into the workplace.

To begin, let us briefly examine the general benefits of microfilm to those responsible for the economical and efficient management of information services. In their original state, paper files are bulky, often irregular in size, and, since they are made of high-acid stock that rapidly decays, generally impermanent. These factors cause various problems for information management personnel. At the very least, those few records of permanent value—usually no more than 1 to 5 percent of the total—must be transferred to a stable medium for preservation. Furthermore, the sheer volume of typical paper file holdings requires costly storage space, shelving, filing containers, and servicing.

The advent of microfilm significantly mitigated, if not eliminated, some of these problems.[3] Through document filming onto silver halide film, records management programs obtain an "archival quality" image (i.e., one that is expected to last one hundred years). With reduction ratios of 24, 42, and even 48 to 1, file drawers of documents could be held in one hand, significantly reducing space requirements for records warehousing, as well as the difficulties involved in the retrieval and transmission of paper records. The costs associated with the misfiling and refiling of documents is also reduced if not entirely eliminated.

As economical as microfilming may initially appear, it is not without costs. Equipment is required for the filming process and for the subsequent use of micrographic records. Since reading microfilm requires machine assistance, this equipment, as well as printers that will produce hardcopy images from film, must be purchased. Finally, a proficient technical staff is required to produce a quality micrographic product. Unless one's organization generates an enormous amount of paper records or operates in an area where warehouse prices are quite high, it is not always possible to demonstrate that a microfilm-based information management program is less expensive to operate than a paper-oriented one.[4] Instead, many users have cited

---

3. I would recommend Joseph L. Kish, *Micrographics: A User's Manual* (Somerset, N.J.: Wiley, 1981), and would next rely upon the references cited in his bibliography. See also Daniel M. Costigan, *Micrographic Systems* (Silver Spring, Md.: National Micrographics Association, 1975); and Daniel Young, "The Commission on Federal Paperwork and Micrographics," *Journal of Micrographics* 11,5 (1978): 305–8.

4. Any work dealing with micrographics in a business environment will attempt to make a case for the cost effectiveness of microfilm and fiche over more traditional, paper-oriented modes of information storage. It is certainly true that microfilming will save space and the cost of storage. On the other hand, dependence on micrographics breeds its own costs. One must invest in equipment for filming source documents, for storing the film and/or fiche, and for reading and producing hardcopy reproductions. Generally speaking, unless one invests in well-trained and experienced personnel to

ease of handling, enhanced document security, and a variety of other non-financial considerations in justifying micrographic applications.

With the growing use of computers in business and government, the micrographics industry identified an area in which there was a strong correlation between microfilming and cost savings. The traditional microfilm process revolved around paper document filming. Even with the best equipment and personnel, this technique is slow and costly. By contrast, the computer output microfilm (COM) process takes the electronic information coming off the CPU and converts it to micrographic images without the intermediary paper step.[5] As a result, COM is economical and fast. It is the most widely employed feature of automated records management found in business and government today. Reduction ratios and image quality are much higher than that of source document work, and master tapes for either film or fiche end products may be run at speeds approaching that of the CPU itself. Furthermore, many COM devices can encode identification markings on the film as it passes through. These markings, usually blips on the film surface, are subsequently employed for the automated retrieval of individual images.

The market for COM devices has grown dramatically over the last decade. This demand has encouraged major COM vendors, such as Datagraphix, Bell and Howell, 3M, and Kodak, to develop new product lines and system enhancements. As a result, customers who at one time relied on service bureaus for their COM work may now choose standalone systems that attach directly to their mainframe computers.[6] In this form, in-house COM processing becomes an ex-

---

run an in-house operation and unless the organization requires a sufficiently large volume of filming to justify such an investment, source document microfilming will not prove cost effective. However, service bureaus can satisfy lesser in-house microfilming demands at fairly reasonable rates. See Pat Molluso, "Micro-Publishing, A Cost-Effective Alternative to Paper," *Information and Records Management* 15,10 (1981): 54, 57; H. G. Suiter, Jr., "COM: The Most Cost-Effective Information Processing Medium for the 80's," *Journal of Micrographics* 14,12 (1981): 16–21; and Joan Ross, "The Great Output Race: COM Joins the Winner's Circle," *Journal of Micrographics* 10,1 (1976): 11–15.

5. As a mature industry, there is no shortage of quality writing concerning computer output microfilm. See W. T. Kidwell, "A User Looks at COM," *Journal of Systems Management* 24,10 (1973): 8–12; Paul D. Snyder, "Computer Output Microfilm," Parts 1-3, *Journal of Systems Management* 25-3-5 (1974): 8–13, 14–21, 33–37; National Archives and Records Service, *Computer Output Microfilm* (Washington, D.C.: GPO, 1975); Isaac L. Auerbach, "Strategies for the Management of Computer Output," *Journal of Micrographics* 10,3 (1977): 127–30; and William Saffady, *Computer-Output Microfilm: Its Library Applications* (Chicago: American Library Association, 1978).

6. Service bureaus afford small RM centers the opportunity to generate COM tapes as needed, without the substantial up-front investment in COM equipment. Only records management programs that can run COM machines on a nearly continuous basis will find the purchase of its own COM equipment cost effective. A service bureau can usually provide COM within a forty-eight–hour period, and charges by the frame for its work. Though COM equipment may be purchased for as little as $50,000, it is unlikely that marginal users of COM will choose to make this initial investment, even though it is approximately one tenth of what these machines cost just a few years ago.

tremely affordable option if the user has sufficient microfilming volume to justify the initial equipment purchase or lease.

Until very recently, industry experts have heralded COM as the records management tool of the 1980s. These prospects are now overshadowed by the emergence of videodisc technology in which a single disc may hold as many as one hundred thousand pages of information, as opposed to a few hundred on a microfiche and a few thousand on a roll of microfilm. However, the widespread use of videodisc systems that can compete with COM on a dollar-per-record level is still a few years away. Although the use of COM in records management may eventually decline, its supremacy is not yet threatened.[7] We will return to the subject of optical disc alternatives to microfilm in the closing section of this chapter.

For the purpose of this discussion, keep the following characteristics of computer output microfilm in mind. First, it is the fastest and most economical form of micrographic production commercially available today. Second, its effectiveness comes from its ability to transform computer-generated data into microfilm. Third, COM can encode identification markings on record screens as they are created in the mainframe or super-mini computer system for automated retrieval on a specially equipped microfilm reader. (At this time, there are no COM devices that run off small computers or distributed information systems.) Finally, COM operates in a batch EDP environment, where vast runs of information are transformed from electronic to micrographic machine-readable images.

Independent of developments in COM technology, the micrographics industry also offers a wide range of information retrieval devices grouped under the acronym CAR (computer-assisted retrieval of micrographics). Whereas COM machines generate output, CAR equipment facilitates access to specific documents.[8] For example, a company might also choose to generate a COM tape of invoices

---

7. See R. Barrett, "Developments in Optical Disk Technology and the Implications for Information Storage and Retrieval," *Journal of Micrographics* 15,1 (1982): 22–26; F. E. Marsh, Jr., "Videodisc Technology," *Journal of ASIS* 33,4 (1982): 237–44; Dick Moberg and Ira M. Laefsky, "Videodiscs and Optical Data Storage," *BYTE* 7,6 (1982): 142–68; William Saffady and Rhoda Garoogian, "Micrographics, Reprography, and Graphic Communications in 1981," *Library Resources and Technical Services* 26,3 (1982): 294–305; S. Suthasinekul, "Microfilming a Storage Medium for Document-Retrieval and Dissemination," *Journal of ASIS* 17,3 (1980): 100–102.

8. For a current review of the micrographics industry, see Coopers & Lybrand, *Information and Image Management: The Industry and the Technology* (New York: Coopers & Lybrand, 1987). See also David Fain and Garrett Gruener, "CAR: The Digital Approach," *Information and Records Management* 13,5 (1979): 21–22; Robert M. Hayes, "On-Line Microfiche Catalogs," *Journal of Micrographics* 13,4 (1980): 15–63 passim; Alan G. Rockhold, "Automating Microfilm Retrieval: Friendly Office Systems Boost Productivity," *Infosystems* 28,12 (1981): 54–56; and Jacklyn Popiul, "Integrating Paper, Microfilm, and Data Processing to Form a CAR System," *Journal of Micrographics* 14,11 (1981): 18–22.

when processing an invoice run that is to be mailed in hardcopy form to its customers. During the COM process, the machine encodes blips on the tape that correspond to the numbers on the invoices. Once the microfilm reel is processed, a user can mount the film on a CAR device, then locate a particular frame by entering the blip code which matches that image. In a similar manner, a library might film its entire card catalog, indexing each micrographic image by author, title, subject, and shelf number, and associating these references with a particular blip code on the microfilm reel. Users could thereafter retrieve individual bibliographic listings through any number of avenues.

Unlike COM devices, most CAR configurations are small, self-contained units. Many are simple machines that have the ability to read little else besides encoded location markings on microfilm tapes. They are usually attached to a standard microform reader/printer and tend to be used in high-production environments, such as accounting or customer service, where there is a demand for rapid retrieval of specific documents. More advanced CAR devices include microprocessors, and even full micro- or minicomputer configurations that allow for the indexing of film frames. These machines match certain document reference characteristics, such as check or invoice number, date, or user department, with the frame's position on the tape. The retrieval data is stored on a floppy or hard disk. A user then mounts both the disk and the microfilm in their respective machines.

Once he or she specifies search criteria on the configuration's computer terminal, the image is retrieved and appears on a separate screen. For example, a university might retain its student records on microfilm arranged by individual identification numbers. The accompanying CAR database would included indexes by student name and number. By accessing either reference point via the CAR unit, a user would obtain the microfilm real and frame number location of the desired record. The user would then mount the appropriate spool of film on a microfilm reader and view the information.

While most CAR systems are not particularly sophisticated, some now allow for Boolean searches of their retrieval databases. Where the volume of requests, time pressure, and anticipated user demand for hardcopy are considerable, a number of micrographic vendors now offer complex microfilm management system configurations that include small computers, video transmission equipment, and a mechanical microfilm cassette retrieval device that operates in the same manner as a jukebox. The purpose of this type of machine is to serve as a remote micrographic retrieval system in which users in distant locations can access microfilm images on their CRTs. If videodisc technology poses a threat to the micrographics industry, it is clearly in this area.[9] CAR equipment nevertheless serves a useful purpose in certain settings and is likely to remain an important component in micrographics systems for the foreseeable future.

Computer input microfilm (CIM) converts micrographic images to computer-readable bits and bytes. CIM is therefore viewed as the reverse of COM. While a number of vendors have promised such machines in their promotional literature, the availability and commercial viability of this hardware are certainly suspect.[10] Furthermore, it is unclear why information managers would want to go to the expense of transferring historical data from film to the computer. On the other hand, some industry experts have suggested that CIM units may provide an archival quality backup to magnetic media machine-readable records. At any rate, the absence of CIM products in the marketplace renders this a moot point, at least for now. Here again, videodisc technologies should replace CIM as both a concept and a reality in the office of the future.

Managing Microfilm

From the standpoint of information management, COM and CAR at least play an important though limited role. Micrographics save space and simplify data handling. If microfilm must be serviced, a CAR system may improve productivity. For its part, a COM configuration is an economical alternative to computer-generated printouts. On the other hand, the widespread use of microfilm media places pressure on MIS resources in ways not entirely dissimilar from those associated with paper-based products. For example, as with more traditional files, micrographics require appropriate storage and servicing. The cost of facilities and personnel may be justified, but the only way to be certain of this is to survey the organization's microfilm holdings and to analyze their immediate and long-term utility.

To assist in this process, I recommend the use of a survey tool along the lines of figure 19. As is the tendency with printed reports and paper files, if micrographic records are not monitored by information services personnel, they will tend to accumulate around the organization. Indeed, because they are less bulky than paper, users

9. See note 7. See also Andrej Tenne-Sens, "Teledon Graphics and Library Applications," *Information Technology and Libraries* 1,2 (1982): 98–110; Gerard O. Walter, "Video Disc for the Storage of Office Documents and Engineering Graphics," *Journal of Micrographics* 15,1 (1982): 12–20; and Dennis Mole, "The Videodisc as a Pilot Project of the Public Archives of Canada," *Videodisc/Videotex* 1,2 (1981): 74–77.

10. J. Ross, "Computer Input Microfilm," *Microdoc* 17,2 (1978): 53–54, 56, 58, 60; J. Ross and B. Royan, "Backfile Conversion Today: CIMera or Chimera?" *Program* 11,4 (1977): 156–65; and R. Holland, "CIM—the Present and the Future," *Microdoc* 15,2 (1976): 52–57.

SAMPLE SURVEY FORM

MICROFILM RECORDS SURVEY: PART I

Location	Record Type/ Medium	Span Dates	Volume Lin. Feet/ # of Rolls	Frequency of Use and Primary Users

Figure 19. Micrographic Records Survey.

MICROFILM RECORDS SURVEY: PART II

Original or Duplicate	Location of Other Copies	Description of File Arrangement	Retention/Disposition Recommendation

Figure 19. (Cont.)

will tend to hold on to microfilm well beyond the useful life of these products. This situation is particularly true in office environments that rely heavily upon COM output. Figure 19 is designed to reveal such circumstances. Part I of the survey form provides room for entering the location, record type (e.g., correspondence, general ledger tickets, monthly reports, and so forth), and medium (i.e., microfilm, microfiche, and aperature card) of each set of images. Span dates of the documents are also called for since these are essential in establishing retention schedules. The holding's size in either linear feet of shelf or drawer space, number of film rolls, or some other standard of measurement is also required. Finally, Part I requires that the surveyor identify the primary users of a given micrographic resource and the frequency with which they and others access these materials.

Part II of figure 19 provides space to indicate whether the microfilm product in question is an original or a duplicate. It also asks for the location of other copies within the organization of that record. Many times multiple copies of micrographic records are produced for operational purposes only to be retained in record storage long after the original requirement has expired. This survey form will promptly surface such inconsistencies. Part II also provides space to comment on file arrangement (e.g., organized chronologically, organized by volume and issue, and so forth), and to list retention/disposition recommendation.

With completed survey forms in hand, information services personnel may slate film for relocation to user areas, for transfer from active to inactive storage, or for destruction (as appropriate). Staff findings will also bring to light unnecessary product duplication, and at times the need for enhanced indexing and servicing. Thus, the survey should conclude in the initiation of two separate sets of assignments for MIS personnel. On the one hand, their inquiries will identify opportunities to rationalize the processes of microfilm production, dissemination, and use. On the other hand, it will point out areas where further investment is required if the organization's rank-and-file are to maximize the utility of these information resources.

The latter assignment will in all likelihood entail the deployment of automated MIS solutions, including COM, CAR, and computerized management tools. For example, perhaps the most intellectually taxing responsibility of the records manager involves the creation of retention and disposition (R&D) schedules for the records generated by the parent institution. As I have already indicated, these R&D schedules often emerge as a result of a survey of all organization paper-based and micrographic-based information resources.[11] With

---

11. Phyllis M. Lybarger, *Records Retention Scheduling* (Prairie Valley, Kan.: Association of Records Managers and Administrators, 1980). See also Michael J. Fox and Kathleen A. McDonough, *Wisconsin Municipal Record Manual* (Madison: State Historical Society of Wisconsin and the Wisconsin Department of Development, 1980).

this information, the records manager must then consider the R&D status of each document category. For retention purposes, the records manager must determine if the papers in question are current (active), noncurrent (inactive), or dead. Active files remain with the user department; inactive files are placed in some type of economical holding facility, such as a warehouse or records center; dead files are discarded.

The records manager will work with the user departments to determine which status applies to their papers. The record center will assume responsibility for noncurrent materials until their final disposition is determined. Up to this point, the only decision reached jointly by the users and information services personnel is that inactive files will be removed from the users' offices to allow more room for active records. Inactive files must remain accessible, however. Furthermore, both law and convention dictate specific retention periods for different categories of documents. Accounting records, for example, may need to be kept for seven years in case of an Internal Revenue Service audit. Other materials, such as those relating to past employees, patents, trade agreements, or organizational history, may have permanent value. It usually falls to the records manager to ensure that the retention and final disposition conforms to the law and the best interests of the parent institution.

Thus, from a records management perspective, the establishment of R&D schedules is a complex, even arduous process. A mistake could cost the parent organization considerable money, embarrassment, and legal problems. Since local, state, and federal laws may govern the disposition of records, the records manager must keep track of numerous regulations and guidelines.[12] In addition, information managers must act promptly and efficiently when it is clear that materials can be discarded; otherwise the organization will end up paying more than it should for records storage. The timely disposal of files will also alleviate some of the clutter in offices and the records center, thus facilitating document retrieval and the filling of user requests.

The computer has a role in all aspects of the R&D process. First, the standardized data elements of a retention and disposition schedule lend themselves to transformation into a machine-readable form. If MIS personnel design their survey forms properly, they will find little difficulty inputting them into an online database. Once entered into an electronic format, the scheduling process will possess all the

---

12. Records retention regulations can be found in all of the following: the Armed Services Procurement Regulation, the Federal Code, the Fair Labor Standards Act, the Interstate Commerce Commission Code, the Federal Insurance Company Regulation, the Industrial Security Manual (Federal Attachment to DD Form 441), and most state codes (especially those portions of codes relating to taxation and accountability).

flexibility lacking in the manual procedure. Staff may, for example, sort the survey information by location, user department, span dates, or record type. If they wish to append retention dates to record categories, they can easily call up all those entries governed by a particular law or convention and process them as a group. The time and effort saved through such an approach are obvious.

Similarly, all of the rules and regulations governing records retention could be entered into the database. Depending upon the type of software employed and the degree to which document categories are standardized, record types could then be matched with their statutory retention dates, and R&D schedules would be generated automatically. Some of the highly computerized records management facilities in the private sector are already doing this.[13] A less sophisticated system could prepare work assignment sheets, listing those files or rolls of microfilm to be collected from user departments and discarded over a given period. It could also produce file and shelf labels, routing slips, and disposition notices that would go to the user department as a final check prior to the destruction of a body of records in film.

To assist in the development of reference and user services, the MIS staff could add the storage location of inactive materials to the database. File inventories could constitute a further set of data elements when detailed intellectual and physical control are required. It would then be a simple matter to produce current inventories of records center holdings by user department, record type, and retention period. Such reports would serve as a helpful reference tool to end users when identifying and retrieving desired records. Furthermore, the computer could assign shelf space to new records center accessions and automatically update the database once the storage allocation is confirmed by records center staff. When auditing center activities, information services personnel would then return to the database for a full inventory and directory listing (even a map) of their holdings. It is likely that such a system will provide a sufficient number of audit trails to significantly curtail the time spent locating misfiled paper or filmed documents.

Indeed, one of the virtues of an automated records center control system is its standardization. Steps follow in sequence and the data

---

13. Typical systems in this area include those of Lockheed, Marathon Oil, IBM, AMP Corp., and Boise Cascade. See Fred V. Diers, "Computer Indexing for a Records Retention Center," *Records Management Quarterly* 12,2 (1978): 21–28, 32; Kay Birula, William Graham, and E. Guden, "An In-House On-Line Information Retrieval System Using a Microcomputer," *Proceedings of ASIC* 15 (1978): 32–34; Jean Carroll, "The End-User Approach to Managing Information," *Records Management Quarterly* 15,4 (1981): 14–24, 32; William Benedon, "Automated Scheduling/Records Center Operations," *Records Management Quarterly* 14,2 (1980): 18–26; and A. Patricia Miller and Susan L. Jenkins, "Automated Retrieval of Project Documentation at Marathon Oil," *Records Management Quarterly* 16,3 (1982): 5–8.

input procedures—whether online or batch—make it necessary that personnel enter all of the key data for the subsequent retrieval of retired files. Manual systems usually do not provide the same degree of structure, nor do they prompt the user to include certain vital information. An automated approach is not error free, and is, in fact, more prone to error due to the multiple levels of data coding involved. However, there are sufficient safeguards in most computerized procedures to at least mitigate some of these problems. Such an automated system would be a powerful and flexible management tool to ensure that the parent institution receives the highest value for the money invested in its information services.

Automated Tools for the Administration of Paper-based Information Systems

To expand further upon my brief review of EDP applications in micrographics and records management, I would now like to examine the potential for deploying computers in the administration of other typical information service activities. From a strategic perspective, the organization should look towards developing integrated information systems. As a practical matter, however, the team may need to proceed in a piecemeal—albeit it methodical—manner. Thus, the team might build a module at a time, insuring that datafile design will afford opportunities for the subsequent merging of MIS products. In this way, the organization can at least embark upon a process of automating its information delivery systems while limiting both its overall resource commitments and financial risk. Due to the limitations of space, my own observations on this complex process will be of a summary nature. Nevertheless, the scenarios that I present here ought to strike resonant chords with those laboring in the areas of system design and implementation.

To identify opportunities for the conversion of manual MIS processes to automated or computer-assisted operations, let us begin by referring back to the resource allocation matrix (figure 5). This tool is designed to isolate discrete information services within one's organization and to correlate the functionality of each process against an array of EDP capabilities. When selecting from this shopping list, focus upon those aspects of office work that are routine, repetitious, and require the least complex and therefore the least expensive automated solutions. The human, EDP, and monetary constraints placed upon the MIS unit by its parent institution will figure prominently in these calculations. If funding is a problem, the project staff might also wish to consider which activities will involve the lowest initial capital investment. It therefore makes sense to start small and build upon initial successes. However, take care to ensure that whatever commitment is made to hardware and software for the sake of economy does not prevent the possible expansion of the system to accommodate future operational requirements. In short, balance immediate needs against anticipated demands upon the new EDP application.

As a starting point, one might establish a single electronic workstation for prototyping and testing. Depending upon one's EDP environment, this unit may be tied to a mainframe computer, operate as part of a local area network (LAN), or function as a standalone personal computer. However, for greater flexibility and better throughput (i.e., the time consumed during input and output that includes the delivery of the final product), the latter option is the preferred one. The configuration should include a printer for the creation of both graphics and letter-quality text output. With these tools in hand, the MIS team may begin developing automated approaches to routine correspondence processing; report and newsletter preparation; in the case of not-for-profit institutions, grants preparation; mailing list administration and production; and so on.

Once fully configured with word processing, graphics, database, and spreadsheet capabilities, MIS personnel may employ their workstation(s) to proceed with these types of simple conversions as time and resources allow. For example, a local historical society or library might use such a system to generate camera-ready copy of publications previously farmed out to vendors for preparation. They could produce their own mailing labels as well. Records management and archives services might use the system to create and update finding aids, shelf lists, and even storage container labels. Other assignments common to any operational area, such as budget and performance report preparation, could also be executed more efficiently and economically with the aid of a workstation configuration. The addition of more sophisticated software will allow the staff to prepare camera-ready forms for existing manual processes and to replace others with automated database alternatives.

Consider the degree to which the most responsible members of your organization must involve themselves in these and other routine office activities by asking: Do the manual tools that we currently employ in these undertakings produce a satisfactory product? Are we or our end users repeatedly asked to revise budgets at the insistence of the parent institution and grant applications at the behest of some foundation or government agency? Do we waste a disproportionate amount of our time making minor revisions to standard documentation, reports, and mailing lists? It should come as no surprise that both MIS and those it serves expend a considerable amount of time on these types of routine projects at the expense of other equally pressing professional responsibilities. Moreover, the quality and usefulness of the manually produced end product does not always justify the total resources invested in its creation.

In making this observation, I do not minimize the importance of these functions. On the other hand, by investing wisely in their automation, the productivity of both MIS personnel and the organization's management team more generally will be enhanced. In addition, clerical personnel may be assigned to customize letters, forms, and legal documents that reside in system memory, thus freeing the senior staff for more creative work. This too may be achieved without any reduction in the quality of corporate performance. Indeed, the customer will be served in a more personalized manner and will credit management for its hands-on approach, even though these tasks are in fact devolving onto personnel of lesser authority. The information processing environment will in and of itself set standards and enhanced throughput. A careful analysis of the costs and benefits of the EDP applications mentioned above will demonstrate the extent to which a given organization will benefit from this arrangement.[14] Whatever its final measure, I have no doubt that the undertaking will pay for itself in no time.

Accessioning and Retrieval Systems

Having justified the institution's initial investment in an automated system on the basis of standard word and statistical processing applications, the project staff should next consider the employment of EDP techniques in more unique information management settings. Again, the approach recommended here is to proceed from simple functions to those of increasing complexity. In most instances, the establishment of database structures is an essential part of this plan. Each operation will have its own data files that are tied to a larger, integrated database. When moving from design to implementation, the team should recognize the fact that the quality of database management system (DBMS) software, the speed of the organization's CPU, and the capacity of its external (magnetic) storage will set certain parameters on overall system performance. The newly automated system should also anticipate the growth in demands for services. Any computerized function that is designed to replace a manual task must operate within these constraints.

---

14. For a strategic approach to the determination of cost-benefits, see C. Warren Axelrod, "The Computer Pricing Process," *Journal of Systems Management* 30,2 (1979): 24–27; and the four-part article by Robert W. Shirley, "Management and Distributed Computing," Parts 1–4, *Computerworld* (In Depth) 14,41–44 (1980): 1–20, 1–8, 1–20, 1–16. See also "NARS: An Accurate Cost Measure of Word Processing for Managers," *Government Executive* 11,9 (1979): 18, 22, 24, 26.

For example, it would prove most unfortunate if the staff initiated a computerized accessioning process that, after a year or two, was found to be incapable of handling the volume of books coming into the library or the number of files coming into the records center or archives. In preparing system specifications, it would therefore prove advisable to consider manual activity over the last three years. With this data in hand, a reasonable estimate of intended use for the next three years could be extrapolated. As a rule of thumb, a system must be viable for at least three years if it is to provide a decent return on the time, money, and effort devoted to its design and implementation. The aforementioned information gathering is therefore essential in making a final determination about a given project.

Obviously, if the organization intends to make a long-term commitment to a particular computer application, the staff may wish to extend its projections further into the future. However, keep in mind that EDP technology will not remain stagnant during this period. If the project team has selected hardware and software based upon the criteria of system expandability and migratability, an anticipated three-year life for an application should suffice. Finally, bear in mind that the operational function to be automated has a life cycle of its own. As the parent institution changes in response to its environment, its basic processes will also evolve, adapt, or disappear. Systems—either manual or automated—will therefore require adjustments to keep pace with the competition and developments in EDP technology.

It therefore follows that after an organization has automated standard office operations, its choices must become more selective. Corporate priorities, as well as sound cost/benefit analysis, will drive the process of selection. For example, in such settings as libraries, research institutions, and archival programs, resource solicitation and collection accessioning activities may be the logical next target for computerization. The organization's staff prepares letters to prospective donors and follows these with further letters, phone calls, and perhaps face-to-face meetings. Once the donor has agreed to make a contribution, his or her lead file becomes a case file. Legal documents are exchanged and so forth.

It is a simple matter to track all these transactions within a DBMS. To account for the presence of key legal documents, provenance statements, biographical sketches of individual donors, and administrative histories of institutional contributors are additional data elements or "fields" that might be included in the database. Thereafter, the system could issue reports that alert staff members to the status of lead and case files and the need for further action as necessary. When it is time to process a donation or merely to announce its arrival, the chronology of the transaction as well as information pertaining to its provenance and history are readily available in the database for transmission in hardcopy or electronic form. With almost no effort, most DBMSs will also generate labels for mailings directed at current and prospective donors.

Like development activities, the book or record accessioning process involves the manipulation of a limited number of discrete bits of information. Most accessioning procedures include recording the size and nature of the collection received, the date of receipt; the name and address of the office or origin, publisher, or creator; the name of the staff receiver; and the physical location of the collection in storage. The design of a DBMS electronic form that deals with these functions is easily accomplished. Since some acquisitions may arrive piecemeal, the form should probably have additional space available for subsequent shipments. Furthermore, the storage assignment data field ought to be flexible enough to indicate when and where a collection has gone, once it has left the stacks for processing.

More sophisticated software packages have the capacity to merge an accessioning process database with a map of the storage facility. Once the staff worker enters the size of the collection in some standard unit of measure (e.g., number of linear feet or storage containers), the computer can automatically search the map for available space. When it locates the shelving section that best fits the collection's storage requirements, the system will assign it to this location and update the database accordingly. Thereafter, the system can generate shelving inventories and storage facility maps upon request. Even a less comprehensive DBMS has the ability to produce a listing of all accessions by their location as needed.

Accessioning tools greatly reduce the problems that are associated with the physical control and handling of incoming materials. For example, within a records center, it will no longer be necessary to store all boxes from a particular office in the same location. A simple report can locate the scattered pieces throughout the facility. Furthermore, the system maximizes the use of shelf space by matching a delivery with available shelving. These new procedures will save considerable staff time, eliminate much of the waste associated with hunting for misplaced collections, and ensure the most economical use of what is always insufficient shelf space.

Similarly, the statistics generated by a records accessioning and processing database might prove most useful to system administrators. By tracing the size of a given collection or information resource against the time it takes for staff members to complete the various stages of processing, management can calculate the average time required to carry out a particular function according to a given unit of measure, such as one linear foot of material. This information could then be converted into workforce and supply cost estimates for the budget process. With this information, the staff can also determine the time it would take to completely process an incoming acquisition and how this translates into the expenditure of institutional resources.

Such estimates can be used to indicate when records center personnel might reasonably be expected to complete the processing of a given collection. These performance measures also provide a quantitative means for comparing the productivity of individual workers over time and of staff members working on similar assignments. Although it is at times difficult to make these types of comparisons because collections vary so widely, the statistical analysis model proposed here will work if properly weighted. MIS managers concerned with demonstrating the worth of their operations and the increasing productivity of their staff should certainly take note of this approach.

When dealing with office files, information services personnel may employ the computer during the last stages of collection processing to produce inventory listings for each storage container. The system should also have the capacity to generate file folder labels directly from the inventory. Much of this same information may very well find its way into the collection guides and finding aids that serve as the culmination of the processing procedure in some institutions. Depending upon the data structures employed, none of this information should need to be entered into the system more than once. After a staff member has keyed it into memory, the listings format may be altered to accommodate labels, index cards, printed pages, or any other output product. By eliminating redundant data entry and report processing activities, the professional and clerical staff will be free for other more productive duties related to collection administration or reference services.

Like accessioning, the management of user access procedures and document copying services is a fairly straightforward task with easily defined data elements. For example, as records or printed materials are released to users, a dated record should be kept of all transactions. All of this can take place online, with the generation of call slips in the stack area or records center as an end product. An integrated version of this system could also track user requests for document reprography.[15] A common database within a microcomputer or mainframe system could easily accommodate these features, and even generate invoices for the cost of copying services. These charges could then be aggregated in yet another report for account-

---

15. The advent of the photostatic copier has made it both inexpensive and convenient for researchers to work from copies of originals, rather than the originals themselves. As a result, reprography is a major operation within many information services programs. See Carolyn Hoover Sung, *Archives and Manuscripts: Reprography* (Chicago: Society of American Archivists, 1982).

ing purposes. The staff might also design the access system so that a user request is checked against materials already in circulation. In this manner, information services personnel and their constituents would immediately know the status and availability of any given holding. This avoids unnecessary research and annoying delays for all concerned.

Yet another application well suited for computer-assisted management is in the area of active file and ephemeral document maintenance. Most offices possess holdings that include news clippings, pamphlets, maps, contracts, reprints of published articles, and the like, but have no systematic means of filing and, hence, retrieving these materials. One method of handling them might be to establish a database for these documents by individually encoding them into the system. They could then be retrieved through a Boolean search mechanism within the DBMS.

Unfortunately, this approach is costly since it requires a considerable amount of inputting. Furthermore, it is questionable that ephemeral materials require such a high level of bibliographic control. A second, and recommended, option involves the development of an effective thesaurus for indexing these documents. Materials would be stored by subject and would be cross-referenced by the system. Staff members could create a thesaurus of their own via a DBMS, or merely adapt a structure borrowed from another institution.[16] Once operational, users could peruse the thesaurus at a terminal and the staff could employ it to file incoming materials and to generate folder labels and hardcopy finding aids.

More sophisticated approaches to document retrieval are available but many of the software products in this area merely provide the facility to generate printed indexes based upon the inputting of file tags. Even the best natural-language (i.e., the most like English) versions of this product are limited and rather inflexible. By comparison, an online query-based system is far superior, since the user may formulate a search, employing Boolean descriptors, that allows the computer to explore the full length of the data file and to return with the specific information requested. The slow and sometimes ineffective step of examining printed indexes is thus eliminated.

---

16. A thesaurus serves the same general purpose as a data element dictionary but also includes functional descriptors and search terminology. See Wilfrid F. Lancaster, *Vocabulary Control for Information Retrieval*, 2nd ed. (Washington, D.C.: Information Resources Press, 1987); Wilfrid F. Lancaster and E. G. Fayen, *Information Retrieval On-Line* (Los Angeles: Melville, 1973): Theodore W. Durr and Paul Rosenberg, *The Urban Information Thesaurus: A Vocabulary for Social Documentation* (Westport, Conn.: Greenwood, 1977); H. S. Heaps, *Information Retrieval: Computational and Theoretical Aspects* (New York: Academic Press, 1978); and Dagobert Soergel, *Indexing Languages and Thesauri: Construction and Maintenance*, 2nd ed. (Los Angeles: Melville, 1978).

When automating this function, the MIS team should take a measured approach. As a first step, continue to prepare detailed inventory lists and related documents on the operating unit's word processor (or electronic workstation), even if the sole purpose of this process is to prepare clean copy for subsequent entry into an online finding aid. Next, select a DBMS that possesses the capacity for full-text searching or at least allows for the unencumbered retrieval of information from designated data fields. Then establish an appropriately formatted screen and data element dictionary. Next, load collection descriptors for all holdings into the system. These might include the name of the document group; its office(s) of origin; its span dates; its points of human, geographical, or thematic reference; and its processing status (e.g., "open to corporate researchers," "open to outsider users," "closed from access," or "in preparation"). Through this database, a user can then obtain a listing of all those materials that fall within his or her area of inquiry. System output could include a printout of file names or document references.

In summary, the process of actually computerizing information services will in all likelihood evolve through stages as part of a larger strategic plan. The first stage encompasses routine office activities, such as word processing and financial management. The success of automating these operations will win end user cooperation and the support of the parent institution's senior management for subsequent undertakings. At the second stage, automation may be introduced into those MIS service areas that pose the least complex management problems while offering the promise of an immediate return on the investment. Accessioning, the control of lead and case files, and the tracking of record groups through various levels of processing are activities that fall into this category. Third, service-related functions that take time away from direct staff interactions with users, such as access control and reprography administration, would be automated.

Next, MIS personnel might begin the more complex process of computer-assisted description and retrieval of ephemeral collections and vertical file holdings. They could then turn their energies toward the cataloging of records, filing systems, and manuscript materials—first on a general collection level and then at a more detailed box, folder, or item level. Ultimately, the system would tie the user directly to specific documents through the development of a microcomputer interfaced with a videodisc player or some other image processing technology. In the end, the organization as a whole will profit from more efficient and responsive information storage and retrieval services. The MIS staff would also benefit in that their jobs would become less mechanical and repetitious, and their capacity to provide more focused assistance to end users would be greatly enhanced.

MIS Networking and the Evolution
of Image Processing

As information retrieval tools become more highly automated and as data sources themselves increasingly reside in machine-readable formats, organizations of all types and sizes will naturally move toward accessing these systems through computer networks. Such an arrangement will lead to greater efficiency in that users will no longer be required to leave the confines of their work areas in search of pertinent information. For its part, the MIS team will find it less difficult to service its constituents, even though it will fall under greater pressure to prepare and train end users in the proper operation of these highly automated information environments.

While established EDP and telecommunications technologies will play a major role in this scenario of linking users with their data resources, the emergence of write-once/read-many (WORM) videodisc systems as an economical complement to the electronic workstation offers new and exciting options.[17] Heretofore, networks carried digitized information from a CPU, over phone lines or coaxial cable, to terminals or microcomputers in user locations. For data to be transmitted via the network, it would need to be stored in hard disk memory or on magnetic tapes. Both media are expensive to maintain and service. Justification for the necessary level of investment to support vast arrays of data stored in this fashion is most difficult, especially if the information in question is accessed only on an intermittent basis. By offering a long-term, stable, and economical storage alternative, videodisc systems open the door to potentially revolutionizing information service delivery. The remainder of this chapter will therefore examine the growing importance of networking and distributed image/data processing as they influence MIS services.

As I have already indicated, many organizations are now finding it essential to deploy data access terminals throughout their facilities. These devices may be stand-alone units that are linked to each other over telephone lines or coaxial cable, or they may operate dependently with processing capabilities that are tied to common memory storage and a DBMS. The typical mainframe-based system will support many terminals, usually configured through controller and communications equipment to service both local and outlying users. For example, in a records center one might allocate terminals or PC work-

17. Donald Newman, "Optical Disk and Micrographic Document Management Systems," *Journal of Information and Image Management* 199 (1985): 15–17; William Saffady, *Optical Disks for Data and Document Storage* (Westport, Conn.: Meckler, 1986); and Mike Befeler, "Combining Image and Text Using CD-ROM Document Delivery Systems," *Information Times* (January, 1987): 12.

stations to the receiving area (for accessioning), to the administrative offices (for word processing, collection development, fund raising, and financial management), to the processing area (for file processing and description), to the stacks (for record retrieval), and to the information center (for user services). Smaller shops may choose to combine office functions at a particular workstation, thus significantly reducing their hardware requirements.

With a networking system in place, the key to its return on the investment is twofold. First, it will eliminate a considerable amount of data duplication through resource integration. For example, even before files arrive from their office of origin, pertinent information concerning the record transfer will enter the system as part of the case-file documentation. When the materials are delivered to receiving, this data may be transferred automatically to the accession record. The expanded online file is then available for viewing by the processing staff and administration who will assign incoming materials storage space and a place in the work queue. As part of the subsequent description process, listings of box and folder contents may be inputted into the database. These same data fields would serve as access points when the time comes for servicing holdings for end users. As outlined here, each records center employee adds to an existing computer record or draws from another database to establish a new information source. In either case, the steps taken save time, effort, and money.

The second and most obvious benefit of networking is that the MIS staff has established a current source of information. As each activity is documented on the system, it becomes part of a database. Rather than weekly or monthly reports on the status of file processing, the location of holdings, or finding aid preparations, records center management will look to the database to know immediately what has transpired. More importantly, since access terminals may be positioned throughout the workplace, the system will speed necessary data to end users in a timely and efficient manner. Furthermore, it will reduce (if not eliminate) the need to maintain paper-based retrieval tools and checkout services. Add to this the benefits derived from the system's performance in routine office work, and one has a powerful justification for the initial investment in and subsequent support of this type of office automation scenario.

For verification of this assertion, one need only consider recent trends in library administration. The networking of automated systems is now at the heart of many library operations. Acquisitions, cataloging, and circulation services are tied together to speed processing and enhance patron services. While local area networks play a role in this scenario, so too do online links to national bibliographic databases, the Library of Congress, and such utilities as OCLC, Inc., and the Research Library Network (RLIN).[18] All of these innovations have reduced costs and improved performance. Similarly, in the private sector, manufacturing concerns are networked so that parts and materials suppliers, the production process, and customers are linked together. This approach has allowed some manufacturers to run without costly inventories, while at the same time, remain responsive to fluctuating market demands.[19]

The widespread use of terminal access to current files is approaching reality in the worlds of business and government. However, many of these systems are too costly to contemplate in relation to the management of inactive records.[20] Indeed, such configurations are only in place today where the need for the prompt electronic delivery of documents overrules considerations of cost. Within the public section, large government organizations will probably be the first to resort to remote information access for archived materials. Two factors converge to make this a reasonable supposition. First, government departments tend to rely more heavily on documentary evidence as an integral part of their decision-making processes. Second, in many instances they are obliged to make their findings and the supporting evidence public. It is for these very reasons that the National Archives of Canada, the U.S. National Archives and Records Service, and the U.S. Library of Congress are all presently pursuing automated document retrieval and videodisc applications.[21]

The interest in optical videodisc technologies is well justified. In the first place, a single twelve-inch videodisc can store 2.6 billion characters (2.6 gigabytes) of information. A typical configuration of

18. See note 2. See also David Bearman, ed., *A Plan for the Acquisition of an Integrated, Generalized, Collections Management Information System* (Washington, D.C.: Smithsonian Institution OIRM, 1984); and Emily Gallup Fayen, "Automated Circulation Systems for Large Libraries," *Library Technology Reports* 22,4 (1986): 385–473.

19. For a thorough discussion of this issue, see Mikell P. Groover, *Automation, Production Systems, and Computer-Aided Manufacturing* (Englewood Cliffs, N.J.: Prentice-Hall, 1980). For product information on inventory control systems, see *Business Systems* magazine.

20. See, for example, Walt Crawford, *Patron Access: Issues for Online Catalogs* (Boston: G. K. Hall, 1987); A. Patricia Miller and Susan L. Jenkins, "Automated Retrieval of Project Documentation at Marathon Oil," *Records Management Quarterly* 16,3 (1982): 5–8; Jean Carroll, "The End-User Approach to Managing Information," *Records Management Quarterly* 15,4 (1981): 14–23, 32; and Patrick Boulay, "Automation in Mortgage Banking: Have Computers Met Their Match?" *Mortgage Banker* 40,12 (1980): 63–67.

21. The National Archives of Canada project is an immense undertaking. The Archives is only in the earliest stages of its development efforts. See Dennis Mole, "The Videodisc as a Pilot Project of the Public Archives of Canada," *Videodisc/Videotex* 1,3 (1981): 154–61. See also R. Barrett, "Developments in Optical Disk Technology and the Implications for Information Storage Retrieval," *Journal of Micrographics* 15,1 (1982): 22–26; Andrej Tenne-Sens, "Telidon Graphics and Library Applications," *Information Technology and Libraries* 1,2 (1982): 98-110; and Clifford A. Lynch and Edwin B. Brownrigg, "Library Applications of Electronic Imaging Technology," *Information Technology and Libraries* 5,2 (1986): 100–5.

discs, commonly referred to as a "jukebox," will hold 166 billion characters for about twenty percent of the cost of the equivalent magnetic disk (DASD) storage. Furthermore, unlike its EDP counterparts, optical disc equipment is more compact and does not require the space, electrical power, and air conditioning necessary with mainframe computer systems. In addition, as I commented in Chapter Three, videodisc technologies are capable of storing visual images, facsimiles of documents and signatures, and even sound recordings.[22]

The storage capacity and economy of these imaging systems suggest that they are potentially well suited for records management, archival, and library applications. In such a scenario, information previously stored on paper, micrographic, and magnetic formats would be captured instead on optical discs. Any number of vendors currently offer equipment capable of this type of information processing conversion.[23] Once the discs have been "mastered," they may be played back to retrieve specific documents. By integrating these devices with a database system running off of a mainframe or even a personal computer, the end user may access records quickly and economically.

A typical configuration might include a number of jukeboxes for data storage linked to a network of electronic workstations, a retrieval database, and an array of printing devices. The user would employ separate CRT screens for database manipulation and document viewing. Before too long, even this accommodation will prove unnecessary as vendors offer screens that will integrate computer and optical disc transmissions. When necessary, printers and plotters would provide copies of documents, photographs, maps, and any other resource stored on disc. Through the use of broad-band transmission technologies, such a system could also send images to remote locations. Thus, a single videodisc library could serve as a resource for a far flung network.

With such a system in place, government publications, bank financial records, retail store customer files, university student records, and any other bulky information source could be reduced to an easily managed and accessed system. The technology is or will shortly be

---

22. See Jeffrey Bairstow, "CD-ROM: Mass Storage for the Mass Market," *High Technology* 6,10 (1986): 44–51; and Ed Schwartz, *The Educator's Guide to Interactive Videodisc* (Washington, D.C.: Association for Educational Communications and Technology, 1986).

23. Not surprisingly, both major computer and micrographics equipment manufacturers are currently involved in image system development and sales, including IBM, 3M, Kodak, Bell & Howell, Filenet, Integrated Automation, Wang, Teknekron, Zerox, Access, and Phillips Europe. For an assessment of the market, see Insurance Accounting Systems' Association Systems Research Committee, "Image Processing: Document Imaging for the Future," *Journal of Information and Image Management* (November, 1986): 10–21, 46–7.

available. Furthermore, it would appear that user acceptance may be easily obtained. In the first place, the retrieval tools that drive these systems tend to be very sophisticated and, at the same time, user friendly. Training does not, therefore, appear to be a problem and acceptance among non-technical users tends to be high.[24] Second, image legibility is quite good, an essential quality in applications where copies of stored documents must be disseminated in lieu of originals. Third, with the system in place, the reduction of paper and the general improvement of overall workflow improves worker productivity and operational throughput. In this regard, fewer documents are misplaced, none are "lost in the mail," and audit trails are easily established. Finally, the merging of data and image processing networks affords the opportunity for a number of users to view the same document simultaneously, speeding research, reducing phone calls, and in general improving problem resolution.

Yet other operational criteria render optical discs an attractive alternative to magnetic storage media. While they have become available only recently, optical media are viewed as physical property and, as such, admissible in courts of law as documentary evidence. The U.S. Internal Revenue Service (IRS), for example, permits the use of optical disc-based documents, as does the U.S. Department of Justice. In terms of shelflife, this medium is extremely stable and does not require the servicing associated with the long-term storage of magnetic media. This means that optical video-discs may legally replace paper, microfilm, or magnetic tape originals, and that their preservation will not require as much cost or effort.

In the final analysis, image processing technologies have the potential to open most organizations to cost savings and greater efficiency. It is for these reasons that the IRS is experimenting with the storing of tax forms, filings, and returns on optical media; that the U.S. Patent Office is employing the technology to archive all filings and patents; and that American Express, Security Pacific Bank, and Prudential Insurance are recording many vital transactions on disc. Other institutions, including the Library of Congress, General Electric, the U.S. National Space and Aeronautics Administration, numerous hospitals, and the state governments of Utah, New Jersey, and New York, have begun videodisc projects.

Admittedly, the aforementioned list includes some of the United States' largest public- and private-sector organizations. This should in no way discourage smaller institutions from examining the po-

---

24. Current applications include McDonnell Douglas, engineering drawings; Library of Congress, card catalog and books; EDS, Saturn component parts ordering and control; SEC, corporate registration documents; Travelers Insurance, policy and account information; New York State, pension plan documentation; St. Vincent's Hospital, patient records; and Bank of America, account documentation.

tential for deploying these technologies within their own office environments. Large agencies may take the lead because they have an immediate need to control their paperflow. Small institutions can learn from these efforts (and mistakes) in selecting appropriate videodisc applications of their own. Furthermore, the reader should bear in mind that 3M, TAB, Cannon, NEC, Hitachi, Infodetics, and many other EDP and micrographic system manufacturers are engaged in the creation and distribution of imaging systems for such a market. All of these systems integrate image and data processing in some fashion. In this regard they are very much like microfilm computer-assisted retrieval (CAR) products. However, unlike CAR systems, optical disc technologies afford transmission via communications networks and support more sophisticated retrieval algorithms.

With the future widespread use of these data/imaging configurations, the focus of information services within most organizations will undoubtedly shift. Today's management concerns will give way to a new host of issues. Perhaps one major area in this regard will entail the administration of the machine-readable records that are coming to supplant paper-based information systems. The closing chapter of this study examines some of these issues in more detail. At this point, I would only stress that in addressing the dynamics of today's electronic office environment, the MIS team will be well served by the methodology presented above. In particular, I would encourage my readers to look to their organization's strategic planning process for guidance when responding to the information needs of their constituents. At the tactical level, a process of ongoing self-appraisal and a willingness to challenge established practices will position MIS to seize technological and operational opportunities as they emerge.

CHAPTER

8

Machine-Readable Records: Management Issues in an Evolving Office Environment

The Environment

As Chapter Seven suggests, EDP and telecommunications technologies afford MIS personnel opportunities to improve and enhance existing services. To achieve the desired results, careful planning and adequate training must precede any new installation. In the long term, those users who are dependent upon information services to achieve their organizational objectives will grow intolerant of MIS delivery systems that are either unresponsive to their needs or outdated in relation to other utilities operating in the marketplace. Ultimately, these users will go elsewhere if in-house MIS personnel do not rise to the challenge. Fortunately, the current trend among MIS departments is towards the expansion and adaptation of user-oriented services, and a willingness to exploit the latest EDP options when developing new offerings.

Ironically, as they begin to deploy automated systems, the MIS team will face yet another challenge: what to do with all the machine-readable records created as a by-product of their its efforts. The issues are complex and not easily resolved. In the first place, these digitized files come in a wide variety of formats, necessitating special documentation and maintenance. Second, servicing these information products is problematic because they all require some type of machine interface before a user may access data. Third, some machine-readable formats are unstable, raising questions about their "archival" viability. Finally, information services professionals as a group have yet to devise techniques for dealing with the preservation of online interactive databases and similar dynamic data resources.

There is no denying the problem. The use of computers and, hence, our reliance on machine-readable records, including data on hard disks (DASD), floppy diskettes, magnetic tape, and optical videodiscs, has grown over the past few years at a staggering rate.[1] As prominent as these types of records have become in the way modern society conducts its business, little, if any, attention has been devoted to the management of machine-readable files once they are no longer of immediate use.[2] Typically, data centers assume responsibility for the creation of backup tapes for the protection of current EDP records. Once a new generation of updated tapes emerges from this process, the staff usually erases the older versions of these records. Thus, information of both short-term use and perhaps long-term research value is lost forever.

To be fair, there are some very good reasons why machine-readable records do not receive the same level of attention enjoyed by paper documents. One may, for example, point to EDP hardware obsolescence, changes in magnetic storage technology, the cost of preserving and storing magnetic tapes, and the ease with which EDP storage media can be erased and reused as justifications for a pragmatic approach to records retention.[3] In short, extremely cogent eco-

---

1. The implications of the growth in the use and importance of machine-readable records have been noted on repeated occasions by leaders within the archives and records management professions. See, for example, J. E. Thexon, "Archival Potential of Machine Readable Records in Business," *American Archivist* 37,1 (1974): 37–42; Charles M. Dollar, "Machine-Readable Archives—Records Managers Neglect Automated Files," *Records Management Journal* 13,4 (1975): 2–8; Lionel Bell, *The Archival Implications of Machine Readable Records* (Washington, D.C.: VIII International Congress on Archives, 1976); Lionel Bell, "The Archival Implications of Machine-Readable Records," *Archives* 26,1 (1979): 85–92; Robert W. Warner and Francis X. Blouin, Jr., "Some Implications of Records in Machine-Readable Form for Traditional Archival Practice," *Archives and Machine-Readable Records*, Carolyn L. Geda et al., eds. (Chicago: Society of American Archivists, 1980), 242–48; and Dominic Nghiep Cong Bui, "The Videodisk: Technology, Applications and Some Implications for Archives," *American Archivist* 47,4 (1984): 418–27.

2. This fact is most graphically demonstrated in a survey of business archives conducted by the Society of American Archivists. See Richard M. Kesner, "Automated Records and Techniques in Business Archives: A Survey Report," *American Archivist* 42,4 (1979) 152–57. Unfortunately, the situation has not improved very much in the last ten years. See also Michael Roper, "The Changing Face of the File: Machine-Readable Records and the Archivist," *Archives* 14 (1979/80): 145–50; and William L. Rofes, "The Archival Snare; Mass and Manipulation," *Archives and Machine-Readable Records*, Carolyn L. Geda et al., eds. (Chicago: Society of American Archives, 1980), 111–17.

3. See *BYTE* 8,3 (1983), which is a special issue devoted primarily to mass storage devices for machine-readable data. The articles and product reviews contained in this volume consider such topics as laser cards, disk memories, random access memory (RAM), bubble storage, and optical disc systems.

nomic arguments exist for the prompt disposal of inactive machine-readable records and the return of magnetic tapes and disks upon which this information is stored to use with active files.

For the present, if an organization requires continued access to a particular set of machine-readable records, it is much less expensive for the data center to convert these into computer output microfilm or even paper printouts. Unfortunately, this approach virtually eliminates the end user's ability to manipulate record contents without rekeying the data. On the other hand, once they have served the purpose for which they were originally created, most data files have only limited usefulness. Agency users and MIS personnel must therefore work together to determine which machine-readable records merit retention. It would then fall to the information services team to establish methods for preserving the residue of these files.

Since the cost of long-term machine-readable record maintenance is so high, it is not surprising that the only well-established archival programs to date are those operating within American, Canadian, British, and other national agencies.[4] The reasons for this are simple enough. First, governmental institutions have to retain files longer than organizations in the private sector because these materials are public property and, as such, are required for the accountability of government officials and projects. Second, the nature of many data-gathering functions in government relates either to the oversight of both private- and public-sector activities or to research funded through tax dollars. Thus, unlike the machine-readable records of a business, government EDP files often possess substantial research value independent of the original reason for their creation. Finally, since government, at least to a certain extent, serves as the memory and conscience of the people, it has both the moral responsibility and the requisite funding to support the machine-readable records component of archives programs at some modest level.

More recently, state and municipal governments and large research universities have also moved toward establishing compre-

---

4. See, for example, Governor's Office of Management and Productivity et al., *Computer and Audio-Visual Records in State Government* (Albany, N.Y.: The State Education Department, 1986); Charles M. Dollar, "Machine-Readable Records of the Federal Government and the National Archives," *Archives and Machine-Readable Records*, Carolyn L. Geda et al., eds. (Chicago: Society of American Archivists, 1980), 79–88; Charles M. Dollar, "Computers, the National Archives and Researchers," *Prologue* 8,1 (1976): 29–34; Harold A. Naugler, "The Machine-Readable Archives Program of the Public Archives of Canada: The First Five Years," *Archives and Machine-Readable Records*, 67–78; Ben DeWhitt, "Archival Use of Computers in the United States and Canada," *American Archivists* 42,2 (1979): 152–57; and Michael Roper, "Machine-Readable Archives and the Public Records Office," *Archives and Machine-Readable Records*, 89–101.

hensive programs for magnetic records retention.[5] The growth in the use of machine-readable records by the administrative units of these institutions, as well as their legal responsibilities to end users, has prompted this response. In many instances, however, they do not individually possess the financial resources and, thus, the pool of technical and managerial expertise to maintain facilities that compare with their counterparts in large government agencies. In response to these circumstances and the high costs of operating a data archives, certain universities have joined together to form the Inter-University Consortium for Political and Social Research (ICPSR). Though member institutions retain their own data archives, this body represents a cooperative alternative to single-institution operations.[6]

As attractive as they may at first appear, neither ICPSR nor the federal models for the management of machine-readable files have applicability elsewhere. Most organizations will need to develop options of their own that reflect the fiscal and MIS constraints that they face. Indeed, I would consider the need to develop programs for the administration of machine-readable records as one of the management imperatives of the 1990s. Too much vital information is now stored in exclusively digitized formats to continue on as we have in the past. While it may be understandable that profit-based organizations would neglect an area that is both costly and, at least in the shortterm, unremunerative, the long-term implications of this neglect must be brought to the attention of the corporate leadership. Through some serious salesmanship on the part of MIS management, the ben-

---

5. See, for example, Kathleen M. Heim, "Social Scientific Information Needs for Numeric Data: The Evolution of the International Data Archive Infrastructure," *Collections Management* 9,1 (1987): 1–53; Margaret O'Neill Adams, "Online Numeric Database Systems: A Resource for the Traditional Library," *Library Trends* 30,3 (1982): 435–54; Alice Robbin, "The Data and Program Library Service: A Case Study in Organizing Special Libraries for Computer-Readable Statistical Data," *Library Trends* 30,3 (1982): 407–34; State Historical Society of Wisconsin, *Archival Preservation of Machine-Readable Records: A Final Report* (Madison: State Historical Society of Wisconsin, 1981); and Thomas E. Mills, "Archival Considerations in the Management of Machine-Readable Records in the New York State Government," *Archives and Machine-Readable Records*, Carolyn L. Geda et al., eds. (Chicago: Society of American Archivists, 1980), 102–10.

6. See Carolyn L. Geda and Erik W. Austin, "An Archives for the Social Sciences," *Archives and Machine-Readable Records*, Carolyn L. Geda et al., eds. (Chicago: Society of American Archivists, 1980), 134–44; Janet K. Vavra and Erik W. Austin, "Inter-University Consortium for Political and Social Research: A Social Science Data Archive Shaped by User Environments," *Databases in the Humanities and Social Sciences*, J. Raben and G. Marks, eds. (New York: North-Holland, 1980), 9–13; Ray Jones, "The Data Library in the University of Florida Libraries," *Library Trends* 30,3 (1982): 383–96; and Inter-University Consortium for Political and Social Research, *Guide to Resources and Services*, 1977–78 (Ann Arbor: University of Michigan Press, 1978). For an interesting discussion of a similar institution, see William J. Gammell, "The Roper Center: A Collegial Structure to Facilitate Social Data Utilization," *Archives and Machine-Readable Records*, 134–44.

efits of an investment in effective retention programs may become more evident over time.[7]

To begin, Chapter Seven considers records management issues pertaining to magnetic media. In this context, I briefly review the characteristics of machine-readable records that cause problems for those charged with their retention. I also discuss how the MIS team should go about surveying their parent organization's magnetic media holdings. My next concern is with those machine-readable files of long-term, archival value and how they are to be identified and preserved. This discussion leads quite naturally to a consideration of how automated management tools might assist in these processes. To conclude Chapter Seven, I move beyond my primary focus on archived records to suggest approaches to the maintenance and preservation of online, interactive, database systems.

Records Management and Machine-Readable Data Files

While many organizations currently maintain an ambivalent attitude toward the management of their machine-readable record holdings, I would not like to leave the reader with the impression that this state of affairs is a product of indifference. Rather, the present malaise stems primarily from the cost and complexity associated with any real solution. Unlike paper files, electronic records possess characteristics that complicate the requirements for their assured survival and usability. First, by definition, machine-readable records involve the use of appropriate equipment to access the contents of these data files. As EDP technologies advance, it is unlikely that the parent organization's computer center will retain the machines to process older generation tapes or disks.

In the case of magnetic tape drives, for example, the equipment that reads formatted tapes at 1600 bits per inch (BPI) is rapidly disappearing in favor of 6250 BPI machines. A 1600-BPI tape cannot run on this new equipment. The data center has the choice of retaining an older machine or converting its tapes to a high-density format for reading on a 6250-BPI drive. Neither of these options is particularly desirable. On the one hand, it is unlikely—indeed virtually impossible—for an active data center to remain state-of-the-art while retaining its outdated equipment. Remember that these facilities are extremely cost intensive. Such centers must maintain special environments

---

7. The dearth of activity in this area is most clearly demonstrated in the professional literature pertaining to the records management and archiving of machine-readable business records. See Richard M. Kesner, *Information Management, Machine-Readable Records, and Administration: An Annotated Bibliography* (Chicago: Society of American Archivists, 1983), 55–88; and "Automated Records and Techniques in Business Archives: A Survey Report," *American Archivist* 46,1 (1983): 92–95.

which usually do not have excess space for idle machinery. Similarly, these units cannot afford to maintain and service EDP hardware that is not in constant production. Their managers would therefore tend to argue that the cost of operating the old hardware exceeds the value of the records in question.

Alternatively, it would be more economical to convert records housed on dated storage technology to new formats than to maintain outdated hardware. In fact, this is often an aspect of the transition from one generation of machines to the next within a data center. The process is not without its costs, however. EDP personnel cannot immediately convert all machine-readable records in their tape library (and off-site storage) to a new format as soon as the records arrive. If they act at all, the first items converted are those records required for current operations. The conversion of backup and archived files may also occur, but often only after pressure is brought to bear on DP personnel by senior management. For its part, the corporate leadership may not be sufficiently aware of the situation to act unless other MIS players prompt it. Typically, it falls to the organization's records management staff to ensure that all records slated for retention are converted.

A second major problem with machine-readable records is their vulnerability to destruction. Though they are sensitive to environmental conditions, I am referring here to the ease with which magnetic media may be accidentally overwritten or erased.[8] Once used, paper records can only be recycled after considerable effort and expense. Even discarding these materials may prove a difficult task, especially if there is a considerable volume. This is not the case with magnetic records. A single disk, floppy diskette, or tape may store thousands of pages of data. Even so, it is a simple matter to erase the old media or to record over them. As a matter of course, computer facilities and PC users alike recycle their magnetic tapes, disk drives, and floppy diskettes with great regularity, disposing of old records in the process.

To avoid the loss of information in digitized formats through this recycling process, information services personnel must schedule magnetic media like paper files. They must also police their handling and disposition—both in their organization's computer facility(s) and in user areas, as appropriate. To be effective in this regard, they must first survey their organization's machine-readable records and there-

---

8. In fact, tests have shown that magnetic media are considerably more resilient than was commonly thought to be the case. See Sidney B. Geller, *Care and Handling of Computer Magnetic Storage Media* (Washington, D.C.: National Bureau of Standards, U.S. Department of Commerce, 1983); and Ellen Shea, "Magnetic Media: The Choices Multiply," *Word Processing and Information Services* 8,8 (1982): 38–47.

after maintain current lists of these holdings. Figure 20 illustrates the type of simple management tool required to complete this process.

Like the other prototypes in this volume, figure 20 differentiates between active records—those in day-to-day use by operations personnel, and inactive records—those in storage and under the care of records management or some other information services unit. The survey format includes columns for the entry of record location; medium (e.g., magnetic tape, floppy diskette, optical videodisc); record type (e.g., general ledger journals, personnel files, patient records); record span dates; and the number of tapes, diskettes, and the like in that particular holding. The far right section of the form provides space for retention/disposition recommendations. By employing figure 20 as a survey document, the MIS unit will quickly identify all machine-readable file holdings within the organization.

This step is not, however, an end in itself but merely a summary review to identify the scope of the management problem. For example, the study will reveal the diversity of magnetic tape and floppy diskette formats in use throughout the organization. It will indicate the types of records stored in a machine-readable format, who is using them, and how long files are retained before they are erased. From a records management standpoint, this information should in turn draw attention to operating units with the largest quantities of machine-readable files, the relative importance of this data to the parent institution, and any issues concerning media scheduling and preservation.

As with paper records, information services personnel will employ their survey findings to schedule machine-readable files in compliance with the law and standard operating procedures. Achieving control over the more established EDP media, such as magnetic tape, should pose less of a problem in this regard because these media are usually stored in a central on- or off-site location. Furthermore, the data center personnel responsible for these files are accustomed to the rigors of scheduling, if not retention/disposition, controls. Microcomputer-based media, on the other hand, more often than not reside in the hands, desk drawers, and filing cabinets of their creators. Because they have grown accustomed to managing their own PC files without MIS assistance, disciplining this wide-ranging user group will prove most difficult. As a starting point, information services might win end user agreement for the enforcement of data backup procedures and a security program for the truly vital organizational information stored on floppy diskettes. Once these practices have become entrenched, MIS could move forward with a more rigorous records scheduling program.

As part of the larger records management program, these and all other machine-readable media should be scheduled as part of the

SAMPLE SURVEY FORM

PART I: MACHINE-READABLE RECORDS SURVEY: ACTIVE RECORDS

Location	Medium	Record Type	Span Dates	# of M-R Medium	Retention/Disposition Recommended

Figure 20. Machine-Readable Records Survey

PART II: MACHINE-READABLE RECORDS SURVEY: INACTIVE RECORDS

Location	Medium	Record Type	Span Dates	# of M-R Medium	Retention/Disposition Recommended

Figure 20. (Cont.)

organization's official retention and disposition timetables. Ideally, these guidelines would be added to the institution's online data library and, hence, accessible to all concerned parties whenever required. Under these controls, active records would remain in the computer room or in user areas as appropriate, with an additional set of back-ups stored separately. A second-generation copy would go off-site for any set of records requiring that level of security. Information services should work closely with both end users and EDP personnel to ensure the survey is comprehensive and that the proper disposition of these records takes place.

In larger operations, it may prove necessary to employ a designated records management coordinator to supervise the uniform application of the scheduling process. In making this recommendation, I do not mean to suggest that data center personnel will prove uncooperative or are incapable of observing R&D guidelines. Rather, one must simply face the reality that the pace and activity of EDP facilities and their production orientation will take precedence over any concern for records retention. This is particularly important when one recognizes the fact that most data centers do not legally own the data they store. Thus, they cannot and should not make any decisions concerning the final disposition of machine-readable records left in their care. They will therefore benefit from, and perhaps even come to appreciate, the assistance of a colleague whose expertise and responsibilities include ensuring that vital organizational files are protected from loss and destruction.

As a practical matter, most data centers do a reasonable job when it comes to backing up their active tape libraries. The real challenge for most information services professionals will not come from this area but, rather, from the handling of inactive machine-readable records. Here one is faced with the vexing problem of what to do about technological obsolescence and its implications for computer access to retired magnetic media. One response to this problem, widely used today, is to "dump" machine-readable records onto microfilm or fiche via a COM process.[9] This may be done during initial processing in-house or through an outside service bureau at a later date. A CIM unit might then be employed as necessary to return the data to a machine-readable format. Unfortunately, this particular scenario relies heavily upon a technology (CIM) of dubious merit.

As a reasonable short-term storage alternative, most organizations rely upon an environmentally controlled tape vault. Holding a tape any longer than one year in this setting without proper servicing,

---

9. See Coopers & Lybrand, *Information and Image Management: The Industry and the Technologies* (New York: Coopers & Lybrand, 1987); and Richard C. Allen, "Storing Computer and Text Information on Microfiche," *Information and Records Management* 15,11 (1981): 48–49.

such as cleaning and rewinding, could result in an unreadable data source.[10] Unfortunately, this approach will not work for archived media where the rate of change in EDP technologies renders machine-readable records inaccessible. In such a situation and where sufficient documentation exists, MIS can work with data center personnel in the conversion of old magnetic files to formats in keeping with the new EDP environment. Otherwise, such records must be discarded as useless.

Videodisc technology may afford an economical solution to both the short- and long-term storage problems associated with magnetic media. Already, the EDP industry can deliver optical videodisc technologies that will provide for the rapid transfer of electronic information to a stable and economical medium for the purposes of preservation and retrieval. Presumably, information dumped from computers onto discs will be accessible in that format. Furthermore, when additional processing is required, users could transmit disc contents back into a computer for manipulation. Indeed, it is conceivable that soon user-driven systems will emerge that incorporate R&D schedules, automatically routing data files to an auxiliary storage tape, COM, or disc as appropriate. While MIS personnel might get involved in such undertakings through systems installation, end users will make the final R&D decisions. In this manner, the mechanical aspects of records management will disappear, to be replaced by more rigorous intellectual, computer-assisted processes. On the other hand, the problems associated with a lack of EDP standards and hardware/software dependence apply with equal force to current optical imaging technologies. That being so, my projections about their deployment in the workplace may appear too optimistic. Whatever the outcome of recent developments in optical systems, information managers must learn to deal with these and other new MIS tools.

Archiving Machine-Readable Records

As an end product of the typical records scheduling process, files are grouped for destruction, short-term retention, or long-term archiving. Those materials that fall into the latter category are retained beyond their period of immediate need because they possess significant administrative, informational, and/or research value. Once they are so appraised by the organization's information services team,

---

10. See Margaret L. Hedstrom, *Archives and Manuscripts: Machine-Readable Records* (Chicago: Society of American Archivists, 1984); and Meyer H. Fishbein, *Guidelines for Administering Machine-Readable Archives* (Washington, D.C.: The ADP Committee of the International Council on Archives, 1980).

these records are preserved and prepared for use by researchers. While the processing of traditional paper records raises a considerable number of problems for those engaged in these archival activities, the administration of machine-readable files demands even greater attention and broader expertise.

First, by definition, magnetic records require machine assistance, that is, the use of an intermediary device (or devices) between the documents and the end user. The initial cost, maintenance, and ongoing availability of such hardware are major problems facing any machine-readable data archives. Second, the user must have the appropriate software and hardware to obtain access to electronically stored information. Here again, advances in the technology could play havoc with the ability of MIS personnel to deliver required services. Third, even with the correct computer equipment, operating system, and applications package in hand, this DP capability will be useless unless one has the necessary documentation for translating the stored magnetic messages into humanly recognizable characters. Fourth, even if one has the codebook to convert the data to an alpha-numeric form, further steps are required to justify the investment associated with long-term preservation of machine-readable files for internal users and outside researchers.

If the digitized records in question merit preservation, proper storage and retrieval facilities must be provided. Typically, these requirements assume a degree of physical and intellectual control beyond the standards set for the processing of paper documents. A consideration of the life cycle of machine-readable media will help to clarify matters in this regard. To begin, most data files come into existence as the end product of a manual data entry process or as a result of a computer program's execution. Inputting often involves the use of a database management system (DBMS), which establishes the electronic structures within which the data will reside. Once data is entered into the system, end users will manipulate and analyze this stored information, often resulting in computer-generated reports. If at that point the machine-readable files retain some usefulness, they are preserved by the data center. On the other hand, if the creator of these records has no further use for them, they are often discarded (i.e., erased) shortly after the final processing session.

Machine-readable records will survive this procedure only if they have been scheduled by a records manager or archivist for subsequent retention and final disposition. Both the office that created the magnetic media files and the data center that processed them play an important role in establishing the criteria for these selection procedures. Together, they decide which tapes or disks are to be erased and which are to be transferred to an environmentally sound storage vault. Only a small residue of records will possess sufficient value to justify the cost of long-term preservation. Even among this greatly reduced population, the information services professional must act as an appraiser if he or she is to separate the truly useful material from the worthless. This procedure begins during retention and disposition scheduling and continues through accessing and collection processing.

The accessioning of machine-readable files is not essentially different from that of paper records.[11] However, the appraisal of these materials requires greater intellectual rigor.[12] For example, to merit preservation, machine-readable files must be unique and not derivative. While from the outset this might appear to be a quality easily determined, the procedure is complicated by the nature of the storage media. It is a relatively simple matter to swiftly create a different "generation" of data, based upon the processing of an original EDP file. Depending upon its formatting, the new generation may not obviously resemble the original and may therefore be retained as a "unique" record in its own right. The MIS team must strive to identify and retain datasets in their raw form and then provide facilities for users to rework the information as their research requires. Unless the uniqueness of newly transferred records can be determined from either system documentation or evaluation, information services personnel will be hardpressed, even at this early stage in the process, to make an accurate determination of value.

The quality of file documentation will, in all likelihood, prove essential to the satisfactory culmination of this effort. This is because even a reading of the files at the machine level is not possible unless MIS obtains all the pertinent technical information regarding the data file's structure and layout, its codebook, and its data entry specifications. The inadequacy of record documentation may render machine-readable media inaccessible and, ultimately, worthless. By contrast, sufficiently documented magnetic records are usable, provided they are physically sound. In most instances, supporting materials are quite extensive, shedding light on how a file was originally created, what each data element represents, and how the information in the file was originally employed.

---

11. For a general description of the accessioning process, see Maynard J. Brichford, *Archives and Manuscripts: Appraisal and Accessioning* (Chicago: Society of American Archivists, 1977): 20–22. For a discussion of the process relating to machine-readable records, see Meyer H. Fishbein, *Guidelines for Administering Machine-Readable Archives* (Washington, D.C.: The ADP Committee of the International Council on Archives, 1980), 9–14, 19–20; and Margaret L. Hedstrom, *Archives and Manuscripts: Machine-Readable Records* (Chicago: Society of American Archivists, 1984).

12. See Charles M. Dollar, "Appraising Machine-Readable Records," *American Archivist* 41,4 (1978): 423–30; and Meyer H. Fishbein, "The Traditional Archivist and the Appraisal of Machine-Readable Records," *Archives and Machine-Readable Records*, Carolyn L. Geda et al., eds. (Chicago: Society of American Archivists, 1980), 56–61.

For example, a typical machine-readable database might include a vast body of data. The original information was collected manually and loaded into the computer through the medium of a database management system (DBMS). The paper form may have included coded information, or those collecting the data may have truncated informational elements to expedite the input process. All of this would most certainly confound a user lacking a thorough explanation of what transpired. Furthermore, the DBMS itself may add locational tags to individual data so the latter may be distinguished by the system. Without documentation, someone coming to this machine-readable file for the first time will not know what software package to use, how the data is configured and tagged, or what is meant by the coding of various fields within the database.[13] It is therefore essential that the appraisal process be based firmly upon the completeness of machine-readable record documentation as well as the physical and intellectual integrity of the medium in question.

In the final analysis, only a very small percentage of machine-readable records merit preservation. Long-term records retention decisions must therefore focus upon the informational or research value of the documents under consideration. This stage in the methodology may operate independently of and should precede technological considerations. Even if the information services team is satisfied with the data files supporting papers and physical "readability," it must ask the age-old question of whether the contents of the records merit preservation for future research use. To make such a determination, MIS personnel will need to broaden their awareness of germane research activities, EDP and statistical analysis, and the potential information requirements of their user constituency. In so doing, the team will develop sophisticated appraisal strategies, perhaps employing their parent organization's automated decision support systems.

Machine-Readable Records: Preservation and Access

Once the organization decides to "permanently" retain a particular data file, the concerns of information services turn next to its preservation and user accessibility. Though not as vulnerable as specialists at one time indicated, machine-readable records do require care-

---

13. Since data file documentation is such an integral part of the appraisal process, all of the works cited in note 12 contain sections on this topic. See also Charles M. Dollar, "Documentation of Machine-Readable Records and Research: A Historian's View," *Prologue* 3,1 (1971): 27–31; Ivor L. Kilmer, "ADP Documentation and Records Management," *Records Management Journal* 10,2 (1972): 9–14; and Harold King and Mitchell Krasny, "A Standard Description for Magnetic Tape Files," *Annals of Economic and Social Measurement* 4,3 (1975): 449–54.

ful storage and regular servicing. Tapes and disks should be stored in a relatively dust-free environment with a temperature of 55 to 60 degrees Fahrenheit and a relative humidity of approximately 40 percent. Fluctuations in temperature and humidity and exposure to any type of electromagnetic radiation must be avoided (if possible). If they are in regular use, magnetic records should be stored on edge, disks rotated every three months, tapes rewound every six months, and both disks and tapes cleaned on a semiannual basis.[14] On the other hand, rarely accessed tapes might suffer damage from repeated cleanings. It is therefore advisable to periodically check on their condition before putting them through a cleaning process. Admittedly, few programs observe these stringent measures and, even so, have not always suffered as a result. Nevertheless, as dictated by organizational needs and resource availability, it is advisable to establish and maintain proper procedures for the storage of these media.

Even the very best maintenance program will be to no avail if the organization lacks access to a facility that can load and run its machine-readable holdings. Unfortunately, major difficulties often stand in the way of realizing this objective. In the first place, the parent institution's data center will be in no position to retain and operate antiquated EDP equipment for the sake of archived media. Similarly, service bureaus can only remain profitable by keeping pace with changes within the industry. They too will rapidly lose the ability to run older magnetic media formats. Thus, unless a program of periodic conversion to current storage technologies is contemplated, one's organization may eventually find that its records will no longer operate on any available EDP equipment. Furthermore, long-term records retention programs should also consider the standardization of storage media to reduce overhead costs and to simplify the tape reformatting process.

Beyond the issue of expense, perhaps the strongest justification for standardizing machine-readable records formats is to facilitate subsequent access to these files and, hence, user services. In this regard, MIS personnel should ensure that all tapes conform to a given bit density (i.e., bits per inch [BPI] of tape), that they are all compatible with the operating environment of their parent institution's or their service bureau's DP facility, and that they run on a common type of hardware. While all of these arrangements are highly desirable, they are not always achievable. Once magnetic tapes are withdrawn from day-to-day operational use, their files are less likely to conform to corporate standards the longer they are kept in storage. If the or-

14. See Sidney B. Geller, *Care and Handling of Computer Magnetic Storage Media* (Washington, D.C.: National Bureau of Standards, U.S. Commerce Department, 1983); and Howard P. Lowell, "Preserving Recorded Information," *Records Management Quarterly* 16,2 (1982): 38–42.

ganization's data center undergoes a major change in its hardware and/or software environment, this too is likely to have an adverse effect on the accessibility of archived media.

There is little that MIS can do (or probably should do) about such developments. Instead, it is essential that the information services unit has in place procedures to measure the impact of these changes and to facilitate an effective response. For example, a tape specifications form with the pertinent technical information will provide all of the necessary information to both administer machine-readable records on a daily basis and to direct data conversion efforts. Figure 21 is a sample of such a form. This simple management tool provides MIS personnel with a checklist of all the essential details, including a magnetic tape's identification number and office of origin, its technical specifications, an EDP provenance statement, a record layout, and a partial listing of file contents. With this information in hand, most tapes may be readily identified, mounted on a tape drive for processing, or converted to a more accessible data format as required. However, for non-sequential files, MIS personnel must also know about the structure employed in originally creating the record. Even then additional documentation may be needed when dealing with software-dependent data files.

As a follow-up procedure, MIS personnel should enter all tape specification information into a common database. Thereafter, this tool will assist them in retrieving individual media from storage when these are requested by users. They can also employ the database to survey holding descriptions when circumstances, such as a major change in their organization's EDP environment, arise. Furthermore, on a proactive basis, they can seek out and correct format anomalies among their archives. With these types of practices in place, information services ought to face fewer problems going forward.

In addition, the latest generation of database systems, at least in theory, offers the advantage of operating independently of the data that the systems manipulate. As long as the files in question conform to a flat data structure (i.e., a file of one record type), they need not possess unique identifiers. Information in such a file is stored sequentially, without any hierarchical structuring of data records. As a result, the information may be accessed without recourse to special algorithms that typically are unique to a given DBMS. Once in the flat data-structure format, the archived tapes ought to require no further changes, because most database systems will be capable of accessing their contents. As long as the user can communicate the file organization and its data field definitions to the system, processing may begin.[15] Unfortunately, the situation is not as simple as preceding

---

15. This type of DBMS flexibility is typical of the so-called fourth generation of

statements might suggest. Some DBMS's, such as dBase III, produce software independent data files by employing file structures with fixed record and field lengths. They then rely upon some type of data dictionary or directory to access the files. To do this, the software must also be in place. Detailed documentation is required if MIS personnel are to develop a conversion program to transfer the data to the control of a different DBMS product. Here again, information services personnel will be well served by a tape specification database in managing these activities.

Taken together, the standardization of archived storage media and the reformatting of outdated tapes and disks should satisfactorily address major problems wrought by technological change. Future developments in systems programming might contribute to a further amelioration of concerns in this area. However, to ensure that equipment obsolescence does not overtake the holdings of machine-readable archives, MIS management must remain sensitive to changes in its organization's EDP operations. This is particularly true (and difficult) in work environments where data processing is highly decentralized. As with all other aspects of information services, close working relationships between the MIS and their constituents are essential for the success of the enterprise.

Automated Management Tools for Machine-Readable Records

To a considerable extent, the administrative needs of a machine-readable records archives resemble those of a traditional paper-oriented repository. Therefore, a similar approach may be applied to automating their operations. At the very least, routine office functions, such as word processing, financial management, electronic mail, fund raising, inventory control, and personnel administration, should be supported by the use of electronic workstations wherever possible. Furthermore, as the use of machine-readable records becomes more widespread and as the servicing of these media merges with paper-based systems management, common automated processes make a great deal of sense. Thus, many of the scenarios already reviewed in Chapter Seven will serve equally well in the context of magnetic media records management. Rather than repeat myself, the following discussion focuses upon additional applications that are unique to machine-readable file management.

---

systems and applications software. All of these products are full relational DBMS with user-friendly English-like query access. They are capable of reading and associating flat files while operating independently of specific data storage formats because they run off of a master data element dictionary. *Datamation* and *Computerworld* regularly carry articles and news releases about these types of products.

TAPE SPECIFICATION FORM

Date _____

Person completing form _____

Institution _____

Address _____

Telephone number _____

Name of study _____

Principal investigator(s) _____

Department/agency _____

Tape # _____

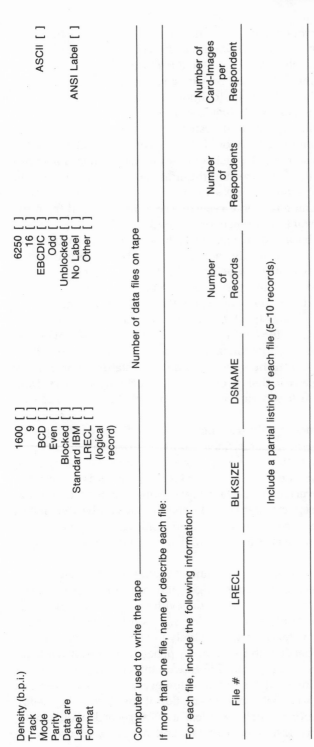

Density (b.p.i.)   1600 [ ]   6250 [ ]
Track   9 [ ]   16 [ ]
Mode   BCD [ ]   EBCDIC [ ]   ASCII [ ]
Parity   Even [ ]   Odd [ ]
Data are   Blocked [ ]   Unblocked [ ]
Label   Standard IBM [ ]   No Label [ ]   ANSI Label [ ]
Format   LRECL [ ]   Other [ ]
                    (logical
                     record)

Computer used to write the tape _____ Number of data files on tape _____

If more than one file, name or describe each file: _____

For each file, include the following information:

File #	LRECL	BLKSIZE	DSNAME	Number of Records	Number of Respondents	Number of Card-Images per Respondent

Include a partial listing of each file (5–10 records).

Figure 21 Tape Specification Form. Whenever a magnetic tape is written, it is imperative to have all of the technical information on how the tape was written in order to access and use the tape efficiently. This tape specification form records the necessary information and should be sent to the recipient of the tape.

In any survey of data archive functions, one characteristic stands out above the rest: machine-readable records tend to be highly standardized. Even complex individual file structures are complemented by support documentation and servicing requirements that are routine and generally predictable. It should therefore come as no surprise that certain aspects of their servicing lend themselves to automated management tools and systems. For example, a magnetic-media preservation program would benefit from a computer-assisted approach to management. In such an operation, considerations must be given to dust, temperature, and humidity control. Each item must also have its own maintenance schedule. This timetable should indicate when machine-readable records are to be removed from the vault, rewound, rotated in place, or cleaned.

A simple database system could be fashioned on a microcomputer to perform these administrative activities. Each DBMS record would include the number of the tape or disk, its shelf location, a list of maintenance functions, and the dates of servicing. If the system allows for formula-driven scheduling, the DBMS will automatically update the file once action has been taken. After a proper interval, it will then flag the item for another treatment. With a DBMS-managed preservation program, information services personnel would have the capability to search the system online for a status report on any particular machine-readable record. More importantly, such a system could produce work schedules (upon request) that list sequenced assignments.

MIS management could use such a tool to direct work-force allocations and to run administrative audits of its maintenance program. If a tape inventory does not correspond to its database listing, the staff could assume that the accessioning process is in error or that they have overlooked certain tapes. Subsequent research and additional DBMS reports might then be required to resolve the matter. This procedure ensures that all archived holdings receive the same high-level care, and serves as a useful check against errors in inventory control.

The appraisal process for machine-readable records suggests another area in which automation might play an important role. The determination of the substantive value (evidential and informational) of office files is certainly as impressionistic as it is scientific. This is because research materials vary so widely in content and format that any effort to standardize the evaluation procedure will prove fruitless. In this regard, there is no difference between the appraisal of paper and machine-readable media. However, automated records also require comprehensive documentation if they are to be useful. This data would address such technical areas as record layouts, data-element definitions, EDP specifications, and magnetic record integrity. A computerized management tool could assist in the administration of these appraisal-related functions.

To begin this undertaking, a formal review and appraisal process must be devised. Since the procedures involved are many and complex, the MIS project team should begin by flow-charting the entire transaction. By way of example, I have included as figure 22 the U.S. National Archives' (NARS) appraisal flowchart for machine-readable records.[16] This schematic drawing lists all the criteria that must be satisfied before the addition of magnetic media into NARS holdings. The reader should note that the approach depicted here is most rigorous and includes both technical and archival (i.e. research or operational value) considerations. At many points during this evaluation process, a given file may be rejected for failing to meet the criteria set by the program.

The flow of procedures within this function may be easily converted to an online computer form which will prompt the information specialist as that person works through the appraisal process. My example (figure 22) is somewhat dated and employs a 1600 BPI standard. The reader should therefore adapt this tool to reflect his or her organization's EDP environment. Figure 22 nevertheless serves a useful purpose by way of illustration. The rigor that one applies will depend upon the circumstances and resource limitations of one's own workplace. Selection criteria should include all those factors that must be present if a machine-readable record is to run successfully on one's system. If these elements are missing, the tape or disk is virtually worthless. A decision-support tool employing a standard database system might be fashioned to facilitate record selection.

A scenario involving such a product might go something like this. When appraising a new acquisition, information services personnel would proceed through the flowchart, indicating on a formatted computer screen all available tape documentation. The software program might be designed to generate a value that represents the completeness of this information. If this score is too low, the system will instruct the staff to reject the acquisition due to insufficient documentation. In addition, MIS may choose to designate certain document components as essential. If these are missing, the collection would be rejected immediately by the decision-support software.

In my view, there is a twofold benefit in automating the aforementioned flowchart model. First, a menu-driven documentation listing serves as an automatic reminder to the staff that a given body of information must accompany a tape or disk into the archives if this data file is to pass its evaluation process. The prompting device within

16. For a full discussion of this flowchart, see Charles M. Dollar, "Appraising Machine-Readable Records," *The American Archivist* 41,4 (1978): 423–30.

the system should eliminate the possibility of staff members mistakenly accessioning a data file that is inadequately documented. Second, this type of decision-making package provides an objective mechanism for the justification of records disposal or retention when there is a difference of opinion among appraisers, or between the office of origin and data archives personnel. Thus, this tool offers both administrative and political benefits to information services when negotiating disposition strategies with records managers or other information officers within the parent organization.

Yet another example of how computers might assist in the management of machine-readable records involves the use of automated systems in reference services. In a traditional information services setting, end users work with the reference staff to identify holdings that coincide with their research interests. Once these materials are located, they are delivered to the requestor for review. The user might at times ask a staff member to copy specific documents, but beyond these services, there is little else required of reference services personnel. Data archives, on the other hand, must provide a wide range of additional support functions. For example, researchers may require that records stored in the data archives be transmitted to some off-site location for processing. They may need copies of tapes, printouts, or COM. In some instances, they may ask the staff to assist in the manipulation and analysis of magnetic media records prior to creating any number of output products.[17]

The complexity of machine-readable records reference services and the costs associated with their delivery are a major challenge for MIS operations entering into this field. As a first step, information services personnel may wish to flowchart their reference activities so as to anticipate user requests. Next, they should establish standardized procedures and pricing for routine services. In many instances, their "customers" will come from within their own organization. MIS personnel may therefore turn to the in-house accounting department to assist them in the development of internal billing mechanisms. To simplify this process, information services could also establish a computer-based reference and accounting system that would tack user activities and associated costs.[18]

---

17. This area is in need of greater exploration and explication. See Walt Crawford, *Patron Access: Issues for Online Catalogs* (Boston, Mass.: G. K. Hall, 1987); Peter A. Baskerville and Chad M. Gaffield, *Archives, Automation, and Access* (Victoria, B.C.: University of Victoria Press, 1985); Laine G. M. Ruus, "Training of Data Services Professionals: Past, Present, and Future," *Library Trends* 30,3 (1982): 455–65; and Theodore Hershberg, "Archival Automation and the Researcher," *Automating the Archives*, Lawrence J. McCrank, ed. (White Plains, N.Y.: Knowledge Industry Publications, 1981), 35–66.

18. References to the financial aspects of machine-readable archives management may be found in Crawford, Baskerville, and Ruus. See note no. 17 above. See also

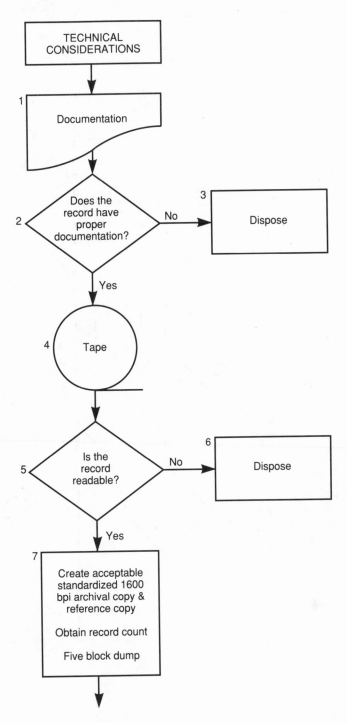

Figure 22. Appraisal Flowchart

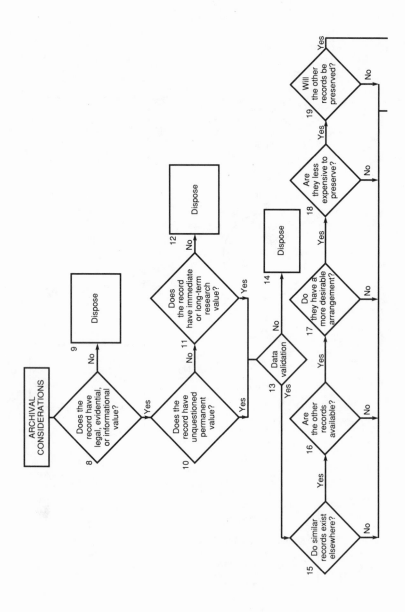

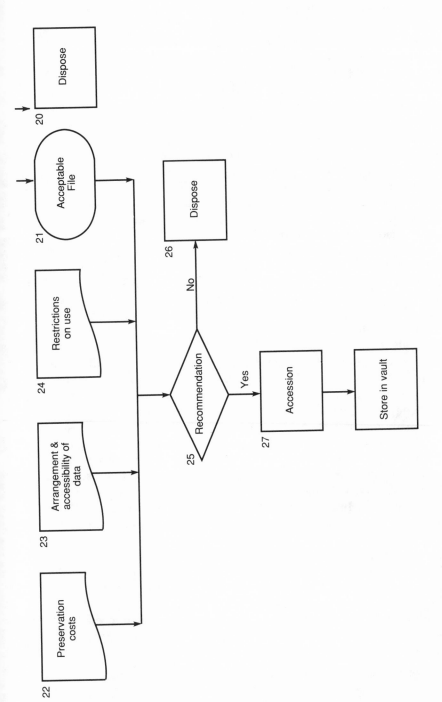

Figure 22.   (Cont.)

In this scenario, all the relationships within the system would be driven by formula. Thus, when a user asks for access to a file, the expense of computer time, processing, materials, and any outside EDP consulting services is automatically computed. A bill for services rendered could then be generated along with system output. Many computer centers already have this type of facility in place. All one need do is modify it to include an expanded list of services. In conjunction with the deployment of such an arrangement, be sure to publicize any changes to the data archives fee structure. Users will appreciate this notice, which may alert them to the hitherto unknown availability of certain services. In this manner, the billing process can be employed as a marketing vehicle as well.

The three examples of automated administrative systems mentioned above fit nicely into a broader management scenario for machine-readable records repositories. Like their records center counterparts, these operations can benefit from office automation. They can employ the computer when accessioning, tracking collection processing, describing holdings, retrieving collection descriptions, and attending to user services. By integrating standardized auditing structures into the EDP components of their services, data archives will have the ability to exercise greater control over the work that flows through their operation. In addition, they will be in a position to employ management modeling tools to assist their staffs in the appraisal of collections and in the evaluation of accompanying systems documentation.

The flexibility and enhanced worker productivity afforded by these automated systems are extremely important because most existing data archives programs are understaffed and inadequately funded. Computers can help mitigate this shortfall in resources. While parent institutions are coming to recognize the need to invest more heavily in magnetic media MIS services, much more must be done if valuable machine-readable information is to be preserved. Unfortunately, at present we are also faced with a chronic shortage of trained people in this field. Here again, nothing will improve until senior management comes to recognize the important role that these services play in the day-to-day operation and long-term survival of most organizations. For this to come about, MIS managers must "educate" their superiors and get them to invest more substantially in the preservation and maintenance of their corporate information resources. Both business and governmental bodies have MIS officials

---

Donald T. Hawkins, "Machine-Readable Output from On-Line Searches," *Journal of ASIS* 32,4 (1981): 253–56; and Ryan E. Hoover, ed., *The Library and Information Manager's Guide to Online Services* (White Plains, N.Y.: Knowledge Industry Publications, 1980).

capable of leading the way. Will they rise to the challenge? It is largely for them to decide and to act.

Protecting Online Data Resources

In concluding this all too brief discussion of machine-readable records management, it is only fitting that some space be devoted to the servicing and protection of interactive databases. These systems currently manipulate the vast majority of all digitized information files. Bibliographic utilities, banks and credit card operations, government agencies, large retail chains, insurance companies, virtually all of the transportation and trucking industries, and even some universities maintain these online data processing facilities. A typical EDP configuration might include one or more mainframe computers, tied to a large number of data storage devices (DASD), and hundreds or perhaps thousands of end user terminals. All of this hardware is driven by some type of complex database management system. While some of these networks operate from a single location, many others serve a national or international constituency.

Conceptually, though they perform a variety of functions, all of these systems function in a similar manner. At their heart, these facilities allow end users to enter, modify, store, and retrieve enormous amounts of data. In the case of a library system, this might be a bibliographic record; in the case of VISA Card, it might be a customer's account statement; and in the case of a city police department, it might be the history of a citizen's traffic and parking violations. In each of these applications, the database has been customized to allow ease of data entry and retrieval. Most if not all information is stored on hard disk systems for rapid responses to inquiries and for the prompt processing of reports at month- and year-end.

However, unlike the data files discussed in the previous sections of Chapter Seven, these online databases are not a stable, unchanging information source. Most are in a state of constant change. Thus, while the end products of an online database system, such as reports, statements, bills, and the like, might be downloaded to paper, magnetic tape, videodisc, or computer output microfilm, the main body of information never leaves the live storage devices within which it resides. The same may be said for those more modest database products (e.g., mailing lists, phone directories, and record inventories) that many of us maintain on personal computers' DBMSs.

There is no denying the importance of these online systems. Without them, many organizations within both the private and public sectors would cease to function. Ironically, it is the very nature of these information services, with their constantly changing data files, that makes them difficult to protect. Generally accepted records management and archival practices do not apply. For example, most on-line operations generate backup tapes of their databases on a twelve- or twenty-four-hour basis. Microcomputer-based system users should copy off a fresh set of data diskettes after each working session with their DBMSs. Unfortunately, either set of procedures can only hope to capture and preserve the complete information picture for no more than a brief period. Once any network participant makes a new entry into the system, the current file and the archived version begin to diverge. In a high-transaction environment, such as that of an airline or a bank, it may only take a few minutes or hours before the duplicate files become irrelevant as a database record.

How, then, can information services personnel protect and preserve online data resources? Despite what I have already said, file backup procedures are an essential first step. If for any reason the primary database is lost, MIS may turn to copies and restore the system. Admittedly, a day or two of work may need to be reconstructed during the restoration process, but that is far better than losing everything. Most data centers will methodically backup all of their live data as part of standard operating procedures. PC users are less likely to demonstrate this sort of discipline. With the proliferation of microcomputers in office environments, it is not possible for MIS personnel to do all of the policing. Instead, they should provide their organization with the necessary policies and procedures, and thereafter rely upon line management to monitor compliance.

As an alternative approach, some MIS departments are establishing PC networks that operate off a common file server (i.e., shared memory storage). There are many operational benefits from such a strategy, but until recently, the necessary hardware and software have not been readily available at a reasonable price. Now that these local area networks (LANs) are more available, microcomputer users—at least in large automated office environments—are employing them. By centralizing data storage in a fixed number of LAN file servers, users may quickly and economically access the same databases. Given the limited number of these units within a LAN configuration, it is much less difficult for MIS personnel to directly supervise backup procedures. Thus, as an additional benefit of PC networking, vital data files may be better protected against accidental erasure.

Unfortunately, unanticipated file destruction is only one category of risk faced by online data resources. As part of a network, these files may be accessed and therefore altered from any node. In some instances, these changes to data may be proper and allowable, but in other instances, they may be mistaken and even malicious. Data security systems were created for the very purpose of preventing

unwarranted or unauthorized access to data files.[19] They exist for
EDP configurations ranging from mainframe-based networks, to LANs,
to standalone PCs. Most involve password access to specific data files
or online transactions, and include administrative reports that identify security violations and their perpetrators.[20] To avoid any appearance of a conflict of interests, MIS personnel ought to remove
themselves from direct participation in data security. On the other
hand, it is, in my view, a responsibility of information services management to ensure that its organization develops and maintains a
comprehensive program.

File backup procedures and data security systems contribute to
the protection of online systems. However, in some instances they
are not in and of themselves sufficient. Where the network in question is extensive and where computer downtime could lead to a
serious loss in business or an abdication of organizational responsibilities, a further step is required. This process may take on many
forms, but is generally referred to as "disaster preparedness and
contingency planning." Its primary function is to anticipate and prepare for any catastrophe that might shut down one's network for an
extended period of time. Such circumstances might include electric
power failures, floods, fires, major snow storms, and any other natural or man-made disaster.[21]

Since one can never tell when adversity might strike, disaster
preparedness and contingency planning (DP/CP) may be likened to
an insurance policy. Senior management weighs the risks to the institution of a major computer system or DP network shutdown against
the cost of a DP/CP program. After deliberations, some organizations
may choose to live with the risk while others will invest heavily in
DP/CP. For example, a distributed network with many processing
nodes may develop a plan for the shifting of work and the rerouting

19. Both manual and automated systems are required to maintain data integrity
and security within a machine-readable records archives. See Ben Harrison, "Data
Security: Plan for the Worst," *Infosystems* 29,6 (1982): 52–62; Randy J. Goldfield, "Rec-
ords Automation," *Administrative Management* 43,2 (1982): 84–85; Eduardo B. Fernan-
dez, Rita C. Summers, and Christopher Wood, *Database Security and Integrity* (Chicago:
Addison-Wesley Publishing Company, 1981); John P. Murray, "Protecting Corporate
Data with Off-Site Vault Storage," *Computerworld* 15,11 (1981): 15–24; New York City,
System Security Standards for Electronic Data Processing, rev. ed. (New York: City
Record, 1981); Donn B. Parker, *Computer Security Management* (Reston, Va.: Reston
Publishing, 1981); and James A. Schweitzer, *Managing Information Security: A Program
for the Electronic Information Age* (Woburn, Mass.: Butterworth, 1981).

20. For the most current data security industry information, see *Datapro Reports
on Information Security* (Deran, N.J.: Datapro Research Corporation, 1987); and Computer Security Institute, *Computer Security Handbook*, 4th ed. (Northborough, Mass.:
Computer Security Institute, 1987).

21. For an excellent summary of the contingency planning process, see John A.
Buckland, *Disaster Recovery in Today's Processing Environment* (Carrollton, Tex.:
Chantico, 1985).

of telecommunications from one location to another at little additional cost. By contrast, centralized DP operations may need to invest in a redundant network and an alternative data processing facility. The MIS leadership will play a major role in these considerations and will most certainly do much of the actual planning and installation of contingency systems.

In some instances, senior management may have no choice in the matter. Regardless of the cost, it must pay for contingency planning as mandated by government regulations.[22] Still others will find that the very nature of their business responsibilities dictates this course of action. Whatever the reason, those contemplating such an undertaking will find it complex and at times daunting. To assist in this process, I have provided my readers with a generic checklist of contingency planning activities (see figure 23). I have purposely framed these program elements in the context of an action plan matrix to encourage the use of the project management tools found elsewhere in this volume.[23]

At the outset, the DS/CP team must establish specifications for the organization's existing data network and requirements for the protection of both telecommunication and online data resources. In part, this survey will entail practical EDP considerations, but it must also encompass operational issues and responsibilities. By way of illustration, it may be acceptable for a toy distributor's customer service unit to be out of action for a day, while it is totally unacceptable for the airport flight controllers' network to be down for even five minutes. Thus, initial DP/CP deliberations must involve senior management and should proceed only after the organizational leadership has approved the broad outline of a plan.

Further data gathering will lead to the framing of both a strategic document and various tactical action plans. For example, team members should examine the current state of data center and networking facilities. Those institutions that are plagued with power outages may decide to include the addition of an uninterrupted power source (UPS) system and a backup generator as part of the program. In the same vein, they may choose to upgrade the physical security and

---

22. For example, in 1983 the U.S. Controller of the Currency decreed that all Federally chartered banks must develop and implement contingency plans as soon as possible. See Jane M. Mintzer, "Disaster Recovery Planning," *Computers in Banking* 3,11 (1987): 51–62; and Donald G. Miller, *Risk Assessment in Financial Institutions* (Rolling Meadows, Ill.: Bank Administration Institute, 1983).

23. Alternative approaches to disaster preparedness and contingency planning may be found in the following publications: *Datapro Reports on Information Security* (Deran, N.J.: Datapro Research Corporation, 1987): IS65–69 ("Disaster Avoidance"); and Computer Security Institute, *Computer Security Handbook*, 4th ed. (Northborough, Mass.: Computer Security Institute, 1987): (Section 4, "Protecting the Data Center"; Section 7, "Disaster Recovery Planning").

Project ID No.	Objective/ Task Description	Task Leader	Date Assigned	Required Resources	Task Status	Planned Dates Start – End		Actual Dates Start – End		Costs Budget – Actual	
CP1.0	Review online DP & contingency plan requirements										
CP2.0	Develop strategic and tactical contingency plans										
CP3.0	Review data center & network facilities & backup requirements										
CP4.0	Select short-term hot site & negotiate contract										
CP5.0	Select long-term cold site & make preparations										

Figure 23. Contingency Planning Action Plan Matrix.

Project ID No.	Objective/ Task Description	Task Leader	Date Assigned	Required Resources	Task Status	Planned Dates Start – End		Actual Dates Start – End		Costs Budget – Actual	
CP6.0	Order and install backup hardware and test										
CP7.0	Order and install backup network and test										
CP8.0	Develop batch applications test plan and test										
CP9.0	Develop online applications test plan and test										
CP10.0	Develop ongoing test procedures for plan and test										

Figure 23.   (Cont.)

Project ID No.	Objective/ Task Description	Task Leader	Date Assigned	Required Resources	Task Status	Planned Dates Start – End		Actual Dates Start – End		Costs Budget – Actual	
CP11.0	Develop disaster recovery procedures documentation										
CP12.0	Review and upgrade CP budgets & org. insurance policies										
CP13.0	Develop & document rebuild program and test as appropriate										

Figure 23. (Cont.)

fire protection systems at their DP facility. They may also decide to reroute phone lines or even build redundant links at key junctures that have experienced problems in the past.

In the extreme case, a contingency plan anticipates the total destruction of the organization's data center. If this were to occur, an alternative processing site would be required. Those operations with multiple data centers may shift work from one location to another. However, most of us are not that fortunate. The team will therefore need to identify both a "hot" and a "cold" site for its DP operations. The hot site would provide an immediate location (within twenty-four to forty-eight hours) from which the organization could resume operations. In the meantime, the team would rapidly prepare the cold site for ongoing data processing services. More often than not, a hot site is obtained from an outside vendor, such as Comdisco in New Jersey and Sun Guard in Ohio, who provides emergency computer room backup.

As part of plan implementation, MIS personnel would work with the hot site vendor to test all systems and to ensure that the redundant network and backup data center can run all applications in a live mode. These activities may take two years to fully implement and must culminate in periodic (e.g. quarterly) tests, where the organization actually runs out of its hot site for a brief period. These arrangements are expensive but are for a limited duration, after which time the organization must relocate its backup operations to a more permanent location. Since the logistics may be formidable, all contingency planning procedures must be thoroughly documented. As the final step in this process, the team should devise a rebuild program to restore the network and its online data resources to a pre-disaster mode. Thereafter, DP/CP system testing, and budget and insurance policy reviews should become established components of MIS operations.

To those of my readers responsible for records management and archives, disaster preparedness and contingency planning may not appear relevant. Perhaps this is true with regard to their current responsibilities. However, as these information services professionals come to address the data file retention and disposition of online EDP environments, they will come to realize that established practices will not suffice. One cannot simply backup interactive system data on a periodic basis. Instead, one must ensure the integrity and ongoing operation of the entire database entity. In this context, tape/diskette duplication and offsite storage have a role, as does a data security program. Ultimately, the online environment itself must be preserved as the only practical means of protecting the associated data files. In so doing, MIS management will fulfill its responsibilities as the keeper of its parent organization's vital records.

Postscript: A Profile of the Information Services Professional

In its opening chapters, INFORMATION SYSTEMS: A STRATEGIC APPROACH TO PLANNING AND IMPLEMENTATION sets forth the premise that modern organizations of all sizes, descriptions, and purposes require information systems to function effectively and economically. It is also argued that the same strategic planning process which drives the parent corporation should provide direction and focus for all MIS functions. To complete this picture, INFORMATION SYSTEMS considers the organizational and environmental context within which MIS professionals must operate. It emphasizes the need for user involvement and leadership in the shaping of information systems. In addition, my recommendations include the establishment of a long-term planning process, opportunities for MIS research and development, and a flexible approach toward the exploitation of EDP and telecommunications technologies in the workplace.

To support these activities, the information services team must demonstrate its ability to design and implement new systems and procedures. My presentation therefore includes a detailed discussion of practical, tested methods, accompanied by a series of simple yet effective management tools. Even so, my readers may be left with a number of questions concerning the role that they and their constituents are to play in this evolving process. In particular, they may wish to ask: Is this volume's model of the MIS professional realistic? If it is, do I fit in? Furthermore, what must I do to position myself within my parent organization to maximize my contribution to the whole? What is the role of my users in the context of these transforming information services and where will it all lead?

In response, I would begin by asking my readers to look around them. Is their office environment or indeed their constituent community standing still? The answer should be obvious. Inexpensive microcomputers and widely dispersed data processing facilities are putting computing power and network communications in the hands of end users. While databases and bibliographic utilities are readily available, paper records, microfilm, and hardcopy publications also abound. CD-ROMs and optical videodiscs may replace some of this paper, but they are more likely to complement it. In short, the organization's information resource options continue to proliferate, increasing office clutter and at times only adding to the confused welter of MIS options.

As has always been the case, information services professionals are required to bring order out of what at times is chaos. They are needed to limit user choices and, indeed, are essential in bringing the end user and the "right" information resource together. In performing these tasks, MIS personnel will continue to specialize. Rest assured that there will always be a need for records managers, archivists, librarians, data network managers, and so forth. The current environment is too varied and complex for the generalist at the line management level. On the other hand, two dynamic forces are converging on these same professions and will transform them over time.

The first of these factors is the information environment itself. Hitherto, one turned to a specific resource for a particular type of data. There was little overlap, and hence the emergence of separate MIS service entities. For example, a user would turn to the organization's records management unit for retired paper files, the data center for database information, and the library for publications. Not surprisingly, developments in the technologies of information processing, storage, and delivery have changed all of this. Paper memoranda are being replaced by electronic mail. CD-ROM publications are supplanting more traditional reference tools. Most importantly, distributed processing and microcomputer networking are making it increasingly possible for a researcher in one location to access diverse sources situated elsewhere. The costs of these services continue to decline even as their integration and responsiveness to user needs improve.

These developments have considerable significance for the information services professional. No longer can the records manager, the librarian, or for that matter the computer center director operate autonomously. Each must be aware of the other's activities and responsibilities. They need not become experts in their colleagues' specialties, but they must learn to speak a common language and comprehend how their area complements those of their MIS counterparts. In short, they must operate as team players, responding to a common set of strategies and work plans. Perhaps these relationships will express themselves organizationally through the establishment of broadly defined information service units led by chief information officers (CIOs). However, a formal structure is not essential to success as long as cooperation, coordination, and (ultimately) integration become characteristics of the parent institution's total MIS environment.

Does such a scenario imply that the incumbents in these positions, as they stand today, are unprepared for the challenges that confront them? In terms of their skills and areas of expertise, I would say that most information services professionals are well equipped to proceed. What may be lacking in some instances, however, is a willingness to adapt or expand one's horizons. To resolve these differences will require leadership. The modern organization needs its CIOs and its MIS research and development units. It requires people with vision and a general commitment to the strategic use of corporate information resources. To begin, the organization's senior managers must set the tone by bringing the consideration of MIS into their own planning efforts. With the recognition that information services must play a central role in the life of the institution, the blending of MIS disciplines will ultimately occur.

A second major factor transforming MIS responsibilities is the evolution of user-driven information systems. These tools, including sophisticated database and communications facilities, allow the end user to define and develop personalized information resources. Furthermore, in many instances these EDP products grant their creators the authority to define records life cycles. Up to the present, the records manager or the archivist has assigned office files their retention and disposition classification. Admittedly, these time schedules have come about with user input and with an eye on government regulations and office traditions. Nevertheless, the final arbiter was, and largely still is, an information services professional.

With electronic files, this scenario may no longer apply. The end user is in a position to erase a record, alter its contents, assign it to archival media, and so forth. By determining the ultimate fate of corporate records, the patron of information services is now being asked to act in the same capacity as a MIS professional. One could argue that this is only proper because the user is in the best position to ascertain the worth of the documents that he or she has created. While I am sympathetic to this argument, I must also point out that in fact most of us do not have the objectivity to appraise our own work in this fashion, nor are we schooled in the laws governing records retention. What is more, few users possess a sufficient comprehensive understanding of their parent organization to recognize the value of their personal information resources to others.

This is not to say that MIS professionals enjoy this level of understanding either. However, they are trained to ask the right questions and, if necessary, to conduct detailed studies pertaining to the long-term viability of a given information resource. It is impractical to expect end users to develop a comparable level of expertise. Be that as it may, the latest generation of automated systems is pressing their users to make these types of decisions. To prepare their constituents for this eventuality, MIS professionals must turn their attention to preparing those they serve for these weighty responsibilities. In this regard, information managers will become less involved in day-to-day data processing and more actively committed to the coordination of information resources and to user training and support.

Who, then, are to be the leading management information systems professionals of the future? First and foremost, they are people schooled in and committed to a comprehensive approach to information services delivery. Though they may possess expertise in a number of specialties, their knowledge of both paper and machine-readable media should be broad enough to recognize the multifaceted nature of most MIS problems and opportunities. They will understand, at least in general terms, electronic data processing and telecommunications technologies. In addition, they will make every effort to keep current of changes in these fields. At the same time, they will not lose sight of the fact that people still love paper and, therefore, that more traditional records management will not go entirely away.

However, given the increasing technological dimension to MIS responsibilities, typical records management, archival, and library functions—as they are known today—will become either highly automated and user intensive or more plainly clerical in nature. Those who fill the high levels of the MIS profession will be satisfied with the challenges that confront them. They will also be well rewarded for their contributions to their parent organization. On the other hand, those who do not adapt, broadening their skill base (and hence their range of activities), will find themselves with poorly paid, largely mechanical assignments. Over the next few years, these trends will become much more apparent. The wise information professional will position him or herself to take advantage of these new opportunities as they materialize. In the same vein, it is most important that this renewed body of specialists be driven by a compulsion to provide outstanding service to its constituents. Here, "service" should include the development of efficient and economical, knowledge-based (i.e., "expert") information delivery systems. Those who ignore these trends do so at their own peril and hasten the day of their replacement by automated information systems and those who service them.

MIS leadership must also change. Integrated information systems should not evolve out of textbook models. Each should reflect the unique operational requirements of its organizational setting and work environment. For this to come about, MIS managers must become much more user oriented. Indeed, I would advise any chief executive officer to look to his or her senior line managers for the person to fill the CIO slot. Technical expertise is desirable but it is not essential.

Support staff and on-the-job training can always fill this gap. What really matters is a MIS executive who is in tune with the parent institution's strategic objectives and its information service requirements. This person must have a vision of the future, but of equal importance, he or she must be capable of convincing others that new MIS procedures and technologies will allow the organization to achieve its goals.

In the end, the best MIS manager will be the person who is perceptive, creative, and above all a good salesperson. EDP technologies are difficult to work with in the best of circumstances. Project planning and implementation are fraught with dangers. But the greatest challenge remains that of convincing one's fellow workers of the need for change and its benefits to the organization. For those ready to seize the opportunities afforded by evolving office and information systems, it will be a rich and interesting life.

Bibliographic Note

In preparing this text, I have taken great pains to provide the reader with both detailed bibliographic and informational footnotes. These notes will direct the reader to additional readings as well as to other appropriate sources of guidance and advice. For those desiring a more structured reference tool, I recommend my volume *Information Management, Machine-Readable Records, and Administration: An Annotated Bibliography* (Chicago: Society of American Archivists, 1983). This work includes nearly one thousand discrete citations arranged according to the following subject categories: periodicals and reference tools, bibliographies, EDP applications in archives, machine-readable records and archives, records management and automation, library automation, information theory and systems, and future directions for archival automation. While much has happened in the years since this bibliography first became available, it does provide general guidance for those seeking greater detail on specific technologies. In particular, more current issues of periodicals listed in its opening section will provide the reader with insights into the latest EDP and telecommunications industry developments.

Index

Richard M. Kesner is Vice-President for Development and Systems at the Parkman Companies in Taunton, Massachusetts. Kesner has also served as vice-president of general services at Multibank Service Corporation and as manager of office systems and services at the Faxon Company. Kesner holds a Ph.D. in history and information science from Stanford University and is the author of several books on information management, including *Automation for Archivists and Records Managers* (ALA, 1984).